Ancient Myths and Biblical Faith

SCRIPTURAL TRANSFORMATIONS

FOSTER R. McCURLEY

FORTRESS PRESS   PHILADELPHIA

———

Library of Congress Cataloging in Publication Data

McCurley, Foster R.
  Ancient myths and biblical faith.

  Includes bibliographical references and index.
  1. Bible—Criticism, interpretation, etc.
2. Mythology. I. Title.
BS511.2.M38 1983   220.6′8   82–48589
ISBN 0–8006–1696–0 (pbk.)

———

9764K82   Printed in the United States of America   1–1696

In gratitude to Susquehanna University
for the honor given to this alumnus

Contents

Foreword

This book attempts to put together some of the pieces of that perplexing puzzle called the Holy Bible. It is an expression of the author's concern that the church teach and employ a theology which encompasses both testaments. While detailed scholarly research on this or that book of the Bible is essential to the interpretive task, equally important is an attempt to synthesize some of the findings of contemporary scholarship. Such a synthesis runs the risk of imposing modern systems on ancient documents, and so care must always be taken in order to ensure the integrity of the pieces while simultaneously demonstrating their interrelationships.

The Bible comes to us from a strange world—a world removed from ours in time and space. Almost two thousand years have passed since the latest books were written, and over three thousand since the earliest pieces left their authors' hands. Furthermore, even though we today cover spatial distances with amazing speed, nevertheless emerging from an airplane in the Middle East presents the traveler with an acute cultural shock.

Recognizing and indeed celebrating the foreignness of the Bible is a key to its interpretation. Rather than disregarding its separation from us in space and time, the twentieth-century reader will benefit far more from letting it be strange, ancient, Middle Eastern, and simply different. In other words, the Bible needs first of all to be understood in its strangeness in order for us moderns to learn from it and hear it address us on the basis of its own integrity.

The Bible developed in a world where a three-storied universe consisting of heaven, earth, and netherworld was simply assumed. The relationships of these three realms were the primary issue in ancient religions. Within the religious systems of the peoples who oc-

cupied the Middle East—what is called the ancient Near East when
speaking of the past—were many stories about the meaning of life
and the means to survival. Such stories, particularly when they tell of
the heavenly escapades of deities, belong to a way of viewing life
called mythology.

It is a basic presupposition of this volume that the writers of the
Bible intentionally employed words and images from these mythological stories in order to communicate in a dynamic way their own
witness to their God. Those ancient stories are strange to us today,
and so we need somehow to grasp a measure of their meaning so
that we can see more clearly how they were used in the Bible. What,
for example, entered the mind of the seventh-century B.C.E. Israelite
when he or she heard that God slew Leviathan in days of old? What
did the Jewish Christian of the first century comprehend when he
heard that Jesus walked upon the sea? Of what significance is the report that God revealed his own name, and later the identity of Jesus,
on a holy mountain?

Words and images make a particular impact on their audiences because such verbal and visual expressions enjoy familiarity. Sharing
that familiarity with ancient audiences determines whether or not we
grasp the impact intended by the author. To use a modern example,
if I say to another person, "I'm making you an offer you can't refuse," the hearer will experience the statement either as a threat or as
a promise. The impact will be one of threat if the person has seen
The Godfather, of promise if the hearer is unfamiliar with that movie
or with Mario Puzo's novel. The addressee will know whether I intend the statement as threat on the basis of any accompanying gestures or words which hark back to the story. To state the case differently, words always convey *some* meaning, but understanding the
intended meaning calls for knowledge of the literary and cultural allusions.

A further complication arises when an allusion is transposed to a
new setting. After seeing *The Godfather* with his woman friend, a
man might say, "I'm making you an offer you can't refuse" as a way
of proposing marriage. The setting, the tone, and the new set of accompanying words and gestures totally transform the significance of
the statement.

This study of mythological allusions in the Bible is based upon this
tension between impact and transformation. What happens to a story
about Baal, a god of the Canaanites, when it is transferred to Yahweh, the God of Israel, who represents in the ancient Near East a

new theological reality? Further, what is the effect of impact and transformation when the words and images from that ancient story, already changed to speak of Yahweh, appear in the New Testament to proclaim the identity of Jesus?

In carrying out this study in the Bible as a whole, I have chosen to use the term *Hebrew Bible* when discussing Israel's involvement in her world and to employ *Old Testament* only when discussing those same Scriptures in regard to the New Testament. While this change of terminology might be confusing to the reader, my concern is to allow Israel's witness to Yahweh to stand on its own, to speak to its own situations, and to guarantee its own theological integrity. Only for the Christian community, on the basis of its confession regarding Christ, does the Hebrew Bible become the Old Testament. This distinction in terminology suffers somewhat because of the appearance of the Septuagint, the translation of Israel's Scriptures into Greek during the third century B.C.E. As a result, I sometimes need to speak of the "Greek Old Testament" because of the use of that text to provide the impact vocabulary for New Testament writers.

This volume is an attempt to synthesize some of my training and experience over the past twenty years. I was trained in Assyriology and Semitic philology generally at Dropsie University by Professor Moshe Held and the late Professor Meir Bravmann. In my early days of teaching at the Lutheran Theological Seminary, Philadelphia, I had responsibilities for courses in Greek New Testament exegesis and Hebrew. Since 1967 I have concentrated on Old Testament theology. The interrelatedness of these disciplines has excited me for some time, and out of the conviction that they are indeed related I make the present attempt at synthesis.

This approach and the insights gained from it are by no means intended as the last word on the scriptural passages examined here. Like every other approach this one is no more than one attempt to comprehend the diversity and unity of the Bible. While each interpreter needs to find some way of stepping into the sandals of the authors of Scripture, we can never completely enter their minds or the mind of God who inspired them to bear their culturally laden witness. The strangeness of the Bible will remain. But we should never cease in our efforts to make those strangers of old a little more familiar so that the Word of God which they addressed to their audiences might be more comprehensible. At the same time the model of their witness might teach us something about communicating the Word of God within a given culture.

The opportunity to prepare this volume came with a sabbatical leave during the academic year 1980–81. For its constant support of scholarship through a generous sabbatical system I wish to thank the board of directors of the Lutheran Theological Seminary. Moreover, the opportunity to carry out research on site, in Egypt and in Israel, was made possible by the generous financial support accompanying the honor of the Franklin Clark Fry Fellowship granted by the Aid Association for Lutherans, and by further financial assistance granted by Lutheran Brotherhood. The support of everyone at the Ecumenical Institute for Advanced Theological Studies in Tantur, Israel, is most appreciated. Particularly helpful to me there was the daily dialogue with fellow residents Professor T. Raymond Hobbs of McMaster Divinity College and Professor Bruce Malina of Creighton University. Finally, for the meticulous typing of the manuscript from my cluttered pages I express appreciation to Ms. Paula Gravelle, a student at the seminary in Philadelphia.

In spite of all this assistance from institutions and friends, the book might fall far short of the contribution which I would hope it could make. Some readers might feel that I have stretched imagination too far, others that I have not stretched it far enough. In any case I offer here what can be no more than one small contribution to contemporary discussion regarding the meaning of Scripture.

Foster R. McCurley
Lutheran Theological Seminary
Philadelphia, Pa.
June 1982

Bibliographical Acknowledgments

The sources which proved helpful in the development of this volume are too numerous to list here. However, those major works which are particularly influential on the present writer, particularly in terms of the extra-biblical materials, need to be cited so that appreciation for their contribution might be expressed publicly.

In regard to mythology and its relationship to the Bible, there exist several classic works. Mircea Eliade's *Cosmos and History: The Myth of the Eternal Return* (New York: Harper & Brothers, 1959) has influenced my approach to the ancient Near Eastern materials. Furthermore, although often criticized for its approach, H. Frankfort's *Before Philosophy*, originally published in 1946 as *The Intellectual Adventure of Ancient Man*, nevertheless contains valuable insights from Frankfort himself and from Thorkild Jacobsen and John Wilson (Harmondsworth, Eng.: Penguin Books, 1959). Of particular importance to the present author were various courses under Theodor H. Gaster, whose own works, particularly *Thespis*, new and rev. ed. (New York: Gordian Press, 1975) and *Myth, Legend, and Custom in the Old Testament* (New York: Harper & Row, 1969) have been a constant resource in understanding mythology. The challenge to discern the differences between ancient Near Eastern parallels and the biblical allusions is most articulately done by Brevard Childs in *Myth and Reality in the Old Testament* (London: SCM Press, 1960, second ed. 1962). Childs's care in defining myth, as well as his explanations of the quality of time and space, enable one to realize the transformation in the Bible due to the new theological reality of Israel's God. The work of Frank Moore Cross, *Canaanite Myth and Hebrew Epic* (Cambridge, Mass.: Harvard University Press, 1973) is especially helpful in demonstrating how the myths actually serve to provide meaning

xi

to Israel's history. His treatment of Yahweh as the Divine Warrior and the interpretations of biblical passages based on that tradition present stimulating reading and a welcome challenge to some earlier approaches.

The interpretation of Mesopotamian myths in this volume is based largely on the works of Thorkild Jacobsen, especially his volume *The Treasures of Darkness: A History of Mesopotamian Religion* (New Haven, Conn.: Yale University Press, 1976). The depth of interpretation, as well as his obvious delight in translating and commenting on the ancient sources, makes this volume an invaluable source.

Without the translations and interpretations of John Wilson, the present writer would have been unable to include Egyptian backgrounds. His contribution to *Before Philosophy* is most helpful in distinguishing Egypt from the others religiously speaking. Further, Wilson's book *The Burden of Egypt: An Interpretation of Ancient Egyptian Culture* (Chicago: University of Chicago Press, 1951) is a comprehensive and sensitive treatment which has yet to be equalled.

The most helpful study of Canaanite religion is that by Hartmut Gese, "Die Religionen Altsyriens" in volume 10 of *Die Religionen der Menschheit* (ed. Christel Matthias Schröder; Stuttgart: W. Kohlhammer, 1970). Gese lists at the outset the various sources for understanding Canaanite religion and with characteristic precision discusses the stories and the deities involved, as well as the characteristics of the cult. In English translation the work of Helmer Ringgren on Canaanite (West Semitic), as well as on Mesopotamian religions, is published under the title *Religions of the Ancient Near East* (trans. John Sturdy; Philadelphia: Westminster Press, 1973). This readable volume provides a plethora of information while never losing sight of its interpretative purpose.

In regard to the first theme treated in the present study, that of order versus chaos, there are three volumes in particular which deserve to be mentioned here. At the turn of this century Hermann Gunkel published his classic work *Schöpfung und Chaos in Urzeit und Endzeit* (Göttingen: Vandenhoeck und Ruprecht, 1902; second ed. 1921). The continuity and discontinuity of Israel and her Mesopotamian neighbors was amply illustrated by Gunkel as he demonstrated in particular how the cosmogonic myth of Marduk against Tiamet from Babylon provided a means for the writers of the Bible to describe the eschatological victory of God over the chaotic forces of evil. Even without the Canaanite texts from Ugarit (discovered in 1929) Gunkel made some brilliant observations. Later works on the subject, particularly O. Kaiser's *Die mythische Bedeutung des Meeres in Ägypten, Ugarit und Israel* (Zeitschrift für alttestamentliche Wissenschaft 78 [1959]), and Bernhard W. Anderson's *Creation Versus Chaos: The Reinterpretation of Mythical Symbolism in the Bible* (New York: Association Press, 1967) have updated the discussion and have provided valuable interpretative insights into the biblical and extra-biblical texts. Anyone familiar with these three works will recognize their influence in the first section of this study.

The sexuality issue is much discussed in contemporary literature. Among these of particular significance is the work by Krister Stendahl, *The Bible and the Role of Women: A Case Study in Hermeneutics* (translated by Emilie T. Sander, Facet Books: Biblical Series, 15. Philadelphia: Fortress Press, 1966). Perhaps the most thorough treatment of the question regarding divine sexuality is Phyllis Trible's *God and the Rhetoric of Sexuality* (Overtures to Biblical Theology, Philadelphia: Fortress Press, 1978). The writer has also appreciated discussion of the issue in a broader sense by Stephen Sapp, *Sexuality, the Bible, and Science* (Philadelphia: Fortress Press, 1977).

In addition to the contributions of Childs (cited above) to the understanding of the mountain's quality, the work of Richard J. Clifford, *The Cosmic Mountain in Canaan and the Old Testament* (Cambridge, Mass.: Harvard University Press, 1972) is a comprehensive study which the present writer found to be especially helpful. In spite of the title, Clifford discusses Mesopotamian and Egyptian sanctuaries as well, arguing that the mountains were not central to the Mesopotamian experience and that Egypt's primeval hill had no influence on Canaan's understanding. From here Clifford launches into his study proper, distinguishing between the functions of El's mountain and those of Baal's, and discussing the appropriate biblical parallels. The entire study is carefully done and of significant scholarly interest.

Introduction

THE IMPACT OF MYTHOLOGY AND
ITS TRANSFORMATION

The word *myth*, even in scholarly usage, has a multiplicity of meanings.

In the first place, myth is a literary category to be distinguished from other literary forms such as saga or legend, fairy tale, fable, novella, or anecdote—all of which are defined in most basic introductions to the Bible. As a literary category, myth is usually understood to be a story about gods, that is, a story which takes place in the realm of heaven where divine beings carry on like actors on a stage. In this sense, myth differs from those literary forms in which human beings occupy the center of the stage.

Second, on a more general level, myth can be used to describe a manner of speaking or writing: a symbolic expression of a real phenomenon which can be expressed in no other way. By this definition any statement about God is a myth, for humans can discuss God only by using certain symbols. To say that God hears and sees and talks is to apply symbolic language to the reality we call God.

Myth in its literary sense occurs rarely in the Bible, which does not explicitly speak of other gods in conflict with God. But it is difficult to ignore references to such antagonists as the sea, Leviathan, Rahab, and even the Egyptian pharaoh. These characters are only a few of those who would overthrow God or who think they can avoid being overthrown by God. On the other side, "sons of God" extol him and gather round him in court, while seraphim sing doxologies around his throne. The Bible, in other words, does recognize other divine beings and powers beside the One who insists on exclusive worship.

1

If the second definition of myth is adopted, then, the entire Bible is myth, for from beginning to end God is the actor who is thoroughly involved in the lives of individuals, tribes, and nations. These actions of God can be conveyed only by human words—symbolic expressions which describe the indescribable.

Myth, then, is no falsehood, but can be understood as a vehicle which communicates truth. J.R.R. Tolkien once responded to C.S. Lewis's claim that myths are lies by saying, "You call a tree a tree, . . . and you think nothing more of the word. But it was not a 'tree' until someone gave it that name. You call a star a star, and say it is just a ball of matter moving on a mathematical course. But that is merely how *you* see it. By so naming things and describing them you are only inventing your own terms about them. And just as speech is invention about objects and ideas, so myth is invention about truth."[1]

Since "myth" can be quite specific or extremely general, perhaps it is more pertinent in a study such as this to deal with "mythology." The "ology" suffix seems to drive the issue beyond a literary category or a means of expression to a more basic issue: a system of comprehension. Mythology refers to a system of comprehending the universe in terms of structural correspondences.[2] In other words, mythology is a means of interpreting life by observing and explaining correspondences between earthly and heavenly realities. These correspondences might be *temporal* in the sense that the time of creation and some contemporary phase of world order are alike. They might be *spatial*, implying that earthly locales and structures are counterparts of heavenly sites. Or finally, the correspondence might be *personal*: the appearance of a human being, usually a king, is like the appearance of a god.

Whether the correspondence be temporal, spatial, or personal, mythology is the process of viewing individual and local phenomena as momentary peeks into eternity. Thus the goal of mythology is to relate the immediate phenomenon to some cosmic and eternal scene. Such a process enables a community to understand the eternal and unchanging order of the universe in such a way that all of life's phenomena are reflections of what always has been and will be. Mythology thus arrests the flight of time and its accompanying fears and anxieties in order to establish the security of order and predictability.

While many biblical passages attest to an awareness of the various correspondences described above, most of the Bible is concerned to show that God's actions are seen primarily in the changes and instability which comprise history. Far from establishing a sense of security in the timeless patterns of nature, the biblical witnesses attest to a God who is never satisfied with the status quo, who constantly changes situations in order to achieve desired goals for humankind. Thus reality itself is understood in the Bible not as an eternal mythological state, but as a dynamic movement by a God who does not himself correspond to any natural phenomenon.

This process of perceiving reality differently—even while employing traditional mythological characters and terms—has sometimes been labelled "demythologization" or "the historicization of myth." In this volume *demythologize* refers to the process of removing correspondences, that is, stripping away the notion that the earth's natural and observable phenomena are reflections of heavenly realities and actions. For example, in Canaanite mythology the god Baal is so intimately experienced in the storm that somehow he and the storm are one: the storm is the earthly reality which corresponds to Baal's escapades in heaven. Against this notion, Yahweh's actions in the Hebrew Bible are not earthly reflections of heavenly realities; rather the earthly experience is itself the reality even when the phenomena of storm are used to indicate his presence (a theophany). Yahweh lives in heaven, but his earthly presence is experienced only when he "comes down" in some way to meet people's needs or to confront those who oppose his will. The actions of Yahweh are essentially earthbound, and so the correspondence is removed. Thus Yahweh himself has been demythologized. (It should be noted here that while the term *demythologize* is usually understood to originate with the work of Rudolf Bultmann, his concern was a different one: to reinterpret the biblical message, encased as it is in a three-storied universe, in such a way that the gospel might be proclaimed to people of a different time and culture.)

As for *historicization of myth*, the terminology is usually applied broadly to the process of using mythological images to describe the acts of Yahweh in the historical life of Israel.[3] It seems, however, that the term should more precisely be employed to describe the application of a particular myth to a given event in history which is similar. That a story about the gods is transmitted in the Hebrew Bible indicates that the historical event serves the function for Israel which the heavenly story served for her neighbors. Such a process occurs, for example, when the prophet Isaiah applies the ancient myth about the invincibility of the sacred mount to the historical siege of Jerusalem by the Assyrian army (Isa. 31:1–9).

More common by far, however, is what I prefer to call "the mythicization of history"—the process by which historical events in the life of Israel are given cosmic or universal dimensions by the use of various mythological allusions. For example, the exodus from Egypt is described using imagery drawn from many traditional stories. In this way, the victory over Pharaoh is given dimensions which extend far beyond those of a local skirmish at a marshy sea.

The difference between these two processes is a subtle one. Essentially the difference is a matter of the starting point: does the author begin with a particular myth and apply it to a similar event in history, or does he begin with an event and mythicize it in order to provide a broader meaning? The former approach justifies the term *historicization of myth*, while the latter is a *mythicization of history*.

The distinction is important for two reasons. First, that there is more than one way to discuss the relationship between myth and history in the Bible indicates that general principles of interpretation do not suffice. Each scriptural passage containing mythological allusions needs to be examined carefully if we are to understand the intention of the author. Above all, however, the presence of these two approaches balances the relative priorities of myth and history: mythology must be historicized lest theology degenerate into the ceaseless rhythms of the universe, but history must be mythicized lest it become devoid of meaning.

The second value in distinguishing between the two processes relates to the question of Israel's uniqueness among her neighbors. The relationship of ancient Israel to her environment can no longer be explained by stating that while the rest of the ancient Near East expressed its faith in terms of myth, Israel based her confession on history. Such a separation of myth and history is too simplistic to be helpful. Indeed, while expressing reality in terms of mythological correspondences, the neighbors of ancient Israel were by no means disinterested in history. Numerous studies, particularly those of Ephraim Speiser and Hartmut Gese,[4] demonstrate that history was an important matter to the ancients, particularly to those who inhabited Mesopotamia over the millenia. For the ancient Sumerians history was essentially a matter of sequence of events, a series of certain kinds of time which repeated itself. For the later Babylonians who lived in the same territory history was a matter of consequence: acts of human obedience or disobedience automatically led to a king's (and his people's) weal or woe. For Israel, on the other hand, history, still far removed from our own concept of cause and effect, was based on the constant movement of the Word of God between promise and fulfillment: that Yahweh accomplished what he had promised or threatened is the quality that distinguished him from idols (see Isa. 44:6–8).

What do these different views of history say to the two processes of relating myth and history in the Hebrew Bible? While Israel based her understanding of reality on God's acts in history, she was by no means disinterested in mythology. Further, other ancient folk living around Israel were not disinterested in history, even though they understood it differently from Israel. Consequently, it was not only ancient Israel but also her neighbors who struggled with the relationship between myth and history. Their various attempts to deal with this tension throw more light on the question of Israel's uniqueness than does a simplistic analysis which identifies Israel with history and outsiders with myth. The following chapters suggest that ancient Egyptians "historicized the myth" of Re and Apophis and that ancient Babylonians "mythicized the history" of Hammurabi's dynasty.

The question of Israel's uniqueness ultimately leads to a consideration of ritual. While this book does not concentrate on comparative rituals in the ancient Near East, one can hardly discuss mythology without paying some attention to ritual. If mythology is the system of understanding the universe in terms of structural correspondences—temporal, spatial, and personal—then ritual is the dramatic activity carried out systematically by the cultic community in order to ensure the continuation of the cosmic order and to guarantee the community's participation in that order. A word of caution is necessary here: the actions of ritual relate to the desired reality not as the effective means but as correspondence. The human does not control the gods in ritual; rather the human participates in the eternal order of things in such a way that the community might be confident of life's continuation. Thus, just as the heavenly and earthly correspond in terms of natural phenomena, so do they also correspond in ritual. (See figure 1, page 6.)

In such a mythological understanding of ritual, the tension between myth and history relaxes in time with the result that history disappears in order to ensure the stability of the myth. In Israel the resolution of this tension moves essentially in the opposite direction: myth tends to take a back seat to history. The result is that Israel's confessing cultic community identifies itself with—corresponds to—

not a heavenly action but a community of earlier days which experienced the saving actions of Yahweh (Exod. 13:8), and a community of the future which will experience the fulfillment of Yahweh's goals. (See figure 2, below.)

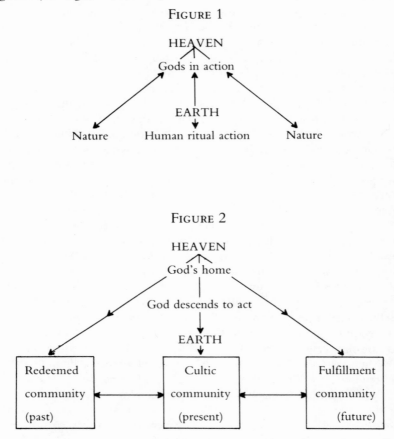

FIGURE 1

HEAVEN

Gods in action

EARTH

Nature   Human ritual action   Nature

FIGURE 2

HEAVEN

God's home

God descends to act

EARTH

| Redeemed community (past) | Cultic community (present) | Fulfillment community (future) |

While we are not at all disinterested in that evolutionary process whereby each culture undergoes common development and thus experiences similar phenomena at certain stages, the purpose of this book is to demonstrate intentionality by the biblical writers in using mythological features from their surrounding culture and thus to make a particular impact on their hearers/readers.[5]

Such a claim for intentional allusion implies, of course, some awareness by the biblical writers of the stories recited by their neighbors. One might select three groups in particular with whom Israel had such contacts as would make her aware of their respective cultures and accompanying expressions of religion: Canaan, Egypt, and Babylon.

The Canaanites, of course, are the people who inhabited the same territory as did Israel from the very beginnings of Israel until about the sixth century B.C.E. The Book of Joshua would have us believe that Joshua's onslaught on the land of Canaan enabled the Israelites totally to dispossess the former inhabitants. Other evidence, however, reveals much more prolonged contact between Canaanites and Israelites. First, the Book of Judges begins with a different account of the land theme, whereby individual tribes and clans carried out both successful and unsuccessful campaigns against the Canaanite inhabitants. While some cities were taken over by groups who later became Israel, in other locations clans and tribes lived side by side with the earlier Canaanite dwellers. Second, even the selection of Jerusalem as David's capital city did not, it seems, necessitate the expulsion of the Jebusites from their homes. Indeed, there is much evidence to suggest that Jebusite traditions played an important role in Davidic royal ideology and perhaps in Jerusalem theology as well. Third, the mission of the prophet Elijah and later of Hosea and Jeremiah attest to the inability of Israelites to choose between Yahweh worship and the Baal worship practiced by Canaanites. Religiously speaking, the people of Israel were constantly attracted to the fertility emphasis of their next-door neighbors and thus became familiar with Canaan's deities, symbols, stories, poetic style, and literary devices. The discovery of the Ugaritic texts in 1929 demonstrated the close ties between the written expression of the two peoples, as well as the accuracy of the Hebrews' knowledge of Canaanite religion.

As for Egypt, it is insufficient to cite the slavery period under Ramses II as the primary source of Israelite knowledge of things Egyptian. Perhaps one needs to begin with the Hyksos invasion of Egypt toward the end of the eighteenth century B.C.E. These Semitic invaders who controlled Egypt for almost two centuries were responsible, it seems, for a great deal of cross fertilization. During this period (1730–1550 B.C.E.) many Semitic gods and goddesses were Egyptianized. Even in texts from a later period the divine names Seth and Baal seem to be interchangeable. Further, during the fifteenth century, Pharaoh Thutmosis III followed his victory at Megiddo with the practice of controlling Syria-Palestine in a benign way. This magnanimity included his permission for the defeated

Syrian princes to rule their former cities, albeit under the nose of Egyptian garrisons. The presence of these soldiers in the land accounts for the discovery there of many artifacts of Egyptian origin and design. Furthermore, one of the features of Thutmosis's strategy was to educate in Egypt the Semitic heirs to the thrones; this practice seems to have made many such future princes extremely loyal to the Egyptian masters. Obviously along with the loyalty came an intimate knowledge of Egyptian life, institutions, art, and religion which must surely have spread beyond the prince himself. One need only look at *The Ancient Near East in Pictures*,[6] pages 160 ff., to see Egyptian symbols on the statues and reliefs of Canaanite deities. The relationships between Egypt and Syria-Palestine during the early fourteenth century B.C.E. are well attested by the Amarna correspondence, letters from the Semitic princes to Pharaohs Amenophis III and Amenophis IV (better known as Akhenaton).

The broad cultural influence of Egypt on the territory of Canaan diminished with the weakening of the Egyptian Empire during the twelfth and eleventh centuries B.C.E., but there are some arguments to suggest that the Davidic-Solomonic court was modeled on the basis of Egyptian patterns. Furthermore, in the tenth century B.C.E. the marriage of the pharaoh's daughter to King Solomon himself and her residency in Jerusalem surely provided some cultural ties. Alliances were made (or attempted) between Egypt and Judah during the reign of Hezekiah at the end of the eighth century B.C.E., and some Jerusalemites fled to Egypt to escape capture by the Babylonians at the beginning of the, sixth century B.C.E. Thus in one direction or the other the ties between the land which Israel came to occupy and the empire of Egypt continued for over a millennium.

The influence of Babylon on the ancient Near East cannot be overstated. From the eighteenth century to the sixth, Babylonian was the official language of the whole area. Even the Amarna letters written from Syria to Egypt are composed in Babylonian. Such a reality implies a widespread cultural impact. The Babylonian Empire of the second millennium cast its cultural and political spell on the Syrian-Palestinian area, and the Neo-Babylonian Empire from the end of the seventh century and continuing until 538 B.C.E. had the entire area indebted. Of importance for biblical studies was the practice of the empire to transport peoples of conquered lands to the homeland. The exile of Jerusalemites from 597 and 587 B.C.E. to Babylon presented, as is well known, one of the most powerful of all challenges to the development of Israel's theology.

Thus Canaan, Egypt, and Babylon are chosen here for the study of mythological allusions and their impact on Israel's religious expression. One can by no means prove that every reference to a mythological image was intentional, but it is the hope of the present writer to demonstrate that the use of mythological allusion was essentially a deliberate process and not simply part of Israel's cultural evolution. The purpose of this intentionality was to make a particular impact on the hearer/reader so that the theme was communicated with particular clarity and emphasis.

The writers of the New Testament lived on the same territory as many of the authors of the Hebrew Bible. Yet by the time of the first century C.E. that Semitic world had become a Graeco-Roman world. The written language of the educated was no longer Babylonian or Aramaic, which became "official" during the Persian Empire, but Greek. Even the Hebrew Scriptures were translated into Greek during the third century B.C.E. Nevertheless, the Jewish people in their own homeland maintained their religious heritage as much as possible. It was out of that faithful group that Christianity emerged.

The New Testament record of Jesus' entire ministry and its significance are described—as one would expect—in culturally laden words and images. Part of the culture which made itself felt in this way was related to those Greek and Roman powers which had controlled the area from the latter part of the fourth century B.C.E. Yet it can never be forgotten that a large segment of the impact vocabulary was derived by New Testament writers from the Scriptures of ancient Israel.

Those traditions of old played a key role in describing the person and work of Jesus. If one intends to communicate that Jesus is God Incarnate or God's Son, then the communicator will of necessity use language familiar to his/her audience. Interestingly, New Testament writers only rarely used the word *God* for Jesus, and even then the usage occurs in passages which are burdened with textual difficulties. Yet the New Testament abounds in titles, images, terms, and stories which describe Yahweh in the Hebrew Bible or in the Septuagint, but which are transferred to Jesus. The impact of the words and images assures continuity between the testaments, while the transformation of the old, familiar images indicates that a new reality has occurred in the birth, ministry, death, and resurrection of Jesus.

Among the many traditions transmitted from the older testament to the younger are those themes from ancient Near Eastern mythology which had already been transformed by Israel's theology. That these terms appear in the New Testament does not imply that the authors had access to the Babylonian, Egyptian, or Canaanite texts. Rather their knowledge was based upon their familiarity with Israel's Scriptures.

The process of transformation in the Hebrew Bible and of retransformation in the New Testament is illustrated in the following pages by the study of three themes. The first is the oft-treated and well-known myth regarding the conflict of the god of order and the chaos of the sea. The second theme seems to develop quite naturally from the first: the rhythm of fertility and sterility in terms of divine and human sexuality. If the first theme represents the temporal correspondence between creation time and the present stage of the natural cycle, the second is related to the personal correspondence of divine and human. The third mythological correspondence, the spatial one, is illustrated by the theme of the sacred mount.

Part One
ORDER VERSUS CHAOS

1
The Cyclical Conflict

MESOPOTAMIA: THE MYTHICIZATION
OF HISTORY

"The land between the two rivers" had a long and complicated history in which various modifications were made from time to time in the religious and political structures. Yet the basic system was an assembly of the gods which ruled over the whole universe and thus over a cosmic state.

The organization of this council in the third millennium B.C.E., essentially the Sumerian period, included three major deities: Anu, Enlil, and Earth. Anu was the sky, and yet in another sense the sky was Anu's home. As sky, Anu revealed power in a peaceful way, and so he was understood as the kindly father of the gods whose authority effected order in the heavens and on the earth. Enlil, second in importance and power, was the god of the storm. In one sense, Enlil was encountered by the worshiper as storm. Yet he was not confined to a particular storm, and so he was the god who caused storms. As such, Enlil was a fearsome deity often called *quradu*, the Warrior. Within the assembly of the gods Enlil's function was to enforce the authority of Anu whenever his will and authority were met with opposition. Enlil's firstborn son, Ningirsu, was a chip off the old block. He was the power in thunderstorms and in the annual flood when the Tigris river overflowed its banks with muddy waters of rain-fed mountain tributaries.

Earth, known most intimately by humans, was experienced in terms of the deities who produced crops and livestock. On the female side was Nintu, the lady who gives life or birth. She was the Mother Earth who caused the ground to become fertile and who increased flocks and herds. On the male side was Enki, lord of the earth (or the earth itself) who was responsible for the supervision of the life-giving waters in rivers, canals, wells, and for the irrigation of the fields. In the divine assembly it was he who excelled in wisdom and who served as arbiter in disputes. These are only a few of the deities who comprised the divine assembly in Mesopotamia, as we know it from the third millennium B.C.E. sources.

This divine organization corresponded to the political structure of ancient Sumer in southern Mesopotamia. No one in this structure had absolute authority. The council met to decide what should be done in this or that situation, and—if need be—to appoint an ad hoc leader to meet an emergency. As with the gods, so it was with the rulers of the city-states of the land. But in the early part of the second millennium B.C.E., the political situation changed, and with it the organization of the deities took a different form as well.

There emerged in the middle of the eighteenth century B.C.E. an Amorite king named Hammurabi. In the thirtieth year of his reign Hammurabi won a decisive victory over King Rim-Sin of Larsa, and thus brought under his control all of what had formerly been ancient Sumer. Having so reunited the land under Babylonian control, Hammurabi elevated his god Marduk to the position of head of the divine assembly.

The Prologue to the Code of Hammurabi (*ANET*, pp. 164ff.), discovered in the year 1902 at the Persian city of Susa (more than two hundred miles east of Babylon), tells that Hammurabi was named by Anu and Enlil themselves as ruler over all the land. This appointment corresponded to the time when those same deities had given to Marduk "the Enlil functions over all mankind" and had made Babylon "supreme in the world." Thus in 1698 B.C.E., Marduk took over the role of the storm god Enlil, the Warrior who was worshiped particularly in the temple of Ekur at Nippur (central Babylonia). It was, therefore, by historical and political event that Marduk became the national deity and new leader in the pantheon. Further, this event established Hammurabi—and presumably Marduk as well—in "an enduring kingship, whose foundations are as firm as heaven and earth." Thus the former political and divine arrangement whereby leaders were chosen ad hoc had given way to an established permanent dynasty.

The mythological explanation of Marduk's ascendancy portrays the matter somewhat differently. The relevant text is one of the most important mythological texts from the ancient Near East. Called the *Enuma elish* ("When on high") on the basis of the first two words, the long story pushes Marduk's supremacy back to the creation of the world, to the time when order first won over chaos. That was the truly important time, the *illo tempore*, as Mircea Eliade and others call it, when the structures of the universe were established.

The story begins when nothing at all existed except a watery chaos made up of Apsu, the sweet waters, Tiamat, the sea, and Mummu, apparently clouds and mist. The scene seems to be located at that point in the Persian Gulf where the sweet waters of the Tigris and Euphrates meet the salt waters of the sea. Out of all this commingling of waters were begotten two gods named Lahmu and Lahamu, who represent the silt deposited by the two rivers at their mouths, making Mesopotamia an expanding alluvial land. The "silt deities" engendered Anshar and Kishar, aspects of the horizon, and they in turn gave birth to Anu, the sky. Anu became the father of Nudimmud, otherwise known as Enki, lord of the earth.

As the gods continued their fertile ways, conflicts developed among the generations, particularly between the young active gods and the older generation. Indeed, the generation gap became wider when the youthful deities held a dance. Such frivolity was too much for old Apsu, and so to his wife Tiamat he expressed his sorrow at having engendered such noisy children and vowed to destroy them. Naturally, when the gods learned of his plan, they panicked—all except the wise one Enki, now called Ea. By reciting a magic formula he cast a spell over Apsu, making the old patriarch fall asleep. Then Ea killed him and established part of the world as it is: Apsu, the sweet waters, sank down, and over Apsu Ea established his abode, the earth. According to Thorkild Jacobsen, this first great victory of the gods over chaos "was won through authority and not through physical force. The myth moves on a primitive level of social organization where dangers to the community are met by the separate action of one or more powerful individuals, not by cooperation of the community as a whole."[7]

Ea engendered Marduk in that new home over the Apsu, and by the time the young hero grew up, Tiamat's allies had persuaded her to avenge the murder of her husband. Again the gods were in an uproar at hearing of the impending disaster, and the several attempts to negotiate by means of emissaries ended in failure. The crisis was immediate, and so an ad hoc warrior was necessary. The leader of the gods, Anshar, proposed to the divine council that the mighty and youthful Marduk lead them against Tiamat with her newly made "monster serpents and fierce dragons." Marduk accepted, but with one condition: that the gods reconvene and grant him authority like that of the leaders of the council.

Endowed with supreme authority and acclaimed as king by the gods, Marduk armed himself with all the weapons of a storm god. Like the former warrior Enlil, Marduk carried bow and arrows, mace, a net, four winds, and seven storms including the *imhullu*, the disease-carrying Evil Wind. He mounted his war chariot and rode off to meet the forces of chaos. Seeing Marduk in all his splendor, Tiamat's warriors were thrown into panic. Only Tiamat herself remained to face the mighty Marduk. After an unpleasant verbal exchange

> They strove in single combat, locked in battle.
> The lord spread out his net to enfold her,
> The Evil Wind, which followed behind, he let loose in her face.
> When Tiamat opened her mouth to consume him,
> He drove in the Evil Wind that she close not her lips.
> As the fierce winds charged her belly,
> Her body was distended and her mouth was wide open.
> He released the arrow, it tore her belly,
> It cut through her insides, splitting the heart.
> Having thus subdued her, he extinguished her life.

> *(ANET, p. 67)*

As the gory action moves on, Marduk crushed Tiamat's skull with his mace and cut her arteries so that the North Wind could carry off her blood to parts unknown. On that happy note Marduk used her corpse for construction work.

> He split her like a shellfish into two parts:
> Half of her he set up and ceiled it as sky,
> Pulled down the bar and posted guards.
> He bade them to allow not her waters to escape.

> *(ANET, p. 67)*

Just as his father Ea had begun the creation of the universe with the establishing of the Apsu, the waters under the earth, and of the earth itself, so son Marduk finished the job by establishing the heavens. Then the victor set up the heavenly constellations and assigned appropriate functions. He next made human beings to do the chores, so that the gods "might be at ease." Finally, he appointed various responsibilities to the gods for the administration of the heavens and the earth. Thus did Marduk found a system for governing his newly acquired kingdom. At seeing all these benefits of his reign, the gods built for Marduk a shrine called Esagila which corresponded to his heavenly home, Esharra. There the Warrior held a banquet for the gods and received their praises in the form of fifty throne names.

In the course of the *Enuma elish*, the political system of the gods developed from an original state of personal initiative to the call of an ad hoc leader by the divine council and finally to a permanent monarchy with far-reaching benefits. Thus, while starting with precreation events rather than the history of the eighteenth century B.C.E., the *Enuma elish* comes to the same point as the Prologue to Hammurabi's Code: Marduk's permanent authority corresponds to that of the enduring dynasty begun by Hammurabi, King of Babylon. At the same time Marduk's kingdom is universal in scope on the basis of his victory over Tiamat, and so by correspondence Hammurabi's dynasty would have been considered in cosmic terms as well.

The battle between Marduk and Tiamat seems originally to have been related to the spring floods caused by the waters from the mountains of northern Armenia. Annually the spring waters of the two rivers flood the plains with the result that the land resembles the primeval watery chaos. When the winds dry up the water, there are left behind rich alluvial deposits. Thus with the proper and orderly control of the rivers, agriculture can thrive, and the community with it. Perhaps the act of Marduk of bidding the guards "to allow not her waters to escape" is related to this desired control.

If such a natural explanation lay behind the present story about the historical and political elevation of Marduk, then it seems likely that in the original version the hero who vanquished the chaotic waters must have been the deity whose functions were given to Marduk. That deity was Enlil, the *quradu* par excellence. Enlil is curiously absent from most of the story, even omitted in the early genealogies. Replaced by a new god of storm, Marduk, Enlil appears only toward the end of the story, where he raises his bow before the gods and lays it down in front of them. This gesture might be an indication that Enlil, fighting on the side of Tiamat, laid down his arms in surrender and submission to the new warrior.

Such a possibility throws us back again into the realm of history. Jacobsen raises the question about the use of Tiamat as Marduk's main antagonist. It is rivers which threaten life in Mesopotamia. The sea (Tiamat), the Persian Gulf to the south, would have played little role in the experience of the average Mesopotamian. Shortly after

Hammurabi's death (ca. 1750 B.C.E.) and continuing for more than two hundred years, the major antagonist of Marduk and Babylon was the "land of Tiamat," that is, the Sealand to the south which comprised the territory of ancient Sumer. That land was eventually defeated by the Babylonian King Ulumburiash, who in 1450 B.C.E. reunited the southern and northern parts of Babylonia.

Whether all the details of this interpretation hold up under the scrutiny of further research, one thing seems clear: *Enuma elish* had a long and complicated development which seems to have included elements of the natural cycle alongside events from the historical and political dynamics of the second millennium B.C.E. Enlil was replaced by Marduk, and as the complicated development continued for another millennium, Marduk gave way to Ashur in northern Mesopotamia. This new hero emerged during the eighth and seventh centuries B.C.E., when the Assyrians universalized their empire by the use of the same story. One cannot ignore the historical and political dimensions of this original nature myth in the development of the *Enuma elish*.

However, it is not so clear that the myth-history combination continued in tension as the years went by. We know from texts of the first millennium B.C.E. that the *Enuma elish* was part and parcel of the Babylonian New Year festival called the *akitu*. That festival was known in the cities of Ur and Nippur, and possibly elsewhere, as far back as the third millennium B.C.E. At what point the *Enuma elish* was incorporated into the *akitu* is not possible to determine at present. Yet in the first millennium B.C.E. the story was recited in its entirety on the fourth day of the festival held at the time of the spring equinox. Excavations at Babylon itself have led to the conclusion that the *akitu* included a certain procession in which the king led Marduk, that is, his statue, from his shrine, moved along the Way to the *akitu* house, being transferred at some point to a ceremonial barge.

Many scholars feel that in the *akitu* house the story of the *Enuma elish* was acted out in ritual and that the entire cult drama of Marduk's battle with the chaos monster was intended to recreate the cosmos annually, to repeat the action of *illo tempore* in such a way as to ensure the continuation of life for another year. In other words, New Year's Day was Creation Day all over again. Since what happened in one realm corresponded to activities and results in the other, then the proper victor in the ritual combat assured the desired outcome of the conflict between chaos and order in the heavenly realm. This result would further correspond to the phenomena of earthly nature on which life depended. By this victory, ritual and celestial Marduk was enthroned annually as the king of Babylon and of the universe. The ritual acclamation *Marduk šarru*, "Marduk is king," corresponded to that of the divine assembly in *illo tempore*.

We saw earlier that the development of the myth consisted of a combination of natural and historical influences. Now it should be acknowledged that the tension between mythology and history dissolved in time as the story took on exclusively mythological significance in the ritual of Babylon.

CANAAN: MYTH AS SEASONAL CYCLE

Among the major traditions discovered at the ancient city of Ugarit, located on the Mediterranean coast in Syria, is the so-called Baal-Anath cycle. Baal is the god of the storm, the position Marduk inherited from Enlil in Mesopotamia. He is also the god of fertility, an aspect of Baal to which we shall return. Anath is Baal's sister, a vicious warrior like her brother, and also a fertility deity of some renown. Individually by turn the brother-sister duo faces a number of opponents, most prominent of whom is Yamm, the Sea (also known as Judge Nahar, the River).

The basic problem in the whole cycle centers around the right to own and live in a palace. El, head of the divine assembly and father of the gods, creator of creatures, old and wise, must be persuaded to give the orders for the construction of such palaces. For some reason the head of the pantheon instructed the master craftsman Kothat wa-Khasis to build a palace for Prince Yamm. Such a decision meant that Yamm assumed kingship over the other gods. At this news the god Ashtar was upset, but the sun goddess Shapsh warned him of El's wrath if he would not cease complaining.

Baal too, when learning of Yamm's fortune, cursed Yamm, but alas, Yamm was only beginning his show of authority over Baal. Prince Sea sent messengers into the assembly of the gods to demand that Baal be given over as slave. The scene is almost comical as it describes the arrival of Yamm's messengers at El's abode on the Mount of Lala. They were instructed not to bow down to the divine assembly but to state the case arrogantly. The messengers arrived as the gods were eating, and the dining divinities responded with fear and trembling at the sight of them. Baal was disgusted with the whole lot.

The gods do drop their heads
   Down upon their knees
   And on the thrones of their princeship.
Them doth Baal rebuke:
". . . I see the gods are cowed
   With the terror of the messengers of Yamm,
   Of the envoys of Judge Naha[r].
Lift up, O gods, your heads
   From upon your knees,
   From upon the thrones of your princeship,
And I'll answer the messengers of Yamm,
   The envoys of Judge Nahar."

                             (*ANET*, p. 130)

   The gods did lift up their heads, but when the messengers reported the message of "Yamm, your lord, Of your master Judge Nahar," then Bull El gave in immediately and answered, "Thy slave is Baal, O Yamm." Needless to say, Baal was annoyed, to the point of trying to smite the messengers. When the action picks up again after some broken lines, Kothar wa-Khasis, the craftsman, promised Baal victory over his enemy and provided the means by which to achieve it. He made two clubs named Yagrush (Chaser) and suggested that they be used to strike the back of Yamm. The opportunity arose immediately, but Yamm was too strong to be overcome. That sent the craftsman back to the drawing board. Returning with two more clubs named Ayamur (Driver?), he suggested that they be planted squarely on Yamm's head. This time Baal succeeded, for Yamm collapsed. Not content with a knockout, the storm god attempted to kill Yamm, but the goddess Ashtoreth "rebuked" Baal to prevent the fratricide. Nevertheless, Yamm was dying, and in his pain announced, "Baal will be king." Having attained supremacy over Yamm, Baal expected a palace from which to rule, but the necessary permission from El was denied for some time until finally Lady Asherah of the Sea persuaded the old leader otherwise.

   The story describes how Baal became the city god of Ugarit. However, it had nothing to do with history or politics. Basically the story represents a conflict between two opposing forces for the rule of the land. The struggle seems to have had its setting in late fall, during the early part of the rainy period in Canaan. At this time Yamm, the Mediterranean Sea, became so rough that the ancients feared to sail. With waves beating against the shore and threatening to flood the lower areas, Yamm was understood to be waging war as a chaotic power. Indeed, Yamm's other name, Nahar, probably re-

fers also to the chaos which results from violent rainstorms or melt-
ing snow turning riverbeds into destructive torrents. The combination Yamm/Nahar would seem to represent all water which
threatens rather than contributes to vegetation and human survival.
On the other hand, Baal, the god of the storm, was bringing the
rains which would result in the growth of vegetation, at least until
summer drought. The battle of the natural forces lasted for some
time, because Yamm was strong (he would not collapse easily). Finally, however, Baal won out, and so a palace for him was indeed
established. While there is no explicit evidence of a ritual related to
this myth, most scholars assume that the myth was celebrated at the
autumn New Year festival in Canaan.

In another text Baal is given credit for vanquishing an opponent
named Lotan, who seems to bear some relationship to Yamm. The
god of death and sterility, Mot, speaks to Baal

> "If thou smite Lotan, the serpent slant,
>   Destroy the serpent tortuous,
>   Shalyat (*šlyt*) of the seven heads, . . ."

> (*ANET*, p. 138)

The description of the opponent indicates one monster, not three, for
common in Ugaritic and biblical poetry is a synonymous parallelism
of three lines (cf. Ps. 29:3, 7–8; 93:3). Interestingly, the defeat of this
monster is claimed elsewhere by Baal's sister Anath. Curious about
the nature of the mission of Baal's messengers to her abode, she asks,

> "Crushed I not El's Belov'd Yamm?
>   Destroyed I not El's Flood Rabbim?
>   Did I not, pray, muzzle the Dragon?
> I did crush the crooked serpent,
>   Shalyat (*šlyt*) the seven-headed."

> (*ANET*, p. 137)

While the list goes on to include other foes vanquished by Anath, it
is not completely clear at this point whether in the last couplet Anath
is answering her own rhetorical question of the first three lines, or
whether there are several opponents listed here. In other words, it is
possible that Yamm, Flood Rabbim, and Dragon are names of the
same chaos deity who is further described as the crooked serpent
Shalyat/Lotan. The possibility would identify Yamm as a serpent,
and thus mean that Baal's opponent Lotan—in the first passage cited
above—might be one and the same as Yamm.

In any case, the victor against the raging Sea is Baal (or his sister), and as a result of that victory Baal is enthroned in his own palace as king. Like Marduk, god of the storm in the Babylonian story, Baal, the god of the storm in Ugarit, rises to the position of supremacy and rules from his temple. Unlike Marduk and the entire creation emphasis in Babylon, neither Baal nor anyone else in Ugarit is a universal creator. Even El, "creator of creatures," (*bny bnwt*), is more of a progenitor than a creator of the world.

EGYPT: THE HISTORICIZATION OF MYTH

In contrast to the Sea or River as a destructive force in Babylon and even more in Ugarit, the only significant body of water in Egypt is the bringer of life. Egypt has appropriately been called "the gift of the Nile," for that river's waters contribute the only significant amount of water for agriculture in the country. The Nile flooded annually in a more predictable and gentle way than the flooding experienced along the banks of the Tigris and Euphrates rivers. Moreover, the Nile's overflow laid down for centuries rich alluvial deposits which make the soil there appear black in contrast to the light sand a short distance from its banks. Thus the Nile was not a chaotic force to be feared but a gift of life worthy of joy and celebration. Likewise, the valiant hero for the Egyptians was not a rain-bringing storm god but the Nile itself and the Sun.

According to the Egyptian view of the cosmos, the Nile River and the sun emerged from the primordial waters of the netherworld called Nun. The Nile poured forth, they believed, from great caverns in the Deep. Wherever ancient divers could not find the bottom of the Nile—as at the point where Elephantine Island is located—they believed they had found the spot where river and deep converged. Now Nun, in addition to lying below the earth (Geb), encircled the flat world as well, and so when the sun rose and set, the solar disk was thought to have come out of and entered into Nun. During the night the sun journeyed through the netherworld in a boat, just as during the day the sun crossed the heavens by the same means of transport. In a mythological sense the sun needed to be reborn every morning on the eastern horizon, just as it emerged from the waters at the beginning of time, the *illo tempore*.

The rebirth of the sun god Re after the nocturnal journey was not automatic. Each night in the darkness Re encountered a serpent named Apophis who attempted to swallow him. Thus did Re, the life-giving one, battle with that force of chaotic darkness in serpentine form. A hymn to the sun god (now merged with the god Amon to form the powerful Amon-Re), dating from the fourteenth century B.C.E., succinctly presents some of these ideas.

> "The sole king, like the *fluid* of the gods,
> With many names, unknown in number,
> Rising in the eastern horizon,
> And going to rest in the western horizon;
> Who overthrows his enemies,
> (RE)BORN EARLY EVERY DAY. . . .
> Thy CREW IS IN JOY
> When they see the overthrow of the rebel,
> His body licked up by the knife."
>
> (*ANET*, p. 367)

In this hymn "the rebel" is not mentioned by name. However, in a text known as "The Repulsing of the Dragon and the Creation," a text which combines myth, ritual, and magical incantation, the dragon-demon is called by the name Apophis. The dragon is represented in history by the enemies of the pharaoh: "Re is triumphant over thee, Apophis—(to be repeated) FOUR TIMES. Pharaoh—life, prosperity, health!—is triumphant over his enemies—(to be repeated) four times" (*ANET*, p. 7). The text dates from the fourth century B.C.E., but it is generally believed to derive from a much earlier period, perhaps preserving language two thousand years older.

Just as this text relates Apophis to pharaoh's enemies, so it also relates Re to the pharaoh himself. Such a relationship is by no means surprising. From the very earliest times in Egyptian kingship, the pharaoh on the throne considered himself to be the sky god Horus, and further, when the king died, he became Horus' father, Osiris. (This relationship was based on an old myth concerning combat between Osiris and Seth, in which the young son Horus finally defeated the antagonist Seth.) By the time of the Fifth Dynasty in Egypt, the twenty-fifth century B.C.E., the pharaoh claimed to be the divine son of Re, the supreme deity. This development was due to the influence of the priests at Heliopolis where the sun god was central. Indeed, one of the five formal titles bestowed on the pharaoh at coronation time was "the Son of Re," and some of the basic images and terms which described the sun were used also of his son. For example, the word *khay* is written in hieroglyphics as the sun upon the primeval hill. The verb means "to shine forth" and so quite naturally was used to describe the sun's appearance at creation and at each rebirth, that is, at sunrise. The same word was used to describe the appearance of the pharaoh at official occasions. Thus, in mythological thinking, the appearance of the sun god and that of the pharaoh, his son, corresponded to each other in such a way that they were virtually the same act.

The divinity of the pharaoh is expressed even more explicitly in certain texts. In a thirteenth century B.C.E. document known as Papyrus Anastasi II, the city of Ramses in the delta is portrayed in glowing terms. In the midst of the city's description it is said of Ramses II, "Ramses Meri-Amon is in it as a god." Further, in the text, these words are put into the mouths of foreign kings as an expression of submission to Ramses: "The will of the god is come to pass" (*ANET*, p. 470). Finally, the conclusion of another text, Papyrus Anastasi III, speaks to Ramses: "O User-maat-Re Setep-en-Re . . . thou god!" (*ANET*, p. 471).

The relationship of this sun worship to the mortuary religion of Egypt becomes clear in a different version of "The Repulsing of the Dragon" (*ANET*, pp. 11–12). Here the god Seth, usually of evil disposition, does a good turn by repelling the abysmal beast so that the sun might cross the underworld and be reborn in the morning. In like manner, it is suggested, "man should survive to make the dead man an *akh,* an effective being."

In other words, to be reborn after death requires that one journey with the sun as he descends the western horizon and travels through the netherworld. Only thus can one join him on the eastern horizon and across the expanse of the sky. Various utterances from the third millennium B.C.E. pyramid texts and from later coffin texts speak of a Lake of Rushes or Field of Rushes through which one must pass with Re on the cosmic circuit. In one such utterance the deceased king speaks: "I have bathed with Re' in the Lake of Rushes." By a reference in still another utterance, it seems that Lake of Rushes and Field of Rushes are virtually the same: "Re' has bathed in the Field of Rushes." This bathwater in some cases seems to be located in heaven, and in other cases in the netherworld. It would seem, therefore, that the water to be crossed with the sun is somehow conceived as the primeval ocean above and beneath the earth, and the goal of the journey with the sun is the Isle of Flame where the sun rose at the creation and where it is reborn every day.

While Egyptian religion was basically mortuary in character, the role of the sun god did indeed have a place in the here and now. Since the pharaoh was the divine son, he was the one responsible for consulting the deity on matters of concern for the effective rule of

Egypt. He was, in other words, the only proper intermediary between humans and gods, and his was the responsibility for learning
the divine will and communicating it to his kingdom. As time went
on, specific means for learning the will of the gods were used,
among them dreams and visible miracles, or simply consultation
with the deity at an appropriate shrine during which an answer of
yes or no was sought from the statue of a god. Among the many
possibilities relevant to our concerns about battles and the role of the
god as warrior, we point to an incident which occurred just after the
death of Pharaoh–Queen Hatshepsut. An alliance of Palestinian-
Syrian princes under the leadership of the Prince of Kadesh on the
Orontes set themselves against the new pharaoh, Thutmosis III. Since
in some oracular form the god Amon–Re promised him victory, the
king rode confidently before his army carrying an image of the god.
Having achieved the promised victory, the pharaoh enhanced the
treasures of Amon–Re in the Karnak temple. Thus did the god play
an important role in the historical battle of the pharaoh, his son.

Finally, there is the distinct possibility that the myth of the sun
god Re battling against the dragon Apophis was used in order to
give a certain meaning to a historical event. From 1730 to 1550 B.C.E.
the land of Egypt was ruled by an Asiatic group called the Hyksos,
whose first king was named Apophis. In a Nineteenth Dynasty document, King Apophis, we are told, served only the god Seth among
all the gods of Egypt. (This is probably due to the equation of Baal
and Seth during this period.) In Egyptian mythology Seth, while oc-
casionally responsible for a good deed, was the storm god who engaged in perpetual battle with Horus, the god incarnate in the Egyptian pharaoh. The serpent Apophis joined Seth and the goddess
Sekhmet as the personalities primarily understood to be hostile forces
in Egyptian mythology. Therefore, one needs at least to raise the
possibility that the Egyptians themselves named the Hyksos ruler
Apophis. He would have represented that serpent of darkness and
chaos who would swallow up Re, the sun god, and thus prevent that
perpetual cycle which assured life for the king, for the people, and
for all the land. If, on the other hand, Apophis was indeed a proper
Hyksos name and not simply an invention by the Egyptians, it is not
difficult to imagine that the indigenous people of the Nile would
have made such a connection on the basis of the impact of their well-
known myth.

Thus, in Egypt as in Mesopotamia and Canaan, the life-giving god
did battle on a regular basis with a serpentine monster who threat-

ens the continuation of life and world order. However, because of the nature of the Nile River—in contrast to the Tigris and Euphrates rivers and to the wintry Mediterranean Sea—the conflict was not an annual or seasonal affair. In Egypt the conflict was nightly with the representative of darkness pitted against the life-giving sun. Yet that victory of Re was the basis of his kingship "over gods and men altogether."

The Egyptian deity and the myth pertaining to him were involved, like that of Mesopotamian mythology, with the rule of the country and with historical battles in which the pharaoh took part. This element was missing in the Canaanite mythological materials from Ugarit, although the legendary King Keret was sent out to battle by El. Finally, there exists the possibility that in Egypt as in Mesopotamia, myth and history were intertwined, for if the suggestion above concerning Apophis has any merit, then in Egypt the Re-Apophis myth was historicized in order to interpret the Hyksos domination of the land. Perhaps by so doing, the Egyptians held out hope for the expulsion of the Hyksos, for according to the cyclical nature of the myth, Re will appear on the horizon as victor and king over the universe.

2

Yahweh, Warrior
and King

The writers of the Hebrew Bible, as might be expected, employed the imagery of conflict between order and chaos that was prevalent in ancient Near Eastern culture. At first glance, it appears that the application of the conflict imagery from the surrounding cultures had a polemical purpose in the Hebrew Bible. If Marduk can defeat Tiamat, so the Deep (Hebrew *tehōm*) will groan at the appearance of Yahweh (Hab. 3:10). If Baal can subdue Yamm, so Yahweh in his indignation can trample the sea (Hebrew *yam*; Hab. 3:8, 15; Job 26:12–13; 9:7). If Marduk's opponent army consists of serpentine monsters and dragons, so also is Yahweh's opponent a serpent or dragon (Isa. 51:9; Ezek. 29:3–6; 32:2–8). If Baal (and Anath?) smites the coiled serpent Lotan, so Yahweh must face the same monster, called in Hebrew Leviathan (Isa. 27:1; Ps. 74:14; 104:25; Job 40:25–41:26). In other words, Yahweh fights and is victorious over the opponents of Marduk and Baal, and over one more villain not yet found in extra-biblical texts: Rahab (Isa. 30:7; 51:9–10; Job 26:12). Each such usage of the old common myths must be examined carefully in order to determine the particular impact which the "monsters" had in the faith of Israel.

CHAOS MONSTERS IN THE PREACHING
OF THE PROPHETS

First, the prophets of the Hebrew Bible used the conflict imagery to convey meaning about Yahweh's opposition to countries and kings of the earth who were hostile to his divine will and purpose. Isa. 30:7 provides an excellent example of how a historical nation was identified with a mythological adversary of Yahweh. The entire chapter contains several pieces which reflect historical events just af-

ter the death of the Assyrian king Sargon in 705 B.C.E. Having suffered under Assyrian domination for some years, Hezekiah, King of
Judah, and leaders of other nations began to talk of rebellion against
the oppressors. As part of this plan, Judean emissaries were on their
way to Egypt in order to ally themselves with and seek the protection of the pharaoh. For Isaiah this alliance was a "covenant with
death" (28:15, 18), made without consulting Yahweh, and so to describe the uselessness of such an arrangement, the prophet speaks:

> "And as for Egypt, (with) worthlessness and emptiness they help;
> therefore I have named her 'Rahab who is vanquished'."[8]

The mythological serpent, smitten by Yahweh, defines the country
on which Judah would place its confidence. Thus, myth and history
meet in the passage. The reality and context of the encounter is a
diplomatic incident which can be dated in time and place with a large
degree of probability. Thus the impact of the myth gives meaning to
the historical event in Israel's life.

Perhaps even more interesting is the combination of myth and history at Isa. 51:9–10. The historical context of the passage is the exile
of the Jerusalemites in Babylon. To those people the prophet known
as Second Isaiah proclaimed the imminent victory of Yahweh which
would result in deliverance and in the reign of God.

> Awake, awake, put on strength, Arm of Yahweh!
> Awake as in primordial days, generations of eternity.
> Was it not you who cut up Rahab, who pierced the dragon?
> Was it not you who dried up Yamm, the waters of great Tehom,
> Who made the depths of Yamm a way (for the) redeemed to pass
> over?

The passage makes clear by the synonomous parallelism in the third
line that Rahab and the dragon (*tannîn*) are one and the same. Moreover, in the fourth line Yamm and Tehom appear as parallels, thus
merging, it seems, the chaotic waters of the Canaanites and those of
the Mesopotamians. All of this mythological imagery is used to
demonstrate Yahweh's strength which occurred "in primordial
days." Like Baal and Marduk, Yahweh was victorious over chaos in
illo tempore. Here the myth remains and is quite explicit. The fifth
line, however, throws the mythical material into tension with history, for the reference to the crossing over of the redeemed can only
be to the Israelites who were brought out of Egypt. Cosmic victory
and historical deliverance are woven in such a way that Yahweh's
battle over the monsters would seem to have taken effect in history

when God accomplished the exodus. Now in the time of Second Isaiah, that same cosmic victory was about to be realized anew as an exodus from Babylon.

More personally, the dragon description is applied to the Pharaoh of Egypt in Ezek. 29:3. Ezekiel is commanded by Yahweh to prophesy against the king of Egypt these words:

> Thus said Adonai Yahweh:
> Behold, I am against you, Pharaoh king of Egypt,
>   the great dragon who couches in the midst of his rivers,
>   who said, "The river belongs to me, and I made it."

The relationship between the river, that is, the Nile, and the pharaoh, son of Re, is well attested to in Egyptian mythology. The Nile and the sun god both came forth from the great Deep, and both were bestowers of life on Egypt. Here, however, Ezekiel identifies the pharaoh and the dragon as one and the same. As dragon of chaos, the text goes on to say, Pharaoh will be destroyed by Yahweh for having failed to support the house of Israel when the people went to the land of the Nile for help. In this passage, then, the roles expected from Egyptian mythology are reversed: now Pharaoh, son of Re, is the representative of chaos rather than order. The judgment to come, the chapter continues, will occur in history when Yahweh gives the land of Egypt into the hands of the Babylonians.

The following three chapters in the Book of Ezekiel continue the prophecy of woe to befall Egypt. In a lament beginning at 32:2 the pharaoh is compared again to "the dragon in the seas" who will be caught in Yahweh's net (compare the netting of Tiamat by Marduk). The gory judgment which follows can be compared to that suffered by the chaos representative in the Babylonian myth. But in a switch to things perhaps more Egyptian, the passage ends by speaking of the darkness which will prevail over the land. It is indeed as if the sun had been swallowed up, and the pharaoh is to blame for the chaos which will befall the land. Yahweh, on the other hand, is the victor, avenging the failure of Egypt to help his people.

In these two texts from Ezekiel the Egyptian myth of Re and Apophis is both reversed and historicized. Pharaoh is responsible for Egypt's forthcoming chaos at the hand of Yahweh.

CHAOS MONSTERS IN THE PSALMS

In the Book of Psalms the mythological imagery is used somewhat more explicitly, although not as frequently as one might expect from such poetic and hymnic expression. When the imagery does appear, the myth seems primarily to serve as evidence of Yahweh's power to bring victory precisely when the people of God were experiencing disaster historically. In the community lament of Psalm 74, for example, the situation described in verses 1–11 points to the destruction of the temple on Mount Zion by the Babylonians in 586 B.C.E. The psalm itself might belong to a specific cultic act in which that disaster was remembered by the community between the time of the destruction and the rebuilding of the temple in 520 B.C.E. In any case, as is typical of such laments, the hymn states the reason why the community has confidence in Yahweh to help. Such motivation in this instance is the mythological victory over the serpents of chaos.

> But God is my king from primordial times,
>   accomplishing victory in the midst of the earth.
> As for you, you split Yamm with your power,
> You smashed the heads of Serpent (*tannîn*) over the waters.
> You crushed the heads of Leviathan;
>   you gave him as food to the sharks.[9]

(Ps. 74:12–14)

The reference here is clearly to the Ugaritic myth in which Baal/ Anath conquered Lotan (Leviathan), the seven-headed serpent related in some way to Yamm. That this victory of Yahweh established his kingship "in primordial days" makes the mythical background even more pronounced. The piece goes on to describe the results in the natural world of God's victory over the serpent, particularly the ensuing lordship over the cycles of day and night and of the seasons. On the basis of this universal reign and by his power manifested in the cosmic victory—the psalm confesses—Yahweh can be trusted to intervene in the historical situation of the sixth century B.C.E. and so to deliver the downtrodden people of Jerusalem.

Explicit use of the ancient mythology is evident also in Psalm 89. The psalm in its entirety consists of three parts: (1) a hymn to the covenant loyalty of Yahweh and to kingship; (2) a poetic form of the oracle given through Nathan regarding the Davidic dynasty; and (3) a lament over the collapse of the Davidic kingdom at the time of the exile. Scholars have debated for some time the interrelationship of these various parts, and while the debate continues it does seem that one need not date the entire psalm in the exilic or postexilic periods simply because the third and final section derives from that time. The first part, our primary concern here, might have been composed much earlier—perhaps even close to the reigns of David and Solomon.

The initial hymn deals first with the unconditional covenant which Yahweh made with David. The covenant is established "for ever" precisely because the continuation of the promise was not dependent on human faithfulness but on Yahweh's covenant loyalty (*ḥesed*). The hymn proceeds in verses 5–18 to relate the kingship of David to the reign of Yahweh. Like the previously mentioned divine assemblies in Mesopotamia and Canaan, the heavenly council in Israelite belief had one deity superior to the others.

> For who in the sky is comparable to Yahweh?
> (Who) is likened to Yahweh among the sons of gods (El)?
> A god venerated in the assembly of the holy ones,
>   great and aweful beyond those who surround him.
> Yahweh, God of hosts, who is strong like you, Yah,
>   and your faithfulness is round about you?
>
> (vv. 6–8)

Then appears the reason for Yahweh's supremacy in the divine council. In terms strongly reminiscent of the victories of Marduk and Baal, the hymn continues

> You rule over the raging of the Sea (Yamm);
>   when its waves rise up, you calm them.
> You have crushed Rahab like a carcass;
>   with the arm of your strength you have scattered your enemies.
>
> (vv. 9–10)

The hymn speaks immediately of the universal claim and acclaim Yahweh possesses on the basis of this victory over the chaotic serpent. Specific mention is made of Yahweh's "throne" as founded upon righteousness and justice, and the hymn concludes with the relationship of the divine reign to that given by Yahweh to Davidic kings.

> For to Yahweh belong our shields,
>   And to the Holy One of Israel our king.
>
> (v. 18)

Thus the first section of Psalm 89 uses the mythological theme of God's victory over chaos and the resulting supremacy in the divine council in order to provide a mythological/theological basis for the election of David and the Davidic covenant by which Yahweh promised an enduring dynasty. The tension between myth and history is here maintained, even though the content of Nathan's oracle tips the scales in favor of history (vv. 19–37). The two pieces are held together both by the references to the Davidic covenant (vv. 1–4 and 27–37) and by the use of mythological imagery (vv. 9–10 and 25). The latter connection is striking indeed. In the first part of the psalm, Yahweh is praised for his conquest of the sea; that authority over chaos is transferred in the second part to the anointed one who, as Davidic king, is the firstborn son of God.

> I will set his hand on the sea (Yamm)
> and his right hand on the rivers (Nahar).

On another level, by the addition of the destruction of the kingdom in the sixth century B.C.E., the mythological victory seems to have taken a peculiar twist. Here again myth and history are held in tension, but the effect of the myth is to illustrate a contrast between Yahweh's splendor of long ago and the apparent lack of such power in the present. Thus in the psalm as a whole the myth seems to have taken a back seat to the terrible reality of Israel's historical present. And yet such allusion to the incomparability of Yahweh in the older piece might have given hope to the people as they asked not "if" but "how long" the apparent absence of Yahweh would continue.

A final example of the use of the conflict imagery is the psalm in the third chapter of Habakkuk. This "prayer of Habakkuk" describes the march of Yahweh from Teman/Mount Paran (cf. Deut. 33:2) as a Divine Warrior armed for battle. Much like Marduk with his radiant glory, Yahweh was accompanied by pestilence and plague (*rešep*, the name of a Canaanite deity who functioned as a warrior). Such an approach made the land of Midian tremble. Then immediately the poem turns to the mythological imagery in verses 8–15. While the Hebrew text is quite obscure and almost impossible to read at some points, studies by W.F. Albright and others have enabled the modern interpreter to make some sense out of the poem. The mythological imagery speaks of Yahweh's anger with Yamm/Nahar, against whom the Lord led his cavalry of heavenly forces (v. 8). Nahar was split (v. 9) and the Deep (*tĕhōm*) groaned as Yahweh charged for the sake of his people (v. 13). Victoriously the Lord crushed the head of the enemy and pierced him with staffs (v. 14). The section ends with Yahweh's trampling of the sea (Yamm), also called "many waters" (*mayim rabbîm*, v. 15). The imagery is almost exclusively derived from the Canaanite conflict of Baal versus Yamm, but the purpose of the imagery here is to describe Yahweh's power as the reason for confidence on the part of the troubled worshiper who waits quietly for the day of Yahweh's wrath on his enemies. The myth is not explicitly historicized here. Rather, it serves the function that it does in Psalm 74: by attesting to the power of Yahweh, demonstrated in his cosmic victory over Yamm/Nahar, the individual and the community who ask "How long?" (1:2) can confidently await the removal of the anonymous oppressor. To put it in other terms, the hope of the psalmist is that the cosmic victory of Yahweh will occur in the realm of history. In this way the myth and the anticipated historical event are maintained in tension.

CHAOS MONSTERS IN THE BOOK OF JOB

The Book of Job contains several references to the mythological conflict. Whether they are incorporated in speeches of Job or of God, the "monster" passages attest to the unfathomable power of God over against the frailty of the human. In Job's opening speech to his friends, the sufferer damns the day he was born and the whole miserable life he had lately been experiencing. As though to highlight his own self-inflicted curse, Job invites others to join him.

> Let those who curse Yamm[10] curse it,
>   Those skilled in stirring up Leviathan.
>
> (3:8)

The precise meaning of the two poetic lines is difficult to determine, but it does seem that the use of magic and spells to curse an enemy was part of ancient warfare. Here it seems that Job is invoking a divine curser against chaos to join him in damning the day of his own birth.

Further, in response to a speech by Bildad, Job admits that to contend with God is futile indeed. God's power, Job says, is reflected in the creation of the universe and in the subsequent command over the heavenly bodies. Job describes the Almighty as one

> who stretched out the heavens by himself
>   and who trampled on the back of Yamm.
>
> (9:8)

Like a victorious warrior, indeed like Marduk over the body of Tiamat, God stood on the back of his vanquished foe, the mythological chaotic force: Sea. As Job continues in his speech, he admits further that it is not possible to stand up to a God who cannot be turned away even by the enemies of chaos.

> God will not bring back his anger;
>> under him the warriors of Rahab bowed down.
>>> (9:13)

Just as Tiamat's army of monster-serpents and dragons was rendered helpless at the appearance of Marduk, so Rahab's army collapsed when Yahweh approached for battle. In the face of such an overwhelming Divine Warrior, the man Job has little chance.

Later on in the discourses, Job again responds to Bildad who seems to have all the right answers. After some initial sarcasm Job points to the incomprehensibility of God's ways by resorting again to creation imagery. Describing the usual cosmogony of ancient times, Job alludes to the establishment of "north" (*ṣāpōn*) over the abysmal deep and to the earth hanging in midair and surrounded by waters. Then occurs the primordial conflict:

> The pillars of heaven kept trembling,
>> and they are panicked at his rebuke.
> By his strength he calmed Yamm,
>> and by his wisdom he smote Rahab.
> By his wind heavens are fair,[11]
>> (by) his hand he pierced the fleeting serpent.
>>> (26:11–13)

The passage is loaded with conflict imagery out of the mythological stories. Not only are Yamm and Rahab mentioned by name, but the description of the "fleeting serpent" in the final line is exactly that of the Ugaritic monster Lotan who was conquered by Baal and by Anath. All together, the description of God's victory, says Job, is only the beginning of God's power.

The final two references to the conflict myth occur in the speeches of Yahweh addressed to Job. In each case God puts Job in his place with a series of questions which demand the answer that only God can do this or that. The first occurs within a description of the creative activity of God.

> Who shut Yamm with doors,
>> when it gushed out from the womb;
> When I made cloud(s) as its clothing,
>> and darkness its swaddling band,
> (When) I set bounds for it,
>> and set barrier and doors,
> And I said, "Thus far you may come and no more,
>> and here shall the arrogance of your waters
>>> be halted."
>>>> (38:8–11)

While the relevant Ugaritic text is badly damaged and little can be learned of Yamm's fate after the decisive blow on the head, it is clear in the Babylonian myth that Marduk set a barrier and guards over Tiamat's waters so that they might not escape their limits.

The second passage describes in almost playful fashion the power of Yahweh over Leviathan. Not Job but only Yahweh can capture the monster, enslave him willingly, play with him, take him for a walk on a leash, and so on. The piece ends with God suggesting to Job

> Lay hands on him;
>   remember the battle;
>   you will not do it again.
>
> (40:25–41:8)

Throughout the Book of Job the references to the mythological conflict are consistently used. The myth here has nothing to do with history, and one should not expect such a connection in a wisdom book. Thus here there is no tension between myth and history. The myths stand on their own as evidence of the unfathomable power of God in contrast to human frailty and limitation.

SOME OTHER ALLUSIONS TO YAHWEH
AS DIVINE WARRIOR

Apart from the direct mention of the monsters, a number of passages in the poetic traditions of the Old Testament describe Yahweh as the Divine Warrior par excellence. Psalm 18, virtually identical to 2 Samuel 22, is a thanksgiving psalm sung to Yahweh by one who had been delivered from distress. The first section describes the situation of the petitioner as "the pits." Calling from the depths of Sheol to Yahweh in his temple, the petitioner experiences the coming of God to his rescue. Verses 7–15 describe in typical Near Eastern terms a theophany, an appearance of God in the phenomena of nature. The combat imagery appears particularly in verses 13–15.

> Yahweh thundered in the heavens,
>   and Elyon gave forth his thunder,
>   hailstones and coals of fire.
> And he sent forth his arrows and scattered them,
>   and lightnings he flashed, and routed them.
> And then were seen the channels of the waters,
>   and there were revealed the foundations of the world,
> at your rebuke, O Yahweh,
>   at the blast of the wind of your nostrils.

Yahweh has marched from heaven with all his power in order to battle the petitioner's enemy in the depths of Sheol. At the appearance
of this mighty God, the adversaries take to flight. Yahweh's rebuke
sends them into a panic, just as occurred when Yahweh encountered
the chaos monsters in Job 26:11–13 (see above). In this case, those
primordial monsters are not named, for the thrust of the passage is
that the enemies of the Divine Warrior are those who oppress the
faithful petitioner. According to the introduction to the psalm, the
enemies were all those, including Saul, who opposed and threatened
David. While it is possible on the basis of orthographic and other evidence to date the psalm from the time of David, it is likely that the
psalm was designed for any Davidic king under threat of enemy attack. The mythological imagery then is used somewhat more exis-
tentially than historically as a way of describing as a cosmic battle
Yahweh's deliverance of an anointed Davidic king.

Since not long after the discovery of the Ugaritic texts in 1929,
scholars have regarded Psalm 29 to be a Yahweh-ized Canaanite
hymn to Baal. The opening call to the divine assembly, "O sons of
El," to give glory to Yahweh is followed by a warlike description of
a storm god who through the usual phenomena of thunder and lightning (theophanic imagery) affects the whole creation. The general
description, as well as specific details, are remarkably similar to a
theophany of Baal in the Ugaritic texts. Finally, in the temple all (the
gods in the heavenly temple, human worshipers in the earthly one)
do ascribe him "glory." The psalm reaches its climax with the enthronement of Yahweh as king, and so some victory over chaos
must be presupposed.

> Yahweh sits enthroned on the primeval sea,
> Yahweh sits enthroned as king for ever.

> (v. 10)

The victorious homeward march of Yahweh, celebrated in true
ritual fashion, is seen most clearly in Psalm 24. The hymn begins
with the confession that the whole world belongs to Yahweh,

> because on the seas (pl. of Yamm) he founded it,
> and upon rivers (pl. of Nahar) he established it.

> (v. 2)

The announcement recalls the creative act of Marduk after vanquishing Tiamat, although the terms used seem more akin to the Canaanite myth. Nevertheless, apparently Yahweh has won the world and
created it, and so the worshipers begin their joyful ascent up the

slope of Mount Zion to the temple. As they move up the hill, the worshipers announce that only the pure of heart shall accompany this procession. Finally, they stand before the gates of the city and sing out,

> Lift up, O gates, your heads,
>   and be lifted up, O doors of eternity,
>   that the King of glory might enter.

This King is then identified as "Yahweh, the Warrior" and as "Yahweh Sabaoth."

Frank Cross points to the problem of the gates having "heads" and being "lifted up." Jerusalem's gates were not opened from above. Cross compares the statement of Baal in the divine assembly of El, issued when the messengers of El caused the deities to droop their heads.

> Lift up, O gods, your heads.

He concludes that the address is to all the gate towers of Jerusalem, personified as the council of divine elders who wait bowed and anxious for the return of the Divine Warrior and his army.[12]

When one combines the return of the Warrior here with such passages as Deut. 33:26–29; Judg. 5:1–5; and Psalm 18 (discussed above), the entire range of Yahweh's activity as a Warrior in myth and in history appears in the belief and cult of ancient Israel.

THE EXODUS EVENT AS YAHWEH'S
COSMIC VICTORY

The first fifteen chapters of the Book of Exodus describe a continuing conflict between Yahweh and the pharaoh of Egypt. On a superficial level the battle seems grossly unfair: a heavyweight against a flyweight, a Warrior with divine power against a mere human king. However, the pharaoh of Egypt was considered to be a god. He was both an incarnation of the god Horus and the son of the sun god Re. Therefore, the conflict in Exodus 1–15 was a battle between two gods: Yahweh, the God of the Hebrews, versus Pharaoh, the god of the Egyptians.

In a very real sense the exodus deliverance occurred as a result of the Passover slaughter of the firstborn of Egypt. This event, reported in Exod. 12:29–32, led to the freeing of the Hebrew slaves and their departure. In Exod. 13:17–21 it is clear that the people had already left Egypt and had entered the wilderness where the action picks up in 15:22 at the Reed Sea, possibly the Gulf of Aqabah (see Num. 33:5–10 and then 1 Kings 9:26). The intervening material at 14:10–15:21 contains a series of accounts about Yahweh's victory over the Egyptians at the sea, all of which seem to be anticlimactic after the Passover night but all of which interpret in mythological terms Yahweh's victory over the pharaoh.

The Song of the Sea: Exodus 15:1–18.

While the Song of Moses has been dated variously by scholars from the earliest periods of ancient Israel's history, it does seem that studies in orthography as well as of typology of language and content point to an early period, perhaps in the twelfth or eleventh centuries B.C.E. Apparently dependent on neither of the tetrateuchal sources combined in Exod. 14:10–31 (J and P) and separated in imagery from other sources, the Song of the Sea would seem to be the earliest of the major accounts. The first part of the psalm, verses 1–12, describes the defeat of the Egyptians at the hand of Yahweh, but no mention is made of the Israelites crossing the sea or of an exodus from Egypt. This section depicts a battle between Yahweh and Pharaoh in order, it seems, to answer the question we had encountered earlier in our discussion of Psalm 89:

> Who is like you among the gods, O Yahweh?
> Who is like you, glorious among the holy ones,
>   awe-ful in praise, maker of miracle?

(Exod. 15:11)

In Psalm 89 the question was answered by remembering Yahweh's victory over the chaos powers (Yamm and Rahab). Here in the Song of the Sea the question is answered by Yahweh's victory over the Pharaoh, a historical king of the nation Egypt. "Yahweh is the warrior" (v.3) who battles not the Sea but not merely a human foe either.

Although historically oriented, the poem contains some allusions to mythological imagery worthy of mention: (*a*) that which covers the Egyptian army are the *tĕhōmōt*, "the floods" (v. 5; cf. Tiamat); (*b*) the *tĕhōmōt* foamed in the heart of Yamm, and waters heaped up "at the wind of your nostrils" (v. 8; cf. Ps. 18:15); (*c*) the drowning of the Egyptians by Yahweh's "wind" recalls the wind which Marduk used to defeat Tiamat; (*d*) it is tempting to suggest (and nothing more) that the drowning of the Egyptian army in the Reed Sea (v. 4) has an interesting mythological twist. The *yam sûp*, the Sea of Reeds,

might be the same as "the Lake of Rushes" in Egyptian mythology;
that "lake" was part of the Way a deceased king would cross in the
company of the Sun god Re in order to reach the eastern horizon, the
Isle of Flame, and thus be reborn. The reader will recall the previously mentioned reference from the pyramid texts in which the deceased king claims he "bathed with Re in the Lake of Rushes" (see
above, p. 23). However, in this battle at the sea where the deeps
raged at the wind of Yahweh, the Egyptians did not bathe but drown
in the Lake of Rushes. While the poet who composed the Song of the
Sea could not have known that long-lost quotation written on the in-
terior of a millennium-old pyramid, it is at least possible that the reference reflects a common Egyptian tradition.

The historical use of the mythological images in Exod. 15:1–12 is
enhanced by the second part of the song (vv. 13–18) which by the
use of mythological terms describes the conquest of Canaan by Yahweh, the Warrior, and the subsequent enthronement of Yahweh in
his own sanctuary.

> May Yahweh be King forever and ever (v. 18).

The universal reign of Yahweh at the sanctuary would correspond to
that of Marduk on the basis of his victory over the Deep and to that
of Baal through his conquest of Yamm.

The Yahwist's Account of the
Sea Event (Exodus 14)

One of the primary purposes of the J writer of the Tetrateuch was
to demonstrate to his audience in the days of David and/or Solomon
how Israel had become such a great people. His explanation was that
the entire history up to this point had been a matter of Yahweh's
faithfulness in accomplishing the promises given to Abraham. Indeed, it seems, Yahweh acted without much human cooperation,
and even in spite of human actions, in order to achieve the desired
goals. The Yahwist's account of the sea event is entirely consistent
with that overall purpose. His version can with some degree of probability be separated from the work of the later priestly writer.

> *v. 10* . . . The people of Israel lifted up their eyes, and behold, the
> Egyptians were marching after them; and they were in great fear. *vv.*
> *13–14* And Moses said to the people, "Fear not, stand firm and see the
> salvation of the Lord, which he will work for you today; for the Egyp-
> tians whom you see today, you shall never see again. The Lord will
> fight for you, and you have only to be still."
> *vv. 19–20* . . . and the pillar of cloud moved from before them and

stood behind them, coming between the host of Egypt and the host of Israel. And there was the cloud and the darkness; and the night passed without one coming near the other all night.

v. 21 . . . and the Lord drove the sea back by a strong east wind all night, and made the sea dry land . . . *v. 24* And in the morning watch the Lord in the pillar of fire and of cloud looked down upon the host of the Egyptians, and discomfited the host of the Egyptians, *v. 25* clogging their chariot wheels so that they drove heavily; and the Egyptians said, "Let us flee from before Israel; for the Lord fights for them against the Egyptians."

v. 27 . . . and the sea returned to its wonted flow when the morning appeared; and the Egyptians fled into it, and the Lord routed (actually "shook off") the Egyptians in the midst of the sea.

vv. 30–31 Thus the Lord saved Israel that day from the hand of the Egyptians; and Israel saw the Egyptians dead upon the seashore. And Israel saw the great work which the Lord did against the Egyptians, and the people feared the Lord; and they believed in the Lord and in his servant Moses.

The historical context for the story is Israel's encounter with the Egyptian pharaoh (presumably Ramses II or possibly his successor Merneptah) sometime during the thirteenth century B.C.E. Thus, the adversaries in the conflict are defined: Yahweh (and Israel) versus Pharaoh and the Egyptians. The meaning of this conflict and of the victory of Yahweh is conveyed by several means, each of which seems intended to convey a particular impact.

First, the scene is described in terms which are virtually stereotypical of holy-war passages:

(*a*) "Fear not, stand still and watch the victory of Yahweh which he will accomplish for you today; . . . Yahweh will fight for you, and you need only to remain still" (vv. 13–14). These words are much like those in the instructions for war given in Deut. 20:1–4, words which are to be spoken by the priest to the people (cf. also Deut. 31:6–8 and more pointedly, 7:17–26; 2 Chron. 20:13–17). Indeed, after the distribution of the land to the twelve tribes, Joshua explained to the assembly of Israel that they had received the land because Yahweh had fought for them (Josh. 23:3, 10).

(*b*) "Yahweh . . . threw into a panic the army of the Egyptians . . . and the Egyptians said, 'Let us flee from before Israel, for Yahweh fights for them against the Egyptians'" (vv. 24–25). A Yahweh-imposed-destruction in the midst of an army's panic is attested also in such battles as that of Joshua against the Amorite kings who "fled" (*nûs*) before Israel (Josh. 10:6–11), of Barak against Sisera who also "fled" (Judg. 4:14–16), and is anticipated in the entire conquest of

the land at Deut. 7:17–26. Interestingly, in the mythologically described theophany of the Divine Warrior in Psalm 18, Yahweh
"routed" the anonymous oppressors of the king. In sum, for the
Yahwist's purposes the holy-war tradition out of the stories of
Joshua and of the judges served well: Yahweh alone accomplished
the victory!

Second, in holy-war battles Yahweh usually employs some natural
phenomenon to combat the foe. In the battle against the Amorite
kings, Yahweh killed the fleeing enemy with hailstones (Josh.
10:11). Against the Canaanites whose land the Israelites dispossessed,
Yahweh would send hornets (Deut. 7:20: cf. Josh. 24:12). In this battle at the sea, Yahweh controls the sea by a strong "east wind" (v.
21). In the Song of the Sea we saw the use of wind as that agent by
which God heaped up Yamm and *tehōmōt*. Yet here the reference is
specifically to the "east wind." From the location of the J writer in
Jerusalem, the east wind was that which came out of the desert. As
such it dried up plants and made them wither (Gen. 41:6, 23, 27;
Ezek. 17:10; 19:12; Hos. 13:15). That it makes a man faint (Jon. 4:8)
can be verified by anyone who has ever experienced the *ḥamsīn*; sore
throats, sleepless nights, irritable dispositions are its gifts. No wonder then that the east wind takes on mythological meaning. Through
this instrument Yahweh brings the plague of locusts on Egypt
(Exod. 10:3), judgment on the wicked (Job 27:21), and on Job's family (Job 1:19). It is the east wind which shatters the ships of Tarshish
attacking Jerusalem (!) and the ships of Tyre (Ps. 48:8; Ezek. 27:26).
Further, just as the east wind saved Jerusalem from attack, so Yahweh uses it to destroy Jerusalem (Isa. 27:8; Jer. 4:11; 18:17).

In only one case does the east wind have a positive effect on people: according to Ps. 78:26–27 it brought the quails as food for the Israelites in the wilderness. The statistics—and impact—of the east
wind lead one to regard it as an evil wind, and this description fits
precisely the Babylonian *imḥullu* by which Marduk defeated Tiamat.
In the Sea event Yahweh used the Evil Wind to destroy the chaotic
force of Egypt which threatened the fulfillment of Yahweh's plans
for Israel.

Third, the battle as described in the Yahwist's version occurs at
night. The emphasis on night and darkness is striking in verses 20
through 24 and reaches a climax at verse 27: ". . . and the sea returned to its usual flow at the appearance of morning" (*lipnōt bōqer*).
One needs to ask about the intended impact of this nocturnal battle.
If one begins with the expression *lipnōt bōqer* (perhaps "just before
dawn"), it seems that a formula of some sort is employed. The He-

brew expression occurs elsewhere in this exact form at Ps. 46:6 (Eng. v. 5). This verse is part of a Zion psalm which begins with an expression of confidence in God as strength and refuge, a confidence which will not be shaken even if mountains shake in the seas and their waters roar and foam. Chaotic forces cannot threaten Jerusalem, the city of God.

> God is in her midst; she shall not be moved.
> God helps her (acts as warrior) at the appearance of morning.

Though nations rage, God needs only to utter his voice (thunder?), and the earth melts. After a confession of faith in the Divine Warrior

> Yahweh Sebaoth is with us;
> the God of Jacob is a fortress for us,

the invitation goes forth to "see the works of Yahweh" who ends war by destroying weapons.

In Judg. 19:26 the expression "at the appearance of morning" occurs with only a slight modification: the addition of the definite article, *lipnōt habbōqer*. Here is told the story of the Levite and his concubine who stayed as guests in the home of an old man in Gibeah. When the household was beset by a mob from the town, the Levite gave them his concubine in order to protect the host's home. The mob abused her all night, letting her go only at the break of dawn. Then "at the appearance of morning" the woman fell at the door of the old man where her master found her "in the morning" (v. 27). Here it is clear that *lipnōt habbōqer* occurs between the "rising of dawn" and "the morning," and so would seem to indicate the time at which the sun makes its first appearance on the horizon.

By this definition one other passage might be examined as a semantic equivalent: Isa. 17:12–14.

> Alas! The thunder of many peoples,
>   like the thundering of the sea they thunder.
> And the roar of nations,
>   like the roar of mighty waters they roar;
> nations roar like the roar of many waters.
> But he will rebuke them,
>   and they will flee at great distance,
> Pursued like chaff on the mountains before wind,
>   and like rolling (plants?) before storm.
> At the time of evening, lo, there is terror!
> Before morning (*bĕṭerem bōqer*) they do not exist.
> This is the portion of our despoilers,
>   and the lot of our plunderers.

The Assyrian armies were Yahweh's instruments of judgment, but before ultimate disaster would occur, Yahweh would suddenly appear as Warrior to drive off the invader (see Isa. 29:1–8; 31:4–9). This theme, among the major ones of Isaiah, is perhaps a new interpretation of an old tradition. Gerhard von Rad, in particular, had argued that a theme about the invincibility of Jerusalem was celebrated in the cult, above all, through such Psalms as 46, 48 and 76. Indeed, it is possible that the tradition reaches back to the pre-Davidic days when Jebusites controlled the city (cf. 2 Sam. 5:6ff.). This old, perhaps mythological, tradition of chaotic waters versus Jerusalem (note the naval attack at Ps. 48:7) could have been taken over by Isaiah and historicized, in order to address the city's people with the immediate circumstance of Assyria's siege. This tension between myth and history is maintained in powerful fashion at Isa. 17:12–14 where the attackers are portrayed as the thundering sea and roaring waters. The battle occurs in the darkness ("at the time of evening") and "before morning" the conflict is resolved.

Finally, while the expressions "at the appearance of morning" or "before morning" do not appear in the narrative account of the actual deliverance from the Assyrian siege (Isa. 36:36–37), the action is the same. An angel of Yahweh went through the Assyrian camp at night (see the parallel at 2 Kings 19:35) and slew much of the army. In the morning their companions found the results of the night's slaughter.

In any case, the passages which contain the expression "at the appearance of morning" or its equivalent exhibit a threefold pattern:

1. Conflict during the night;
2. Resolution of the conflict "at the appearance of morning";
3. Third party observation of the result of the resolution in the morning light.

While the passage at Isa. 17:12–14 does not include the third component, the observation of the corpses of the Assyrian soldiers at 37:36 seems to fill out the pattern in the Book of Isaiah. With the possible exception of Judges 19, all the pertinent texts have their origin and purpose in Jerusalem.

In the final unit we will discuss the probable background of the defense of Zion on the basis of Canaanite mythology. There is, however, in the Canaanite texts nothing known at present of a *nocturnal* battle; likewise in Mesopotamia such a conflict is unknown. Only in Egyptian mythology does the beneficent deity, the Sun god Re, battle an adversary during the night. The breaking of dawn on the eastern horizon and the subsequent appearance of the solar disk indicate his victory over Apophis and, as seen by all the world, lead to joyous praise and acclamation of his kingship.

The threefold pattern seen in the passages studied above is evident as well in the Yahwist's version of the sea event. The battle between Yahweh and the Egyptians occurs in the darkness; the Egyptians were drowned "at the appearance of morning"; the people of Israel "saw the Egyptians dead upon the seashore." The victor in the battle is Yahweh—not the expected conqueror of nocturnal battles, the Sun god Re, but Yahweh, the God of the Hebrews, appears victorious in the morning light. The old myth has been used, it seems, with a reverse effect, and by the impact of that mythology, the conflict between the God of Israel and the god of the Egyptians comes to a decisive end.

Perhaps it is not unreasonable to suppose that this twist on things Egyptian was related to Solomon's marriage to the daughter of the pharaoh as part of a political alliance (1 Kings 3:1). Solomon brought his blushing bride into the city of David itself (v. 2) until he had built for her a house like his own Hall of Throne (7:8–9; cf. 9:24). The presence of the princess and her entourage in the city would doubtless have made those in court circles familiar with Egyptian customs and religion. It would also have angered those who felt that such marriage alliances with foreigners were contrary to the will of Yahweh (see 1 Kings 11:1–8). Thus the historical-political situation in Jerusalem might have had an impact on this author's version of this cosmic event, just as in a similar way circumstances in Babylon in the second millennium B.C.E. contributed to the present form of the *Enuma elish*.

The Priestly Account of the Sea Event

Having separated the Yahwist's material from the total narrative at Exod. 14:10–31, the following remains as the work of the priestly writer whose work was accomplished either in Jerusalem or, more likely, in Babylon during the exile of the sixth century B.C.E.

> *v. 10* When Pharaoh drew near . . . the people of Israel cried to the Lord. *vv. 15–18* The Lord said to Moses, "Why do you cry to me? Tell the people of Israel to go forward. Lift up your rod, and stretch out your hand over the sea and divide it, that the people of Israel may go on dry ground through the sea. And I will harden the hearts of the Egyptians so that they shall go in after them, and I will get glory over Pharaoh and all his host, his chariots, and his horsemen. And the Egyptians

shall know that I am the Lord, when I have gotten glory over Pharaoh, his chariots, and his horsemen."
   v. 21 Then Moses stretched out his hand over the sea; . . . and the waters were divided. *v. 22* And the people of Israel went into the midst of the sea on dry ground, the waters being a wall to them on their right hand and on their left. *v. 23* The Egyptians pursued, and went in after them into the midst of the sea, all Pharaoh's horses, his chariots, and his horsemen.
   vv. 26–27 Then the Lord said to Moses, "Stretch out your hand over the sea, that the water may come back upon the Egyptians, upon their chariots, and upon their horsemen." So Moses stretched forth his hand over the sea. . . *vv. 28–29* The waters returned and covered the chariots and the horsemen and all the host of Pharaoh that had followed them into the sea; not so much as one of them remained. But the people of Israel walked on dry ground through the sea, the waters being a wall to them on their right hand and on their left.

The continuing conflict of Exodus 1–15 is crystallized here by the repeated aim of Yahweh to get "glory over Pharaoh and all his army, his chariots and his cavalry." The particular act which results in the necessary victory is the splitting of the sea, so that Israel might walk across the sea between two walls of water. This feature alone will occupy our attention here, because it differs from the drying-up action of the Yahwist and from the drowning of the Egyptians thrown overboard in the Song. Indeed, the "cleaving" act in the Priestly story is more grandiose and dramatic precisely because it results in two walls of water between which the Israelites walked but which collapsed upon the pursuing Egyptians. The notion of "cleaving" the sea already existed in the preexilic period as the use of the verb in the same sense at Ps. 78:13 demonstrates. In addition, the term appears later than P in the historical survey at Neh. 9:11. Thus the image seems to have had its own history of development.

When one considers the historical situation of the Priestly writer, however, it is difficult to imagine the impact of "cleave the sea" apart from the gory act of Marduk in the *Enuma elish*:

"Then the Lord paused to view her dead body,
That he might divide the monster and do artful works.
He split her like a shellfish into two parts. . . ."

(*ANET*, p. 67)

Thus began the new creation of the cosmos, the king over which was Marduk. In other words, while the term *bāqaᶜ* did not originate with the exilic author, the priest might have chosen that image out of other possibilities because of a polemical purpose against the Babylonians who paraded Marduk's statue in victory every New Year's

Day. At the same time, the ascription of the act of cleaving chaos to Yahweh proclaimed to the exiled Israelites that their God was powerful enough to repeat once more—not cyclically but one more time in history—the exodus of the chosen people from bondage in a foreign land. Far from simply a recollection of the past, the formulation of the priest carried a powerful message clothed in myth for the historical present.

Summation of the Sea Event in Exodus 14–15

It seems that a consistent interpretive principle was at work regarding the deliverance from Egypt. The historical formulation "Yahweh brought us out of the land of Egypt"—so frequent in Israel's liturgical formulations—was mythicized again and again in order to convey a particular meaning to the Israelite people in the various circumstances of their historical existence. In the old Song of the Sea the battle did not include an exodus; however, the victory over the Egyptians in the surging sea provided the background for the victory over and the conquest of the land of Canaan, where Yahweh was enthroned as king. In the Yahwist's seemingly "natural" description of the event, mythological features out of several backgrounds—Canaanite, Mesopotamian, Egyptian—are merged in a holy-war formula to settle the dispute between Yahweh and the Pharaoh. And in the Priestly record the Mesopotamian parallels stand out most clearly—as one would expect of a writer during the Babylonian Exile.

Finally, when all the pieces are combined in Exodus 14–15, there results a powerful mythicized interpretation of the historical deliverance from Egypt. As we saw earlier in the preaching of the prophets and in the psalms, several mythological stories merge in one passage as though the ancient Hebrews had an entire storage room of illustrations from which to draw their own portrayals of the cosmic battle, particularized for them in history. Such amalgamation of originally separate stories out of the ancient Near East further enhances the impact of the combined tetrateuchal sources. For example, it is at the Lake of Rushes where the Egyptians longed to bathe with the sun god and to accompany him on a journey through the netherworld's darkness to the place of rebirth (sunrise); yet here in Exodus 14–15 the Sea of Reeds is the spot where the power of Egypt is vanquished by the Divine Warrior named Yahweh. Moreover, to include the Priest's itinerary in the complex of these traditions is to make the polemics even broader. According to that writer, the battle at the sea took place in the vicinity of Baal-zephon (Exod. 14:2). Baal-zephon was a place of worship in the Egyptian delta for the Canaanite deity who vanquished the chaos force of Yamm and who erected his palace on Mount Zaphon. While this Egyptian site is not the Canaanites' mountain of Zaphon, nevertheless the place was a locale for the worship of Baal. According to the Priest, then, right under Baal's regal nose Yahweh used Yamm to vanquish his chaos opponent, the pharaoh and god of Egypt.

CHAOS AS THE OBJECT OF
YAHWEH'S REBUKE

Used as a technical term in the conflict between Yahweh and agents of chaos is the word "rebuke" (Heb. *gāᶜar*). In the extra-biblical conflicts the cognate appears only in Ugaritic. When the gods in divine assembly drooped their heads at the sight of Yamm's macho messengers, Baal "rebuked" his colleagues for showing such weakness. It seems that his action was directed at those who were responsible for the decisions to maintain order but who clearly were willing to allow the agents of chaos to have their way. In another case, Baal himself is the object of another deity's rebuke. When the victor tried to kill the wounded Yamm, Lady Asherah "rebuked" Baal. This wife of the chief god El had exercised her authority over one of their sons in order to protect another son. In each of these cases, it seems that one who has authority or soon will have authority rebukes someone of lesser degree in order to bring control into a certain situation.

In the Hebrew Bible persons other than Yahweh attempt to rebuke someone else, but only Yahweh possesses the authority to do so. Jacob rebuked his son Joseph for his dream about the family bowing down to this one son (Gen. 37:10). As father he should have had the authority to rebuke, but the story itself demonstrates that his action was inappropriate. In the time of Jeremiah, Shemaiah had written to the exiles in Babylon that they should have rebuked Jeremiah for his prophecy that the exile was not some fleeting phase, but since history confirmed the prophet's words, such an action would have been inappropriate (Jer. 29:27). Boaz was wise enough to instruct his workers not to rebuke or reproach Ruth but to allow her to glean the sheaves (Ruth 2:16). Only in irony, it seems, can Isaiah suggest that the rebuke (RSV "threat") of a few will cause a thousand to flee; like the old holy-war schemes, a small number possessing authority will cause masses of opponents to flee (Isa. 30:17). The only case in which humans seem clearly to have authority to rebuke others occurs at Sirach 11:7; after investigation of facts in a case a person may rebuke (Greek *epitimān*) another.

Yahweh, on the other hand, clearly has the authority to rebuke, and the objects of that act are those who would thwart his orderly plans: the primordial waters, chaos forces attacking Jerusalem, and Satan.

Yahweh's Rebuke of Primordial Waters

As in mythology in general where the established structures of the universe originated in *illo tempore*, the exclusive right of Yahweh to "rebuke" is founded in the cosmogonic act. The beautiful hymn, Psalm 104—often believed to have been based on the Egyptian Hymn to the Aton—describes in dramatic fashion the creation of the heavens and the earth. Having "stretched out the heavens like a tent," Yahweh organized clouds, wind, fire and flame as his instruments. Then he turned his attention to the earth.

> You established earth on its foundations,
>   so that it should not be moved for all eternity.
> Deep (*tĕhōm*) covered it as a garment,
>   above (even) mountains stood waters.
> At your rebuke they fled,
>   at the sound of your thunder they took to flight. . . .
> A boundary you established,
>   so that they might not trespass,
>   so that they might not return to cover the earth.
>
>   (Ps. 104:5–9)

Thus the original rebuke of Yahweh occurred at creation when Yahweh established order out of watery chaos and provided the means by which that order would continue. All that the Divine Warrior needed to make the enemy flee (see the discussion of Exod. 14:27 above, pp. 40–42) was his authoritative word of rebuke which remains exclusively his for all eternity.

Hereafter, the exercise of divine authority over the chaotic force of water continues the principle of relating the cosmic battle to historical events. At Nah. 1:3b–5 a theophany description typical of a storm god introduces the account of Nineveh's downfall in 612 B.C.E.

> In whirlwind and in storm is his way,
>   He rebukes the sea (*Yamm*) and makes it dry,
>   and all the rivers (pl. of *Nahar*) he dries up. . . .

The effect of his awesome appearance is that fruitful mountain ranges wither and mountains quake. This powerful God who thus effects order by prevailing over primordial chaos now moves against the capital of the Assyrians who had been causing chaos in Israel's life for more than a century. Thus the cosmic "rebuke" of Yamm takes effect in history where the Divine Warrior demolishes the enemy of his people.

In a similar way reference to Yahweh's "rebuke" of the sea (Yamm) provides the means by which the Warrior drives off the enemies who attack the kings of the Davidic line. Psalm 18 celebrates the king's deliverance from his enemies who were routed by Yahweh. In theophanic splendor—mountains quaking, storm clouds, thunder and lightning—Yahweh answered the cry of distress.

> Then the channels of the sea (Yamm) were visible,
>   and the foundations of the world were revealed,
> at your "rebuke," O Yahweh,
>   at the breath of the wind of your nostrils.

> (Ps. 18:15)

The baring of the earth's underpinnings caused by Yahweh's rebuke corresponds to the effect of the Warrior's wrath upon everyone who would prevent the orderly reign of the Davidic king, the Messiah.

Since the cosmic rebuke against Yamm effected judgment in history on the Assyrians and on any opponents of the Davidic dynasty, that same "rebuke" became a powerful proof of God's power to judge Babylon and thus to deliver the exiles. At Isa. 50:2 Yahweh answers his own rhetorical question about his ability or inability to redeem by citing his cosmogonic act.

> Lo, by my rebuke I dry up Yamm,
>   I make rivers (pl. of Nahar) a desert. . . .

Much like Nah. 1:4 the object of Yahweh's rebuke is explicitly Yamm, the Sea. In this instance, that proven authority established in the cosmic realm provides the basis for confident expectation that Yahweh will again assert his authority and reign.

The use of "rebuke" in these cases maintains that tension between myth and history which we observed earlier in studying the "monster" imagery. There is one instance of the rebuke of Yamm, however, in which the mythical aspect is removed. In Psalm 106, a hymnic description of Yahweh's relationship with Israel from the exodus through the wilderness, his rebuking authority is transferred from the cosmic realm (Nah. 1:3) to the local and historical arena.

He rebuked the Sea of Reeds, and it became dry;
   he brought them through the deeps (*těhōmōt*) as through a desert.

(v. 9)

Here it is not the cosmic rebuke of the sea which proves Yahweh's power to act in history; the historical event at the Sea of Reeds itself establishes his right to receive Israel's praise.

Yahweh's Rebuke of Chaos's Forces
Attacking Jerusalem

It is only a short step from the rebuke of the sea which corresponds to Yahweh's judgment on those who attack Zion's king (Psalm 18) to the actual rebuke of the enemies of Jerusalem themselves. In Psalm 76, a Zion psalm much like Psalms 46 and 48, such an attack on Jerusalem serves as the scene for the Divine Warrior's awesome effect upon the enemy. The opposing warriors are rendered helpless after their weapons are shattered.

By your rebuke, O God of Jacob,
   rider and horse are stunned.

(v. 6)

While the similarity with the fate of the Egyptian army at the exodus is interesting, there is nothing in the psalm to suggest that scene as the intended reference. It seems that the mythological rebuke of primordial waters is the background of this imagery which proclaims and celebrates Yahweh's defense of the city.

In a quite similar way the preaching of Isaiah at the time of Assyria's siege of Jerusalem utilizes the same imagery. The event in 701 so resembled the chaotic sea's attempt to wrest control from Yahweh that the attacking Assyrians are compared to the roaring of many waters,

but he will rebuke them,
   and they will flee far away.

(Isa. 17:13)

Thus, as in Psalm 76, the object of Yahweh's rebuke is the historical nation, not the sea. Yet that nation corresponds to the sea of the cosmic conflict and so is appropriately rebuked.

In the final unit we shall return to consider in more detail Yahweh's defense of Zion, the hill of his holiness. Here it is sufficient to observe that Yahweh's rebuke is directed against those historical nations who threaten the order of his authoritative reign from Jerusalem.

Yahweh's Rebuke of Those Who Attack
the Oppressed

Psalm 9 provides a worshiper in the Jerusalem temple (v. 9) with the means to give thanks for Yahweh's deliverance from the wicked.

> You rebuked nations,
>   you destroyed (the) wicked;
> their name you wiped out forever and ever.
>
> (v. 5)

In contrast to the fate of the wicked, Yahweh is enthroned as king over the cosmos. With such authority he alone has the power to rebuke, and he exercises that cosmic power not only for chosen kings and the elect city but also for the poor and the needy who live in this hope (v. 18).

Yahweh's Rebuke of Satan

In the Hebrew Bible the term *sātān* is used for anyone who acts as an adversary to someone else. Yet in three cases the non-specific term appears with the definite article; there "the adversary" is rendered as the proper name Satan. In the first chapter of Job (the prologue) Satan is portrayed as one of "the sons of God" in assembly whose function is to challenge the faith of someone considered to be righteous. God acts according to the arrangement suggested by Satan, but ultimately Satan is proven wrong in his accusation against Job's faith. The "adversary" here is not particularly an evil figure; he is something like a prosecuting attorney—a necessary but unpopular role in the court. At 1 Chron. 21:1 Satan is cited as the one who incited David to commit the sin of taking a census, an act which in the earlier tradition at 2 Sam. 24:1 was attributed to Yahweh himself. Thus one cannot with certainty identify Satan here as a power opposed to Yahweh; he might simply serve as Yahweh's agent—as in the Job story.

However, in the third chapter of Zechariah, when Satan plays his assigned role as "devil's advocate," he seems to have gone too far. This fourth nocturnal vision which Zechariah received from the Lord portrays Satan as an agent of chaos standing in the way of Yahweh's plans.

> Then he (Yahweh) showed me Joshua, the high priest, standing before the messenger of Yahweh, and Satan (the Adversary) was standing at his right hand to be his adversary. And Yahweh said to Satan, "May Yahweh rebuke you, O Satan; may Yahweh who elected Jerusalem rebuke you. Is not this one a firebrand delivered from the fire?" (Zech. 3:1–2)

The Joshua mentioned here is the son of Jozadak who was chosen to be high priest in Jerusalem during the time of restoration from the exile in Babylon. The vision thus describes the heavenly court scene in which Joshua ben Jozadak was confirmed as high priest in Jerusalem. This chosen one stood before Yahweh's messenger (angel) and beside Satan. For a reason not stated in the vision report, Satan contests the election. Yahweh, however, convinced of the qualifications of Joshua, describes him as a "firebrand delivered from the fire." This metaphor might be a reference to the rescue of a few (even perhaps Jozadak) when the Babylonians slaughtered the priests years before (2 Kings 25:18–21).

The functions which Yahweh intended to fulfill in the office of this High Priest are listed by the angel: rule Yahweh's house, have charge of the courts, and possess "right of access" (v. 7). These functions seem to combine in Joshua the offices of priest and of Davidic king, since they relate to temple, court, and a right which can be both priestly and royal. The priestly function of "drawing near" to Yahweh in the Holy of Holies for the atonement of the people's sins seems to be confirmed by the divine promise to remove the guilt of the land in a single day (Day of Atonement). On the other hand, following the tradition at Jer. 30:21, the "right of access" might indicate the royal function of sharing the throne with Yahweh; such intimacy with the Ruler of the world can be shared by a Davidic king/prince only at the risk of his life. The reference in v. 8 to the royal metaphor "the Branch" (cf. Jer. 23:5), however, seems to make a distinction between Joshua the priest and some other person to fulfill the royal function. According to 4:1–14 that other person is Prince Zerubbabel, who along with Joshua the priest, represents one of "two branches," that is, "two anointed ones" who together stand beside Yahweh (see also 6:9–13). Thus, the vision at Zechariah 3 includes both the high priest and the Davidic prince. In the priestly "branch" the Day of Atonement would be accomplished (v. 9); in Zerubbabel, the royal "branch," the shalom of the Day of Yahweh would be realized ("on that day," v. 10). The functions of these two branches seem to make the two days simultaneous events.

It is small wonder, then, that Satan was rebuked by Yahweh. By challenging the qualifications of Joshua ben Jozadak as high priest/ Branch in Jerusalem, Satan played the same role as those forces who had earlier attempted to attack Jerusalem and to wrest control from Yahweh's anointed one, the Davidic king. When others had tried to bring chaos to Yahweh's established order in Jerusalem, the Divine

Warrior exercised his authority. Yahweh's rebuke corresponded to the action of the Divine Warrior on enemies of the Davidic king (Psalm 18). Now Satan challenges Yahweh's elect one by whom the guilt of the land will be removed in a single day (Zech. 3:9). And so, once again chaos is brought under control by the authoritative rebuke of God.

THE ESCHATOLOGICAL DEFEAT
OF CHAOS

In our discussion of the Reed Sea event above (pp. 37–42), we saw how the Yahwist used characteristics of a holy-war scheme in order to describe the exodus from Egypt. At Exod. 14:30 the account is concluded with the summary statement that Yahweh saved Israel "on that day" from the hand of the Egyptians. That seemingly innocent temporal phrase is itself a characteristic of holy-war descriptions. It occurs in combination with other elements to relate the attack of the tribes on Benjamin for the crime of inhospitality (Judg. 20:15, 21, 35, 46). The phrase appears twice in the account of Samuel's leadership of Israel against the Philistines (1 Sam. 7:6, 10) and three times to report Jonathan's victory over the Philistines at Michmash (1 Sam. 14:23, 24, 31).

Because of its use in citing and celebrating Yahweh's victories over Israel's enemies in bygone days, "on that day" eventually was projected into the future to introduce Yahweh's victory over oppressors. At first, it seems, such a view led to a false optimism about "that day," but the prophet Amos corrected the idea by telling Israel in the mid-eighth century B.C.E. that the day of Yahweh was darkness and not light (Amos 5:18). Not only the nations but Israel and Judah themselves would experience the attack of the Divine Warrior. From this point on in Israel's prophecy, what happened "on that day" was both judgment and restoration for Israel. It was the time at which Yahweh would destroy all peoples and powers which stood in the way of his establishing his kingdom. In the course of this development the chaos monsters of the cosmogonic act would be vanquished once and for all on the eschatological "Day of Yahweh."

The classic example of the projection into the future of the conflict between Yahweh and the chaos forces is the single verse Isa. 27:1. Variously dated by scholars from the sixth to the third centuries B.C.E., the "Apocalypse of Isaiah," chapters 24–27, looks forward to the day on which Yahweh will be victorious over heavenly and earthly enemies and thus be enthroned as king on Mount Zion (see

24:21–23). This day of victory will include a festive banquet on the holy mountain (25:6–8), resurrection of the dead (26:16–19), and restoration from the lands to which the people of Israel had been dispersed by the Assyrians (27:12–13). In that context appears the prophecy of the cosmic battle.

> On that day Yahweh, with his hard and great and strong sword, will
>   visit (punishment)
> upon Leviathan, the fleeting serpent,
> upon Leviathan, the crooked serpent,
> and he will slay the dragon which (is) in the sea (*yam*).

The parallelism of the three lines describing Leviathan indicates that the object of Yahweh's wrath is not three serpents/dragons but one who is described by synonyms. On that basis one cannot but compare this passage with that piece from Ugarit where Baal is described by Mot as having conquered the serpent.

> "If you smite Lotan, the fleeting serpent,
> Destroy the crooked serpent,
> Shalyat of the seven heads."

The similarities between the descriptions of the serpent Lotan/ Leviathan (the same word) in the two passages can hardly be coincidental. While it is difficult to determine the precise line of transmission from the fourteenth century B.C.E. text to that in the Isaiah Apocalypse a millennium later, the use of some of the details seems to indicate a continuing tradition which had at some point been transferred from Baal to Yahweh. Particularly striking about this process is the transformation of the slaughter of Lotan/Leviathan to the *future* day of Yahweh when the Lord would establish his kingship on the basis of victory over the powers of chaos. The reinterpretation takes the victory over the serpent out of the realm of cosmology and thrusts it into the realm of eschatology.

Not unrelated to this entire development is the appearance in Daniel's vision of monsters who emerge from the "great sea" (Dan. 7:1–8). The beasts in this passage correspond to worldly empires, but though they represent the kingdoms of this world over against the immanent kingdom of God, they are not portrayed as particularly hostile to Yahweh. It seems that in apocalyptic thinking time must run its full course before God's new era can begin. Further, Behemoth and Leviathan at Job 40:15–24; 41:1–34 continue their development in the intertestamental literature to the point where they are seen as having been made originally as food and reserved for the menu of the final days (Eth. Enoch 60:7, 24; IV Esdras 6:49ff.; Syr. Baruch 29:4).

SUMMARY OF CONFLICT IMAGERY IN
THE HEBREW BIBLE

Throughout the Old Testament there does not seem to have been a single approach to the mythological imagery of the conflict between order and chaos. As one might expect, the long history of the traditions, as well as the different types of literature involved, produced a variety of approaches to the ancient myths. The poetic wisdom of the Book of Job provides the least transformed, that is, least historicized, use of the monster imagery. Sea, Rahab, and Leviathan are the means by which Job himself spoke of the power of God and of human powerlessness in face of such a warrior (Job 9:8, 13; 26:11–13) or by which God himself humbled Job for his plea to contest his suffering in a court case (Job 38:8–11; 40:25–41:8).

The references in the Book of Psalms to Yahweh's victory over chaos and kingship over the world likewise point to his power. Usually cited in community laments, the might of God, so manifested in the primordial time, provides the reason for confidence in the present time of distress (Ps. 74:12–17; Hab. 3:8–15) or the reason why the community in the present time wonders about the ability or concern of the Lord to repeat that powerful deed (Psalm 89). In one case, the victory of Yahweh and his ensuing kingship provide the theological explanation for the election of the Davidic dynasty and the unconditional covenant with the kings of that lineage (Ps. 89:1–18, 19–37). The study of the term "rebuke" in reference to the conflict imagery demonstrated a display of Yahweh's authority to calm the raging forces and so to deliver the oppressed people from their afflictions (Ps. 9:5; 18:15; 68:30; 76:6). In one case, the "rebuke" of the waters remains completely in the realm of creation without reference to deliverance (Ps. 104:7), and in one case the term is completely historical since it describes the exodus from Egypt (Ps. 106:9).

It is in the poetic and narrative descriptions of the exodus event itself that a major reinterpretation occurs. In the Song of the Sea at Exodus 15:1–12 the poet used the battle imagery in a rather moderate way in order to provide a particular impact for the Reed Sea event. The Yahwistic writer, gathering traditions and editing earlier works during the Davidic-Solomonic reigns in Jerusalem, described the defeat of the Egyptians at the sea by using a variety of images which we have observed in the stories from the Babylonians, Canaanites, and Egyptians (Exod. 14:10–31). The Priest, dealing with the traditions and addressing an audience of exiles in the sixth century B.C.E., found the Babylonian mythology particularly timely as a way of setting forth hope for the people (Exod. 14:10–31). Thus, the Hebrews interpreted a historical event—an escape from slavery in Egypt—as the act of Yahweh, and the composers of the narratives of that event (oral and then literary) recounted the battle in mythological terms in order to interpret the impact of the event for the life and faith of Israel. By this transformation Yahweh defeated the representatives of chaos (the pharaoh) and paved the necessary way for his rule.

That process of transformation, begun in describing the exodus, provided the prophets with a useful hermeneutical principle for their preaching. Just as the pharaoh and the Egyptian armies represented the chaos forces opposed to Yahweh's purposes and rule, so the same kind of identification could be made by the prophet Isaiah (30:7) and Ezekiel (29:3; 32:2) to speak respectively of the vanity of Egypt's help in war or of her refusal to help Israel in time of need. The impact of these passages becomes clear when one recognizes that the person of the pharaoh or the nation of Egypt have been mythicized in order to interpret the events of 705 B.C.E. and of 597–586 B.C.E. Yet the prophet who mythicized history perhaps more than any other was Second Isaiah. Closely combining the primordial victory of Yahweh and the exodus event, that prophet in the exilic period proclaimed the return from Babylon in the sixth century B.C.E. as a new cosmic victory/exodus (Isa. 51:9–10; also 43:14–21). Indeed the authoritative rebuke of chaos in the primordial time is Yahweh's own proof text for his ability to accomplish this new victory (50:2).

Yet the mythicization of history, that is, the interpretation of a historical event in mythological terms, was not the only approach to the relationship between myth and history. The prophet Isaiah in the eighth century B.C.E. was most responsible for a historicization of myth. A major motif in his preaching was the protection by Yahweh of Jerusalem. On the basis of that motif in the so-called Zion psalms (especially Psalms 46, 48, and 76) which seem to predate the prophet, Isaiah addressed the immediate historical problem of the invasion of Jerusalem by the Assyrian armies under Sennacherib. In other words, already existing in the city's traditions was the mythological motif of invincibility. It was known in the Jerusalem cult and practiced in ritual for centuries, but now the motif was used to address a specific moment in history. This process, it seems to the present writer, is

different from that described above, namely, starting with a historical event or person and then finding the mythological traditions to
interpret the event for the readers/hearers. Both processes exist side
by side in the prophetic books of the Hebrew Bible, as Israel's
preachers struggled constantly with the necessary tension between
myth and history.

It is at this point that ancient Israel differed from her neighbors. It
is true that the myths of the Babylonians and the Egyptians originated in some cases with historical events and that the monster of the
myth of the Sun god and Apophis was identified as a hostile king.
Yet the tension between myth and history was dissolved in time, and
only the mythic cyclical role was retained in ritual. For Israel, on the
other hand, the historical event was determinative in the cult but
needed to be understood by the community on the basis of traditional mythical imagery. As a result, Israel's neighbors mythologized
nature in ritual while Israel herself mythicized history in the cultic
life of the community.

It was just before and during the Davidic-Solomonic reigns that
history was mythicized in order to interpret the new theological reality of Yahweh and the divine role in Israel's formation. Struggling
with the implications for life and worship of this deity who did not
correspond in true mythological fashion to a particular natural phenomenon amidst other such deities, Israel's "theologians" needed to
communicate a different kind of god by the use of stereotypical religious expressions. The rise of David and the cosmopolitan reign of
Solomon forced the theologians to struggle with the tension between
myth and history. This struggle gave rise to some polemics against
the foreign influences brought into Jerusalem itself. In this setting the
Yahwist wrote his mythicized version of the exodus event, and the
psalmist based the Davidic covenant on the cosmic victory and reign
of Yahweh (Psalm 89).

Yet most of the passages in our discussion date from the end of the
seventh and from the sixth centuries B.C.E. Both prophets and psalmists in this period of international involvement used the conflict imagery in the ways outlined above. This period was one in which an
archaizing trend was evident in the whole ancient Near East. At the
same time, this was a time in which the power and supremacy of
Yahweh was severely challenged by the apparent successes of other
national deities, and so prophets and psalmists extolled the victory
and rule of Yahweh in primordial times as the means by which Israel
could hope for deliverance from her present distress. As Israel

waited, the tension between the power of Yahweh in the past and a concrete demonstration of that power in the present was particularly acute. It was only when Second Isaiah saw the immediate end in sight that the tension was resolved by virtually identifying the cosmic victory of former times with the new exodus about to occur in history (Isa. 51:9–10).

Finally, the study of the term "rebuke" demonstrated that Yahweh alone had the authority to calm and put in place the forces which would threaten his purposes and his reign. Only Yahweh had the authority to rebuke, and he exercised that authority over the forces who opposed his reign and threatened his peace and his purposes. Thus the objects of his rebuke include the primordial waters Deep and Sea, the enemies who attack Jerusalem or the king, and Satan.

On the day of the Lord, when all such opposing chaotic forces shall be vanquished, Yahweh's reign of order will be established universally for all. Such is the hope of the oppressed when chaos seems to prevail in history. In this hope God's history would reach its ultimate goal.

3

The Son of God Versus Chaos

The synoptic Gospels and the Book of Revelation continue the imagery of the cosmic conflict as the means by which the eschatological victory of God is achieved and his kingdom established. In the synoptics this victory over chaos forces is won in the ministry of Jesus, while in Revelation the battle is described in typical apocalyptic fashion as the otherworldly clash of opposing forces.

THE TESTIMONY OF THE SYNOPTICS

The most pointed use of the conflict imagery from the Hebrew Bible occurs in connection with the verb "rebuke." Moreover, all three synoptics utilize the verb *epitimān* (used in the Septuagint for the Hebrew *gāʿar*) in such a way that only Jesus can serve properly as its subject. While Mark cites three cases in which someone other than Jesus rebukes (8:32; 10:13, 48), Jesus himself makes clear that they have acted or spoken inappropriately. Just as Yahweh alone had the authority to rebuke in the Hebrew Bible, so Jesus stands alone in the New Testament with the authority of God to control chaos. It is above all in Mark that Jesus exercises this divine authority to bring under control an array of chaotic forces much like those in the Hebrew Bible: Sea, the unclean spirits, and Satan. By so rebuking these adversaries of old, Jesus is identified as the Son of God in whom God's reign is dawning.

Jesus' Rebuke of the Sea

The fourth chapter of Mark concludes with a story which has as its punchline a rhetorical question about the identity of Jesus. The precise wording of the narrative itself answers in advance that question for the reader.

58

"On that day, . . . he (Jesus) said to them (his disciples), 'Let us cross
over to the other side.' . . . And there was a great storm of wind, and
the waves beat into the boat with the result that the boat was already
filling. And as for him, he was in the stern, sleeping on the cushion; and
they aroused him and said to him, 'Teacher, doesn't it matter to you
that we are perishing?' And waking, he *rebuked* the wind and said to the
sea, 'Peace! Be still!' And the wind ceased, and there was a great calm.
And he said to them, 'Why are you afraid? Do you not yet have faith?'
And they feared a great fear and said to one another, 'Who then is this
that even the wind and the sea obey him?'"

(Mark 4:35–41)

The explicit object of Jesus' rebuke is the wind, while to the sea he
utters the command to be still or quiet. Does the structure of the sen-
tence indicate that wind and sea are independent of each other, causing the rebuke and the command to be separate acts? It seems the use
of the wind and sea in synonymous parallelism in the Hebrew Bible
enables the interpreter to conclude they belong together as the concept "storm." Indeed, in Psalm 107, a passage which many feel to be
the background of the Marcan account, "stormy wind" and "waves
of the sea" are parallel; there Yahweh stills the storm and silences the
sea's waves (vv. 25, 29). Further, the rebuke and the stilling acts are
used together to describe the cosmic battle at Job 26:11–13. Moreover, in the parallels to Mark 4:35–41, Matthew and Luke make a
modification in the wording by which wind and sea are combined as
the object of the single verb "rebuke" (Matt. 8:26; Luke 8:24). Still
closer to home, the first chapter of Mark reports that the action of
rebuke consists of the words "Be silent, . . . !" (Mark 1:25). Thus not
two actions but one are intended by Jesus' rebuke of the wind and
command to the sea at 4:39.

Jesus would seem to be identified in the story as possessing the authority of Yahweh to bring under control the raging sea whose
waves can bring chaos to human life. Since only Yahweh possessed
such authority to rebuke in the Hebrew Bible, the use of that image
is either blasphemy or a confession that Jesus is the Son of God. In
Psalm 89—apart from the verb "rebuke"—Yahweh's power to rule
the sea (in parallel to stilling waves) in the primordial time is transferred to the Davidic king who immediately thereafter is said to be
the firstborn son of God the Father (Ps. 89:25–27). Moreover, the
reader of Mark's Gospel has already encountered the Son of God title
three times before this story; clearly for this author the conflict imagery represents a confessional statement. "Who is this . . . ?" has already been answered for those who read the account as the author

narrated it. Jesus is the one with the authority of Yahweh; he is God's own Son (1:1, 11; 3:11).

At the same time, the words "on that day" which introduce the story seem to relate the rebuke of the chaotic sea to the eschatological battle anticipated in the Hebrew Bible. This evangelist is well known for his redactional phrases which he prefixed to received traditions. He is responsible for such temporal phrases as "in those days" (1:9), "after some days" (2:1), "immediately" (fifteen times), and others. It would seem to be so here too with "on that day" (Greek *en ekeinē tē hēmera*). This redactional phrase is precisely the one used in the Septuagint to speak of the Day of Yahweh when God would accomplish his cosmic victory and establish his kingdom. Indeed, *en ekeinē tē hēmera* appears in the Septuagint at Isa. 27:1 to introduce Yahweh's eschatological victory over Leviathan, the dragon in the sea.

The relationship between "on that day" and the kingdom of God can be supported by the literary context in which the story appears. Preceding the account is a collection of Jesus' teachings about the kingdom of God. The chapter begins by setting the scene for the parable of the sower "by the sea" where a large crowd gathered to hear him. Later, alone with the disciples, he explained that to them have been given the secrets of the kingdom of God, but to others he speaks in parables. Without informing the reader of a change in scene or audience, the evangelist gathers here several more parables about the kingdom of God (4:21–32). In this setting of kingdom parables taught by the sea is recorded the rebuking event "on that day."

Similar in meaning to this story of rebuking wind and sea is the account of Jesus' "walking on the sea" at Mark 6:45–52. After feeding the multitudes with a small amount of food, Jesus "immediately" sent the disciples off in a boat on the sea. Jesus stayed behind to dismiss the crowd, after which he retreated alone to the mountain. This sudden action on Jesus' part is difficult to interpret as Mark relates the story, but perhaps the parallel at John 6 throws light on Mark's account and on that of Matthew as well. According to the Johannine version, the crowds in the desert were so enthused by Jesus' miracle of the feeding that they attempted to "take him by force to make him king," causing Jesus to withdraw to the mountain (John 6:15). His miracle had incited the Zealots to find in Jesus the leader they needed for a rebellion against Rome. The Gospels of John, Mark, and Matthew all report the same succeeding event: the disciples, adrift on the sea, were threatened by a storm wind, but Jesus approached their tossing boat by "walking on the sea," and the storm ceased. The Greek chosen for this miracle varies in the evangelists' accounts only in regard to grammatical construction and sequence. Matthew's version reads *peripatōn epi tēn thalassēn* (14:25); Mark has *epi tēs thalassēs peripatounta* (6:46); John similarly reads *peripatounta epi tēs thalassēs* (6:19).

The terminology chosen for this act is striking, because in the Septuagint the same words describe the vanquishing of Yamm in the cosmic battle. It is Yahweh, of course,

> who alone stretched out the heavens,
> who walked on the waves of Yamm (*peripatōn hos ep' edaphous epi thalassēs*).
>
> (Job 9:8)

The Hebrew text of Job 9:8 can be translated literally, "who trod upon the backs of Yamm," and thus, like the same words at Deut. 33:29, indicates even more precisely Yahweh's conquest of enemies (see also Hab. 3:15). With this background in mind, the terminology at Mark 6:46 and parallels might have been chosen to repeat the proclamation at 4:35–41: Jesus subdues "the sea," the symbol of chaos, when it threatens the lives of his followers.

A relationship between the miracle of feeding the multitudes and the control of the sea is indicated in the story itself. When Jesus climbed into the boat after walking on the waves, the disciples— strikingly—"were utterly astounded, because they did not understand about the loaves, . . ." (Mark 6:51–52). One would think the miracle on the sea would have been on their minds at this point, but the narrator reports their confusion over the feeding miracle instead. What is the relationship between the two events? If John's account can be used to interpret Mark's, then it seems that Jesus sent his disciples away from the feeding scene so that they would not be caught up in the Zealot's fervor. By staying behind to calm the crowd and by retreating to the solitude of the mountain, Jesus rejected the role of military leader against Rome in order to wage God's eschatological battle against the cosmic enemy, the sea.

Taken together, the accounts of Jesus' rebuke of the storm in Mark 4 and of his treading upon the sea in Mark 6 indicate that the battle of the final days is taking place in the ministry of Jesus. The sea, the symbol of chaos in the mythologies of Mesopotamia, Canaan, and Egypt, indeed the adversary of Yahweh himself, is rebuked and subdued by one who is confessed to be the Son of God. Yet just as the chaotic sea was represented in the earlier literature by various forces, so in the New Testament does chaos have its representatives who cause havoc in people's lives.

Jesus' Rebuke of Unclean Spirits

Already in the first chapter of his Gospel, Mark introduces the reader to the term "rebuke" in the context of kingdom preaching. The first fifteen verses provide an introduction to the whole Gospel, culminating in the summary statement of Jesus' preaching in Galilee: "The time is fulfilled, and the kingdom of God is at hand; repent and believe in the gospel" (Mark 1:15). This sermon is the content of "the gospel of God" (v. 14) and serves as the key to Jesus' entire ministry. He announces that the *kairos* is fulfilled, that is, the expected time has arrived. Such a message can refer only to the dawning of the eschatological "Day of the Lord" when God would achieve his victory over chaos and establish his kingdom. Immediately following this introduction, Mark reports the call to discipleship of Simon, Andrew, James, and John. The newly formed group entered the town of Capernaum on the shore of the Sea of Galilee. There on the sabbath Jesus taught and amazed his hearers with his authority.

Then "immediately" Jesus had opportunity to exercise his authority when he was confronted by a man with an unclean spirit. This spirit called out to Jesus the characteristic response to a threat of authority: "What have you to do with us, Jesus of Nazareth? Have you come to destroy us? I know who you are, the Holy One of God!" (1:24). Of course he came to destroy them, for the unclean spirits represented chaos in people's lives rather than the order which comes with the kingdom. And so, "Jesus rebuked him, saying 'Be silent, and come out of him!'" (v. 25). This authoritative command to exorcise the demon is the same as that addressed to the sea at Mark 4:39: "Be still!" The response of the crowd was again—as with his teaching—to express amazement at Jesus' authority. The chapter continues by citing repeatedly the interconnection between Jesus' preaching/teaching and his exorcising/healing; both give testimony to the kingdom of God breaking into history in the ministry of God's Son.

The unclean spirits continue to be rebuked by Jesus, according to Mark's Gospel. At 3:12, again by the sea where the crowds pressed in on him, Jesus "rebuked" the unclean spirits, ordering them to keep silent about his identity as the Son of God. In the ninth chapter is the account of the man who brought to Jesus his epileptic son. When the man had expressed his faith and a crowd was gathering, Jesus "rebuked" the unclean spirit (9:25) and restored the boy to his family. The disciples wondered about their inability to exorcise that demon, but Jesus indicated that "this kind" could be driven out only by prayer.

Immediately following the account of Jesus' rebuke of the sea at the end of Mark 4, the evangelist includes another exorcism account, that of the man who lived among the tombs in the country of the Gerasenes. This story likewise conveys cosmological significance even without the use of the technical term "rebuke." Here the author accomplishes the same effect by relating the exorcism to the sea: first, by the literary context itself; second, by the use of sea to destroy the enemy. After the customary "What have you to do with me, Jesus, Son of the Most High God?", the infamous Legion tried to dissuade Jesus from destroying them. Jesus allowed them to enter a herd of swine, but when they did, the herd rushed down the steep bank "into the sea and were drowned in the sea" (Mark 5:13). One can only wonder if the author intended to call attention to the drowning of the Egyptians in the sea at Exodus 14–15. Since the sea plays a cosmological role in the story which immediately precedes the exorcism in Mark 5 and will again serve in that capacity in the walking-on-the-sea episode in Mark 6, such an impact from the exodus story seems probable. Like that event from Israel's history, the drowning accomplishes a deliverance from bondage, the subjugation of hostile powers, and leads to the reign of God. Furthermore, here as in the exodus event the sea itself is not the adversary of God but rather the means by which the adversary is destroyed. Interestingly, in Luke's account of Jesus' exorcism of Legion, the body of water is called "the abyss," thus highlighting even more the cosmological intention (Luke 8:31).

When one notes the relationship of Jesus' exorcisms with the term "rebuke" on the one hand and with the sea on the other, it seems that the unclean spirits represent the armies of chaos which threaten human life and stand in the way of God's plans for his reign. As such, these forces must be subjugated by God's authoritative command in order for his divine reign to be realized. That Jesus is the one who possesses authority to rebuke such enemies testifies to his identity as the Son of God. The battle with chaos is not yet complete, however, for Jesus must finally demonstrate his authority over Mr. Chaos himself: Satan.

Jesus' Rebuke of Satan

The relationship between the unclean spirits and Satan is established by the words of Jesus in Mark 3:23. While the Q version of this saying (Matt. 12:25–26; Luke 11:17–18) is not as clear on the identification, Mark's account equates Beelzebul, prince of demons, and Satan. Having heard reports of his exorcisms, Jerusalem scribes charged,

> "He is possessed by Beel-zebul,
>   and by the prince of demons he casts out demons."
>
> (Mark 3:22)

Jesus responds "in parables": "How is Satan able to cast out Satan?" (3:23). Since the days of Elijah, Baal-zebub, the god of Ekron, was one to whom Israelites turned for healing instead of to Yahweh (2 Kings 1:2–3). Thus for almost a millennium he had been a god to whom Yahweh had been opposed. That Jesus should be charged with conspiring with the enemy was a serious claim by the scribes: Beel-zebul, the chief demon, was the means by which Jesus exorcised demons. Jesus' response seems to be twofold. On the one hand, Satan is not capable of driving himself out, thus Satan and the demons or unclean spirits are one and the same. On the other hand, if Satan is indeed rising up against himself, then his house is weakened and his kingdom will fall. The time has come for a new kingdom to be established. Indeed, not only Jesus himself but an appointed army of twelve apostles has been commissioned to wage the eschatological war (3:13–15).

The encounter between Jesus and Satan began in the very first chapter of Mark's Gospel. "Immediately" after his baptism at which God announced to Jesus that he was God's "beloved Son," the Spirit drove the Son of God into the wilderness where he was "tested" (Gr. *peirozomenos*) by Satan (1:12–13). Mark's account of the temptation is almost nonchalant compared with the Q version at Matthew 4:1–11 and Luke 4:1–13. Moreover, in Q the tempter is called not Satan but "the devil" (*ho diabolos*). In Mark alone is it Satan who plays the role of tester, the function which God himself performs in the Hebrew Bible: God tested the faith of Abraham (Gen. 22:1) and that of the people of Israel *in the wilderness* (Exod. 15:25; 16:4; Deut. 8:2). Consistent with his function in the Job story, Satan seems here to carry out the work of God.

Why then does Satan become identified with the demons in Mark 3? Why is the end of Satan's house accomplished in Jesus' exorcism of demons? Why is Satan the one who takes away the word of God which is sown (Mark 4:15)?

Perhaps the answer lies in Mark's concern to demonstrate that Yahweh's eschatological rebuke which corresponds to the universal reign of God is fulfilled in every possible way. Like Yahweh in the Hebrew Bible, Jesus rebuked both the sea and the armies of chaos who brought disorder to people's lives. Yet to complete the authoritative rule over chaos, Jesus must rebuke Satan, as Yahweh did at the installation of Joshua ben Jozadak.

That final rebuke occurs in the eighth chapter of Mark on the road to Caesarea Philippi. Peter had just confessed to Jesus, "You are the Christ" (8:29). Immediately Jesus began to talk about the necessity that the Son of Man suffer, be killed, and after three days rise again (v. 31). So plainly did he speak that Peter took issue with Jesus. Suffering and death did not fit the picture of the Messiah which Peter had inherited from his tradition. The Hebrew Bible never assigns suffering to the Davidic ruler to come! With tradition on his side Peter committed the inexcusable act: he presumed authority to rebuke Jesus (v. 32). With that indiscretion came the divine response: Jesus *rebuked* Peter and said, "Go behind me, Satan! For you are not concerned with things of God but with those of humans" (v. 33).

By acting as he did, Peter played the same role as did Satan in Zechariah 3: he stood in God's way of fulfilling the plan Yahweh had determined for the person of the Messiah in the city of Jerusalem. Indeed, when one considers the details of Zechariah's vision regarding Joshua, the comparisons with Mark's Gospel are striking. Not the least of these parallels is the name itself: Joshua in the Septuagint is *Iesous*.

Zechariah 3	*Mark*
Characters:	Characters:
Joshua	Jesus
Satan	Satan
angel	—
Joshua nominated as high priest/"Branch" (Priestly)	Jesus confessed to be Messiah
Joshua's special relationship to Yahweh: right of access	Jesus' special relationship to God: Son of God/Messiah
Through Joshua's office comes God's atonement	Through Jesus' office and person comes God's forgiveness
Atonement to be accomplished in Jerusalem	Forgiveness to be accomplished in Jerusalem
Satan rebuked for standing in God's way	Peter (Satan) rebuked for standing in God's way

The parallels break down at two significant points. First, unlike Joshua ben Jozadak, Jesus has the authority to rebuke Satan. In Zechariah's vision it is Yahweh who rebukes Satan for challenging Joshua, but since that divine authority had already been transferred to Jesus in order to control sea and unclean spirits, Jesus is both the object of Satan's challenge and the subject of the rebuke of Satan. By serving as the "fall guy" for this necessary rebuke of Satan, Peter is given a new understanding of the Messiah, a Christ who suffers and dies. Second, the difference between Zechariah's report and the Marcan account is that Mark is not recording a vision of the future but an accomplished reality. The expected eschatological moment when God would combine the Day of Atonement and the Day of Yahweh has already occurred in the death and resurrection of Jesus. Yet both these differences serve Mark's purposes precisely: to announce that in Jesus, the Son of God, the kingdom of God had dawned. This announcement was achieved by Mark in several ways, one of which was the use of the authoritative "rebuke" to cover the range of chaos forces which Yahweh controlled in the Hebrew Bible.

Mark's exclusive concern to include this entire range can be illustrated by the synoptic parallels. Both Matthew and Luke retain the verb *epitimān* in reference to Jesus' command to the unclean spirit in the epileptic boy (Mark 9:25; Matt. 18:18; Luke 9:42). The same two evangelists make a similar modification in the story about the raging sea and vicious wind: they combine the two to serve as a compound object of rebuke (Matt. 8:26; Luke 8:24). However, Matthew drops the "rebuke" of Peter by Jesus, probably because of his concern to elevate the apostle's confession (see Matt. 16:23), and Luke removes the entire debate between Peter and Jesus concerning the suffering of the Messiah (see Luke 9:18–22). Finally, Luke (but not Matthew) retains the word *epitimān* for the first unclean spirit to meet Jesus in Galilee (Luke 4:35) and adds the term where Mark does not use it: the healing of Simon's mother-in-law (4:39; see also v. 41). Thus, while the three synoptists use the "rebuke" of Jesus against storm and unclean spirits as agents of chaos, only Mark insists that Satan too was rebuked by Jesus. By completing the entire image from the Hebrew Bible, Mark clearly establishes an impact on the reader: Jesus is the Son of God who exercises the divine authority in order to accomplish the eschatological victory necessary for the reign of God.

The power of that message is felt particularly when one realizes the cosmic dimensions of the victory. Never is Jesus content with local skirmishes, that is, with fighting earthly armies or historical nations. The battle is never historicized in the sense that the chaos forces are identified as particular kings and nations. The enemy which Jesus faces remains the mythical one: the sea, the demons, and Satan. Yet the historicization occurs on the other side: the Son of God has become human in a man named Jesus in order to wage the cosmic battle. [13]

THE FINAL BATTLE

The author of the Book of Revelation addressed his letters to the seven churches in 95 c.e. This was the time when Domitian, emperor of Rome, was carrying out the customary role of persecuting Christians. Literary style, imagery, and content combine to characterize the book as apocalyptic, an "unveiling" of the secrets of the end time. Such "unveilings" occur repeatedly when the historical realities of life become unbearable. Hope can be offered only by means of the visions of what will be, for reality demonstrates that no confidence can be placed in the present.

Strikingly, the revelation to John, like the Book of Daniel in the Hebrew Bible, offers us apocalyptic in moderation, in contrast to more extreme books which were not included in the canon. In this book, however, there are several visions depicting a battle in which the forces of chaos are vanquished. To some extent, the visions look back from 95 c.e. to the crucifixion and resurrection of Jesus; in another sense, they look forward to the fulfillment of the new age of victory which had already begun in the death and resurrection of Christ.

The second major section of the Book of Revelation, chapters 12–19, develops in vivid terms the traditional dualism of apocalyptic. The war between light and darkness, good and evil—so common in the writings from Qumran—is set forth in these chapters by the use of various mythological motifs.

At Revelation 12 begins the cosmic battle between the forces of order and those of chaos. Unfortunately the chapter is difficult to analyze, primarily because of scholarly disagreement on the relationship between verses 1–6 and 7–13. It does seem likely that verses 7–13 represent an earlier—even Jewish—tradition which has been incorporated into the rest of the material. The story tells of a heavenly conflict between the good and the evil: Michael, the protector of Israel, along with his angels versus the dragon and his angels. The victory the desert to Pella, both prior to the fall of Jerusalem in 70 c.e. In either case or both, the events of history are mythicized in order to interpret the times as the apocalyptic end.

The vanquished character is further identified as "that ancient serpent, who is called the Devil and Satan, the deceiver of the whole world" (v. 9). The reference to the "ancient serpent" might allude to Genesis 3, particularly because of the description as "deceiver of the whole world." More likely, on the basis of the mythological battle scene, the serpent recalls that representative of chaos whom Yahweh vanquished in primordial times and whom he would again defeat in the eschaton. Strikingly that chaos monster of old is identified here with Satan, once a responsible functioning member of God's divine assembly (Job 1; Zech. 3:1–4) but now a rebel excommunicated from heaven because of his presumption to sit beside God's throne (II Enoch 29:4–5; Book of Adam and Eve 9:1; cf. the attempt of "Day Star" in Isa. 14:12ff.) or because he allowed his accusing role to get out of hand (cf. v. 10).

The victory of order over chaos results, as one would expect, in the acclamation of the reign of God (v. 10). At the same time, that heavenly conquest places the angry Satan on earth where he will literally raise hell, "because he knows that his time is short" (v. 12).

If this much of the story originated in Judaism where Michael's adversary role was clearly established, the account has been christianized, or better christologized, by words and phrases in verses 10–11: "and the authority of his Christ," "by the blood of the Lamb." The latter expression clarifies for the Christian community that chaos is not overcome by angels, even Michael, but by the cross of Christ.

The reference to the cross in verse 11 is the only historical allusion in the chapter. Set in the present context of Revelation 12, the excommunication of Satan follows immediately a "sign" in heaven (vv. 1–6). Introduced as the sign is a woman clothed with the cosmic garments of sun, moon, and stars. Pregnant with child, the woman represents the heavenly counterpart of the ideal Zion to whom is born the Messiah (see Mic. 4:9–10; 5:2–4 as one example of the image). This heavenly birth does not describe the earthly delivery of Jesus but an eschatological fulfillment of the Messianic hope. Like the Davidic kings enthroned in Jerusalem, this Messiah will rule all nations with a rod of iron (v. 5; cf. Ps. 2:9). Every attempt by the chaos monster, "a great red dragon, with seven heads and ten horns" (like Lotan/Leviathan), to devour this Messiah will end in failure. All that is left for the cosmically defeated dragon is to vent his wrath "on the rest of her offspring, on those who keep the commandments of God and bear testimony to Jesus" (v. 17). It is possible to understand this reference to Jews and Christians: Jews who fled to Jabneh with Johanan ben Zakkai, and Christians from Jerusalem who fled through the desert to Pella, both prior to the fall of Jerusalem in 70 c.e. In either case or both, the events of history are mythicized in order to interpret the times as the apocalyptic end.

The warning given to sea and earth because of Satan's excommunication from heaven (12:12) is appropriate indeed, for as the chapter ends, the dragon stands on the sand of the sea. Then out of the sea itself arises a beast, likewise decorated with ten horns and seven heads (13:1). To the beast was given the power, throne, and authority of the dragon with the result that people worshiped both dragon and beast, saying "Who is like the beast, and who can fight against it?" (v. 4). To those faithful who knew their Bible, what we call the Old Testament, such a rhetorical question should have had a powerful impact. For centuries the worshiping community of Israel sang hymns which recalled Yahweh's victories over chaos and asked rhetorically,

> For who in the skies can be compared to Yahweh?
> Who among the sons of gods is like Yahweh?
>
> (Ps. 89:6)

On the basis of that victory over the chaotic sea, the same question was asked after the drowning of the Egyptians in the Sea (Exod. 15:11) and after the deliverance of the weak from the strong (Ps. 35:10). Thus "who is like the beast?" are fighting words, because both Israel and the church know who he is: the Divine Warrior who defends his people from all the representatives of Chaos.

But who is this beast? If the dragon is the heavenly opponent of God, the beast out of the sea would seem to be identifiable as some earthly representative, just as the monsters of chaos were often represented by kings and nations in the Hebrew Bible. The description of the beast as having ten horns, an appearance "like a leopard," feet "like a bear's," and mouth "like a lion's" seems to sum up the characteristics of all four beasts who rise out of the sea in Daniel 7. In that earlier apocalypse, the beasts represented the kingdoms of the Neo-Babylonians, Medians, Persians, and Greeks—all kingdoms which must tick away on the cosmic clock before the kingdom of God is given to the faithful Saints of the Most High (apparently the Maccabean martyrs). In Rev. 13:1–2 all these characteristics describe one beast, the Roman Empire with its succession of psychopaths and egotists who claim to be divine and thus demand worship (13:4). Prototype of such lunacy was Nero who by suicide in 68 C.E. received a mortal wound (13:3) and who in myth was expected to return in order to continue his atrocities (13:12). In connection with this beast's authority against the faithful, the author issues his "call for the endurance and faith of the saints" (13:10).

This seven-headed beast out of the sea, while impossible to identify as any particular Roman emperor, seemed mythologically to represent the monster Leviathan. That identification is strengthened when one encounters in the second half of Revelation 13 a beast "which rose out of the earth" (v. 11). This monster seems to represent the mythological Behemoth, a land animal. Together the two are mentioned for the first time at Job 40:15–41:34, but the terrible duo continues in apocalyptic tradition. At 1 Enoch 60:7–8 the two are assigned their respective locales, Leviathan to the watery abyss and Behemoth to the wilderness waste places. These same homes are mentioned at IV Ezra 6:49–51 where the two are reserved as food for the eschatological day, as indeed Leviathan was devoured in the primordial days (Ps. 74:14). Perhaps most interesting in regard to Revelation 13 is the prediction of II Baruch 29:4 that each monster will arise from the sea and land respectively at the revealing of the Messiah; the faithful people who survive the battle of the last days will eat the meat of Leviathan and Behemoth. Thus, beginning at Job 40–41 there developed a mythological tradition in apocalyptic literature which is further transformed by John the Seer in order to describe the monster adversaries of God's elect people. Further, that their appearance was to coincide with the Messianic age is useful for John in his portrayal of the imminent era of victory.

It is the historical identification of this second beast which has caused a great deal of scholarly debate and popular interest. It seems that the key to understanding his identity lies in the number 666. However, agreement on the interpretation of the number is by no means achieved, particularly because of a textual variant 616. While most scholars argue for Nero on the basis of gematria (each letter of the alphabet has numerical value), others suggest the more symbolic interpretation that three sixes indicate thrice lack of perfection (777). That the Seer introduces his number for the beast with the warning that "this calls for wisdom" (v. 18) serves to remind us that he has not provided the key to interpret the imagery; such secrets are reserved for the initiated few in apocalyptic tradition. In any case, the beasts of Revelation 13 seem to have something to do on a historical level with the Roman Empire. While some scholars identify particular Roman emperors or even Roman sympathizers like the Jewish historian Josephus with either of the beasts, a responsible approach might simply be to suggest that the Roman Empire itself developed in such a way that the signs of the apocalyptic end were in sight. God was accomplishing his victory over heavenly and earthly forces in order to thus establish his reign over the cosmos (see Isa. 24:21–23). Thus was the history of the times mythicized by various and sundry images in order to introduce the cosmic battle.

The lines for battle are clearly drawn. On the one side is the dragon with his beastly friends, the ten-horned beast from the sea (13:1) and the two-horned beast from the earth (13:11). On the other side, standing on Mount Zion is the Lamb along with 144,000 on whose foreheads are written the names of the Lamb and his Father (14:1). Later this opponent of the dragon is a Warrior on a white horse; he is the Word of God on whose robe is the name "King of kings and Lord of lords" (19:11–16). On the basis of the adversaries involved, the issue at stake is clearly the dominion of the cosmos: either chaos or order will reign after the battle.

Finally, in Revelation 20 the adversaries become completely cosmic: an angel versus Satan himself. The battle ensues when the angel comes down out of heaven, bringing along the key to the bottomless pit, the Deep. Immediately "the dragon, that ancient serpent who is the Devil and Satan" (compare 12:9) was bound and thrown into the pit. To keep him there for a thousand years, the door was shut and sealed over him, just as Marduk once bolted the door and set guards so that Tiamat's waters might not escape (20:1–3).

At the end of the thousand years Satan will be loosed from his pit, gather the evil forces for battle, and attack Jerusalem. But just as Yahweh had defended his city from the chaos forces of the past (Isa. 17:12–14; Ps. 48:4–8; 76:1–6), so will the enemy again be driven off. Satan will be thrown into the Lake of Fire, to be joined by Death and Hades themselves (20:7–15). This is the cosmic hope for those who suffer under the persecutions of Rome and under such representatives of chaos throughout history.

The final battle complete, chaos subdued once and for all, the Seer begins his final vision: "Then I saw a new heaven and a new earth; for the first heaven and the first earth had passed away, and the sea was no more" (Rev. 21:1).

Part Two

DIVINE AND HUMAN SEXUALITY

4

The Rhythm of Fertility and Sterility

In the first chapter we observed a continuing conflict among the natural forces representing order or life on the one hand and chaos or death on the other. The forces of life-giving storms needed to prevail against the flooding of the land in order for the crops necessary for life to grow; the life-giving sun needed to rise over the Nile valley in order to cause the fertile ground to give its food. Human survival, in other words, was the key to the consuming interest in the orderly functioning of nature. In this same regard it is essential to the understanding of the respective mythologies to consider the specific relationship of the deity's welfare to the fertility of crops and animals. What caused the seed to grow? What happened when the crop had been harvested? What caused animals and humans to be fertile on some occasions and infertile—or disinterested—on others? How could one ensure the development of the seed so that life might continue?

MESOPOTAMIA: DUMUZI AND OTHER LOVERS

From as early as the fourth millennium B.C.E., the people of Mesopotamia worshiped the gods as providers. While later literary evidence is necessary to support the scanty artistic evidence from that early period, it is clear that life-sustaining activities bore special significance and devotion.

While sexual and marital experiences of many divine couples are attested to in the myths and rituals of Mesopotamia, the stories from the Dumuzi cult offer abundant information which enables us to understand this aspect of the religion. In a general sense, one can speak

74

of Dumuzi in terms of the young god's courtship and marriage, his early death, and a search for his body in the netherworld. In actual fact, this whole range of action appears neither in a single text nor in a single cult. The various representations of Dumuzi and the essential events are related to each community's basic economy—date growing, barley raising, shepherding.

In one community Dumuzi is known by the form Dumuzi-Amashumgalana, the power in the date palm to produce new fruit. In this cult his partner is the goddess Inanna, who represents the storehouse for the dates. The story of their marriage is depicted on a fourth-millennium B.C.E. vase from the city of Uruk and is related in poetic form in various texts from the following millennia. That the power of fertility is wed to the storehouse for the dates indicates in the life experience of the Mesopotamian that the whole community can enjoy food and drink and know the security that Inanna will "take care of the life of all lands." The story thus represents a date harvest ritual, and since in mythology what happens in the heavens corresponds to an event on earth (or vice versa), the sacred marriage is portrayed in ritual. One text reports that the role of Dumuzi-Amashumgalana is played by the king and that of Inanna by a queen or high priestess.

> "The king goes with lifted head to the holy loins,
> goes with lifted head to the loins of Inanna,
> Amashumgalana goes to bed with her."[14]

Other stories, originating in different economically based communities, expand the blessings of fertility far beyond the date palm to include those for farmers and shepherds alike, as well as for hunters and for wildlife in general. On the other hand, Dumuzi could be separated from date palms altogether and could become the deity responsible solely for the generative power in livestock. Here, too, of course, the spring growth is necessary for food but that blessing is short-lived in contrast to the success of animal mating. In this mythology the sexual act is emphasized even more than that of the date palm economy, and so the narratives and the accompanying rituals are much more explicit and frank. In other words, here fertility rites become even more important than those harvest rites which emphasize bonds of marriage and security in mutual love.

The shepherd's view that crops are short-lived over against the blessings of livestock is amply confirmed by numerous versions of

the death of Dumuzi, corresponding to the passing of fertile spring
and the onset of the hot and dry summers of the Middle East.
Dumuzi's death is described in various ways, even in one story by
the deliverance of Dumuzi to the owners of the netherworld by his
own wife Inanna, so that she herself might escape that terrible fate.
Normally, his death leads to much lamentation by his wife, his
mother, and his sister, which is enacted ritually by mourning rites of
the worshipers. Part of the divine lamentation involves a search for
Dumuzi's body in the netherworld, particularly performed jointly by
his mother and sister or by his sister alone. Indeed, also reported is
the descent of Inanna herself into the netherworld, which seems to
suggest the dwindling of food supplies in the storehouse and the un-
certain continuation of human life.

In only one composition is the return of Dumuzi reported. In his
form as Damu, the power in the sap of trees and vegetation, the god
is lamented ritually at a sacred cedar tree in the temple compound at
Uruk. This tree represented the god's mother and marked his birthplace. By proper ritual lamentation the worshipers could go on to
experience the revival of the sap which was dormant in the trees and
rushes in the dry season but which became visible with the rise of the
Euphrates river.

Apart from Dumuzi cults and myths, the god Enlil—whom we
met earlier as the storm god of springtime—was active as a sexual
partner for his wife Ninlil, a grain goddess. Enlil's relationship to
fertility can be seen in the description of his throne as "the holy
mound" which reflects the storage pile of grain and wool. Further, in
a text called the "Hymn to Enlil," the deity is described as having
such power and authority over fertility and sterility that without his
consent animals could neither lose their young at birth nor could
they deliver their offspring. It seems that by a mythological interpretation of wind pollination, Enlil rapes Ninlil, the grain, and dies as
springtime passes.

Another divine pair worth noting is Enki and Ninhursag. Enki
represents the power in the sweet waters of rivers which makes seeds
grow as well as that power in male semen which fertilizes the animal
egg. Ninhursag is the mother of all wildlife as well as of all gods and
humans. In a myth about the relations between the two, the proper
lady will consent to intercourse only if Enki agrees to marriage. The
resulting offspring is "Lady Plant" who, upon reaching young wom-
anhood, is seduced by Enki, causing his daughter to bear another fe-

male offspring. This process recurs again and again until finally Ninhursag warns the fourth daughter about her incestuous father. Eventually this showdown results in a reconciliation between husband and wife. Yet far from being a tale of morality (or lack thereof), the story seems to be a fertility myth celebrating the generative power—as well as the inconstancy—of river water.

The ritual theme of the sacred marriage is difficult to trace from the Sumerian period (third millennium B.C.E.) through Mesopotamian religion. However, on the basis of information from seventh-century B.C.E. Babylon, it seems that the sacred marriage was an essential ingredient of the *akitu*, the New Year Festival on the fourth day of which the *Enuma elish* was recited and dramatized. The king, representing the fertile and victorious god, escorted the goddess (in human form) into a hut where the marriage was consummated. This ritual act, along with the victorious combat of Marduk, ensured fertility and order, indeed sustained life itself for the ensuing year.

As the Sumerian period passed over into the Babylonian and Assyrian times in Mesopotamia, the names of deities changed, or—as we saw earlier in the transition of power from Enlil to Marduk—new deities took over roles of the older ones. The goddess of fertility par excellence—formerly Inanna—became Ishtar, goddess of love and war. Her reputation as a lover was attested to by quite a number of divine partners, although she never seemed to have recovered from the rejection by the divine-human figure Gilgamesh. At any rate, that her welfare had direct bearing on the fertility of the earth is seen clearly in the text called "Descent of Ishtar to the Nether World" (*ANET*, pp. 106–109). Like her predecessor Inanna, this goddess of fertility descended to that abode from which there is no return: the realm of the dead. Although the reason is not clear, Ishtar was apparently visiting her sister Ereshkigal, Queen of the netherworld. Ereshkigal, however, was not all that pleased with her unexpected visitor, and so Ishtar was locked up, perhaps even killed. When news of her descent reached the gods above, a divine messenger reported the effects to King Ea:

> "Since Ishtar has gone down to the Land of no Return,
> The bull springs not upon the cow, the ass impregnates not the jenny,
> In the street the man impregnates not the maiden.
> The man lies down in his (own) chamber,
> The maiden lies down on her side."

> (*ANET*, p. 108)

Thus by the incapacitation of the fertility goddess, animals were impotent, and humans were disinterested. Apparently the soil was infertile too, with seeds locked in the ground as was Ishtar herself.

Not to demean the poor lady when she is down and out, it is interesting to note that Ishtar, like Inanna before her, was the goddess of harlots, and herself a harlot. This claim to fame was probably related to the belief that she was the goddess of the morning and evening stars: when the evening star came out, so did they, disappearing again like the morning star in the light of the sun.

This brief survey demonstrates that the gods and goddesses of Mesopotamia were active sexual beings. While some of the stories might seem simply comical or perhaps vulgar from our perspective, many of them are myths which interpret nothing less important than the sustenance of life itself. The sexual activities of this or that deity, portrayed in more or less detail, correspond to the fertility of the earth's seed and of human and animal seed as well. Ritually, the texts demonstrate the need for the sexual act to be enjoyed by the king representing the god and some divinely endowed human woman representing the appropriate goddess. This ritual "sacred marriage" corresponded to the heavenly consummation and thus ensured the fertilizing of all sorts of seeds on earth. Whether or not the sexual act was enjoyed by others in addition to royalty in Mesopotamian liturgy and ritual is difficult to determine, but in a religious culture based so fundamentally on fertility, one can probably assume more general involvement.

Yet it would be misleading to give the impression that sex for the ancient Mesopotamian was strictly a religious affair. On the contrary, sex was a quite natural and joyous human activity, consistent with the harmony of the cosmos. Beautiful—and explicit—love poems indicate an openness to include sex as part of a normal and healthy life. In those human poems, as well as in some of the myths discussed above, male and female share with eager participation in the sex act and in the pursuit of joys thereof.

As with every other area of life, sex was part and parcel of that branch of Mesopotamian "science" related to omens. All kinds of fortunes and misfortunes are explained by the sexual activities of humans. Sex performed regularly during afternoon siestas will enable a man to have a personal god and be happy. Yet disaster will befall a man who, after having intercourse, experiences an emission during a dream; if intercourse does not precede that emission, he will enjoy good fortune and success. Furthermore, the "missionary position" seems to have been the most beneficial, for if a woman mounted a man, the virility of that man would be lost for a month. While this last example might provide evidence of a lack of equality in love-making, the entire range of possibilities in these omen texts suggests a naturalness and even an openness to experimentation in sexual activity. The consequences for good or ill were not determined by morality but by magic.

Indeed it is by magic that one could gain (or regain) potency, an important quality for male and female in a society where begetting children was essential to family economy. The rituals and incantations for potency are as vivid in expressive detail as any contemporary X-rated film. Yet in their context this language was by no means lewd; it was a natural expression related to the continuation of life and to the joys of sexual activity.

CANAAN: FERTILITY AND INFERTILITY OF BAAL

Alongside the theme of the conflict between Baal/Anath and Yamm, in the Ugaritic texts, that of the conflict between Baal and Mot ("Death") represents a mythological interpretation of the natural cycle. While the battle against Yamm takes place during the late autumn/winter storms, the struggle against Mot has its setting in the summer when the scorching sun and drought cause the vegetation to wither. Thus Mot represents not only the death of animals and humans but the passing of vegetation as well. Yet in fairness to this deity who is sometimes referred to as "the darling of El," some scholars have suggested that the word *môt* means basically "maturity." In other words, this deity might play a role in the maturing or ripening of the fruit on the vine for which Baal's wintry rains provided the impetus. However, as we all come to know too well, too much maturity leads ultimately to demise, and so Mot seems to represent the sterility of seed. Indeed, just as Mot lives in the netherworld beneath the earth, so do seeds go underground until Baal provides the necessary rain for their return.

Therein lies the nature of the myth. Following the defeat of Yamm by Baal, Mot, it seems, had been assigned to the subterranean regions. In a speech to the victor, Mot invited Baal to descend to the netherworld where "Death" would swallow up the fertility deity. The correspondence between Baal's descent into Mot's ravenous gullet and the annual death of vegetation is explicit in these few lines of the poem.

One lip to earth and one to heaven,
  [He stretches his to]ngue to the stars.
Baal enters his mouth,
  Descends into him like an olive-cake,
  Like the yield of the earth and tree's fruit.

(*ANET*, p. 138)

The news that the master of fertility had been lost to the realm of sterility was reported to King El by messengers who claimed they had found Baal dead. Immediately El left his throne to begin the mourning ritual consisting of pouring dust on his head and donning sackcloth, gashing his body as a plow harrows a garden, and crying out that Baal was dead. When Baal's sister Anath discovered the body, she too lamented in the same fashion, then buried her brother on his own Mount Zaphon where she slaughtered animals as tribute to Baal.

This mourning ritual of the deities El and Anath corresponds—as one would expect in myth and ritual—to the activity of the human prophets of Baal in their so-called contest with Elijah on Mount Carmel (1 Kings 18:26, 28–29). After slaughtering a bull, the devotees called on Baal all morning long (perhaps imitating thunder to which their yelling was to correspond); this crying was accompanied by a limping dance around Baal's altar. More pointedly, they "gashed themselves with swords and lances *according to their custom* (ritual), until blood spurted on them." The reason for all this activity was clearly related to the information already given in the story that a drought was in its third year (cf. 1 Kings 17:1 and 18:1). In the Canaanite religion such a drought indicated that the rain god was dead, and so indeed "there was no thunder; no sign of life" (18:29; cf. 2 Kings 4:31).

Indeed, as the story continues in the Ugaritic texts, El described the corresponding effects on the ground rather precisely. El had just seen a vision of the resurrection of Baal and the fertility of the land, but in reality he discovered and declared,

"Parch'd is the furrow of Soil, O Shapsh;
  Parched is El's Soil's furrow:
  Baal neglects the furrow of his tillage."

(*ANET*, p. 141)

Just as the ritual corresponds to the mourning of El and Anath, so the earth itself dies in correspondence with the demise of its lord.

Ultimately Baal appeared on the scene, demonstrated his renewed strength by beating off a few enemies, and ascended to "the throne of his kingship." His real test occurred, however, with renewed combat against Mot. After a fierce struggle between Fertility and Sterility, Baal vanquished his opponent, and so the summer drought had come to its end!

The various correspondences between the action among the deities and the natural cycle clearly define the story as a fertility myth. In addition, many scholars find various pieces of the story explicable only by viewing it as a cultic drama in which rites and actions in worship accompanied the recital.

While there is no indication in the Ugaritic texts or in other West Semitic evidence to suggest that the kings of the city-states were considered to be divine, they were considered to be El's sons and his representatives on earth. Thus it is interesting to note that in two epics from Ugarit the death of a royal person leads to the breakdown of even the natural order. In the "Legend of King Keret" the severe sickness of the king is related to sterility of the land, exhaustion of the grain, wine, and oil reserves, and the need to pay tribute to Baal by an offering. "The Tale of Aght" reports that after King Daniel's son Aght was killed by Anath in order to obtain his bow, the royal father anticipated in a lament that

> "Seven years shall Baal fail,
> > Eight the Rider of the Clouds.
> No dew,
> > No rain;
> No welling-up of the deep,
> > No sweetness of Baal's voice.
> For rent
> Is the garment of Daniel the Rapha-man,
> > The vestment of Ghazir [the Harnamiyy-man]."
>
> > > > > > > > > > (*ANET*, p. 153)

The myth of Baal has not yet introduced the theme of sex related to fertility, as indeed was so explicit when the Babylonian Ishtar descended to the netherworld. Such escapades do in fact exist in the literature, although even the intimacy of Baal and Anath is difficult to place in sequence with the myth already described. Quite distinct perhaps is the story which tells of a passionate affair between brother and sister. Represented in several places with the horns of a cow, Anath is spied by Baal, mutual foreplay is described vividly, and the result of the embrace is that ultimately Baal receives "godly tidings" announcing the birth of a wild ox (*ANET*, p. 142). The text might suggest a sacred marriage, particularly because a related text states (euphemistically?) that Anath eats the flesh of Baal without a knife and drinks his blood without a goblet.

The most explicit sexual poem in the Ugaritic texts is that called "The Birth of the Gracious Gods." There it is the god El who is responsible for the fertility of two young women who bear him the sons "Dawn" and "Sunset." Interpretations of the myth vary considerably. Theodor Gaster interprets the story in terms of a Canaanite festival of first fruits in which sacred marriage played a key role. For Gaster El's virility is evidenced by the allusion to his "hand as far reaching as the sea." Other interpreters, particularly Marvin Pope, interpret El's "hand" euphemistically and argue that while long, El's penis kept drooping while he was trying to seduce the women.[15] Finally, however, the virtual impotence of El was overcome by magical rites, and the deity succeeded in causing the women to conceive and bear sons. Whatever the view of El in the story, it is interesting to realize that the text is full of ritual rubrics, at least stage directions, and the drama seems to be enacted in the presence of royalty. Thus, it is quite possible that the king and queen played a ritual role in the sacred marriage. In such a case, the sex act between the human partners would correspond to that of the divine figures in the drama and thus likewise result in fertility.

In addition to Baal and El, other deities played important roles in the fertility cults of Canaan. Though assigned no role in the mythological texts of Ugarit, Dagan was probably the original vegetation deity whose son Baal later took over that function. Mentioned in the Hebrew Bible as the grain god of the Philistines (Judg. 16:23; 1 Sam. 5:1–5), Dagan had a temple in Ugarit and thus was a major deity there alongside Baal, his son. We have already seen that Anath played an active sexual role, and so, like her Mesopotamian counterpart Ishtar, she was goddess of both love and war. While often called in translation the Virgin (*'lmt*), she certainly does not fit that description. Further, the goddess Asherah—the estranged (?) wife of El—is portrayed more as a matriarchal figure than a sexual partner like the younger and more vigorous Anath.

The Hebrew Bible serves as an important source for understanding Canaanite religion, particularly in terms of the fertility emphasis in that society. Living in the land side by side with Canaanites, the people of Israel were well acquainted with the enticing religious practices of their neighbors. We have already noted the fertility role of Baal and the mourning ritual on Mount Carmel. Yet the same role is evident in architecture as well as in ritual: as the source of procreation par excellence Baal was frequently represented at cult sites by a "pillar" (*maṣṣēbâ*; 1 Kings 14:23 and often). Anath does not appear in the Hebrew Bible as a deity, but Asherah takes on the youthful form of a fertility goddess, who was worshiped in a house (temple) of male cult prostitutes (see 2 Kings 23:7, also v. 14; cf. 1 Kings 14:23–24; 22:46). Apparently this deity was represented at various high places as a fruitful tree, either natural or manufactured (Hos. 4:11–14; 1 Kings 14:23; 15:12). That cultic prostitutes played a role in the worship of Canaanite deities provides further evidence of the correspondence between myth and ritual; such sexual activity, it seems, was not restricted to king and queen, as one might conclude from the scanty information available in the Ugaritic texts.

All this suggests that for the Canaanites sex was deeply rooted in a theological and religious concern for life itself. While the prophets and others, such as the authors of Deuteronomy, depict this sexual activity in a negative light, it must be realized that for the Canaanites sex was nothing less than a vital force to maintain the life of the community. That such activity in ritual corresponded to the actions of the gods did not make it any less enjoyable, to be sure, but their enthusiasm for sexual activity and resulting progeny was both natural and necessary for life in an agricultural economy. Without texts describing the non-cultic place of sex in the life of the average Canaanite, one can assume an openness to lively participation by this society which made no distinction between the sacred and the secular.

In that light, the means by which infertility was overcome are strikingly mild in contrast to the vivid sexual maneuvers prescribed in some Mesopotamian magical texts. On the one hand, young women of marriageable age participated in sex with a representative of the fertility god in order to ensure progeny for a prospective husband. This ritual act, performed in the temple precinct with some stranger, allowed the woman to display publicly by means of certain jewelry or even well-placed scratches that she was no longer a virgin but initiated into the powers of fertility. Thus, proof of premarital cultic sex was desirable for a man to find in a prospective bride. On the other hand, the practice of kings who were son-less was to sacrifice to the god Baal, for by appeasing him the king could look forward to the blessing of progeny from El. By this means both Keret and Daniel were successful in their bids to provide male heirs to their thrones (*ANET* pp. 143, 149f).

EGYPT: DENIAL OF DEATH
AND STERILITY

The place of sex in the divine assemblages over the Nile valley was not so explicitly described as it was in Mesopotamia and Canaan. This difference can be explained in part by the absence of epics and dramatic texts which would relate such fertility myths. In other words, the stories for such activity simply do not exist; there are preserved no tales of the exploits of fertility gods and goddesses who make love in order to ensure that infertility or sterility might not take control. But the absence of such stories is itself a symptom and not the cause of differences between Egypt and its Semitic neighbors in the area of sex. Just as Egypt's concept of the conflict between order and chaos was based not on the precarious seasonal combat of natural forces but on the regular nocturnal and consistently won match between sun god and serpent, so that same regularity and that same confidence in victory eliminated the need for the struggle between fertility and infertility among the deities. The consistent flow and overflow of the Nile River and the daily appearance of the sun enabled the Egyptian to assume the natural cycle of sowing and harvest.

Nevertheless, fertility was indeed a vital—though not worrisome—issue in the Nile valley, and evidence for that concern mythologically can be seen in the very ancient myth of Osiris. Born to the grandchildren of the Creator God, Osiris and his brother Seth vied for supremacy of the universe. The idyllic age established by Osiris was destroyed by Seth who likewise murdered and "cast down" Osiris himself, in fact cut him in pieces. The now widowed Isis put together again enough of her husband that she was able to conceive a son, Horus. When that divine offspring grew up, he became the avenger of his father, but the battle between Horus and Seth lasted so long that even the other gods tired of the monotonous disturbance in the universe.

Since mythology is based on correspondences, it is necessary to interpret the story in terms of earthly existence. Seth is destruction and chaos; storm, earthquake, and the deadly desert wind are his manifestations. Osiris represents the grain who at harvest time is cut down and whose seeds go underground (actually, underworld) for a time. Like Baal in the Canaanite stories, Osiris was retrieved by his sister-wife and mourned by both Isis and Nephthys. Yet unlike Baal, Osiris never seems to have been resurrected as a mighty power; indeed, Osiris remains a passive deity, a symbol of inertia and death, even identified as the place of the dead, the pyramid. It is Horus the son who becomes the active one, the deity incarnate in the pharaoh. It is he who has responsibility for the growth of the crops, so that Osiris might again live—in the grain and in the life-after-death of each deceased king who by becoming "an Osiris" is transformed into a living soul. As long as Horus is incarnate on Egypt's throne, nature itself and royal humans can expect immortality.

The role of sex in the myth and ritual connected with Osiris is difficult to perceive. Even Horus is assigned no sexual role, except perhaps in his form as Min. Venerated chiefly at Coptos, Min is consistently portrayed standing upright with penis in full erection. While his virile splendor is not described in any stories, the fact that the annual harvest festival was held in his honor confirms the obvious role which the visual image of this deity suggests. Moreover, a relief of Min appears on the wall of the "Birth House" of Amenophis II, part of the temple of Thebes (modern Luxor). Thus this deity seems to have been responsible for fertilizing both crops and humans.

The structure and interpretation of the details of the Min festival are by no means completely clear. Any attempt to interpret the evidence, however, seems to be based on the identification of Min with the god Horus who ruled by incarnating himself as the pharaoh. The harvest festival, then, seems to have reaffirmed that the procreative power of Min—and indeed the god himself—was incarnate in the pharaoh. The office and person of the king guaranteed the development of the new seed for one harvest after another. Further, some scholars have suggested hints of a sacred marriage in the description of the festival: perhaps the pharaoh—acting as the ever-ready Min—impregnated the mother of royal princes, one of whom would succeed his father as the new incarnation of Min-Horus.

The female counterpart for Min-Horus would seem to be Isis, his mother. The notion that a god caused the conception of a god through his own mother presents a cycle which is somewhat baffling. Yet in all probability this concept was one way of expressing immortality. The epithet most commonly used for Min is Kamutef, "Bull of his Mother." Usually "Bull" implies the spouse who impregnates his consort-wife-mother. Thus, in a peculiar way, since Min-Horus is perpetually incarnate on the throne of Egypt, the god recreates himself to all eternity.

The strange triangle just described takes an interesting twist in another festival, the Opet, which was celebrated at the neighboring temples of Karnak and Thebes (Luxor). In this festival—perhaps patterned after the *akitu* in Babylon—the mighty god Amon-Re left his magnificent temple at Karnak and was escorted by joyous procession as he traveled on a barge to the temple at Thebes. There he joined his consort Mut for a week of blissful visitation. The offspring of this divine couple was the Karnak deity named Khonsu. Interesting is the description of Mut as a serpent who wound herself around her "father Re." Thus, Mut is both daughter of Amon-Re as well as the mother of his son. The triangle of father-mother-son through an incestuous affair must likewise have something to do with the immortality issue.

The sexual activity of the deities of Egypt is thus quite different from those of their counterparts in Mesopotamia and Canaan. While there is constant conflict with Seth, the victory over death and destruction is guaranteed by the rule of the pharaoh, Horus-on-earth. Thus there is no real threat to the continuation of the cycle of seedtime and harvest. Indeed, in the so-called mortuary religion of Egypt, death and sterility are virtually denied in favor of a static and consistently argued notion of immortality. Thus sex among the gods has as its major purpose the immortality of the deity who rules in the person of the pharaoh.

As for the sexual activity in the ritual descriptions of Egyptian temples, it must be admitted that there is no clear evidence. The participation of worshipers in cultic prostitution—common in the religions of Canaan—does not seem to have played a role in Egypt. The function of maintaining the growth of crops and animal life, to say nothing of human progeny, was the responsibility of the pharaoh alone. Even the role of the king in the sacred marriage—if indeed the pharaoh played such a part—would have been understood differently from that of his royal counterpart in Babylon. In Mesopotamia the king took the part of the god in a sacred marriage at the New Year festival; in Egypt the god reaffirmed his incarnation as the pharaoh in the sex act as in every other aspect of life. Sexual intercourse between Egyptian king and queen—even at a festival—reaffirmed what already existed: the immortal relationship between the god and the reigning pharaoh. In that relationship the prosperity of the land was assured.

Indeed so all-inclusive was the power of the divine king that in some texts the royal person is described as androgynous and thus self-sufficient in the role of fertility. An inscription from the tomb of Rekhmire provides a clear example. "What is the king of Upper and

Lower Egypt? He is a god by whose dealings one lives, the father and mother of all men, alone by himself without an equal."[16]

Yet in the midst of all the emphasis on immortality of the pharaoh and his all-encompassing sexual role, the ancient Egyptians by no means denied the joy of sex. While explicit texts are rare, it is noteworthy that the great sun god Re himself claimed responsibility for the gift of earthly sex. "I am he who made the bull for the cow, so that sexual pleasures might come into being" (*ANET*, p. 13). Thus it would seem that human sex too was the gift of a god who himself knew its pleasures, even if only at annual festivals.

EXCURSUS
SEXUAL ROLES OF MALE AND FEMALE

Little can be said about the roles played by men and women in Canaanite society. The major source of information about religion and social life, namely the Ugaritic texts, offers little help. On the basis of the understanding of the religion and culture in terms of fertility, one might assume that both male and female were regarded as highly and equally significant, for without such a heterosexual partnership, the necessary fertility could not be achieved. Indeed the emphasis on the female and her reproductive parts in art and iconography indicates almost a veneration for female deities and ideally—by correspondence—to human women. One wonders, however, whether the importance of women in the area of fertility had any bearing on other areas of the society.

In Mesopotamia one can hardly speak of the equality of the sexes. Women were regarded as inferior to men, as is evident from law codes and other literary sources. However, the famous law code of Hammurabi demonstrates a protection of women in cases of rape and divorce, allowed women to own property and engage in business, and recognized the right of a woman to deny her husband sexual intercourse. Further, Babylonian law allowed a woman to obtain a divorce, and punished equally a couple caught in the act of adultery.

While the situation in Babylon was better than that in Assyria, it was nevertheless the exceptional woman in the right time and place who managed to gain power during the long history of Mesopotamia.[17] Only one woman gained supreme power in Mesopotamia; according to the Sumerian King, List Ku-Baba "became king" in Kish and ruled a hundred years. Other women, because of their relationships to the king, acquired power, influence, and respect. In the eighteenth century B.C.E. Zimri-Lim of Mari married a woman named Shibtu, who over the years demonstrated such administrative skill that she was entrusted with governing when her husband was off on military campaigns. Almost a millennium later, the woman Sammuramat, wife of Assyrian king Shamshi-Adad V, became legendary for her power and influence. A century later Zakutu, wife of Sennacherib and mother of his successor Esarhaddon, exalted herself by assuming power during the reign of her son. Finally, most powerful of all and lauded by the historian Herodotus was Adad-guppi, the mother of Nabonidus who ruled Babylon from 555 to 539 B.C.E. This woman played a significant role in acquiring the throne for her son, after having attended such kings as Nabopolassar, Nebuchadnezzar, and Neriglissar. While she lived during the first nine years of her son's reign, Adad-guppi seems to have exerted considerable influence based on keen intellect and much experience at court.

It is noteworthy in these cases that not only were the women exceptional in ability and in opportunity but, with the exception of Ku-baba, gained prominence only through their relationship—as wife or mother—to the reigning king. Such opportunities were not open to women in general or even to all royal wives. Thus while one can cite women of prominence, one can hardly speak of sexual equality in Mesopotamia.

The roles and importance of women in Egyptian life and society is amply attested to in the early periods. Even in the Old Kingdom (2750–2250 B.C.E.) Egyptian queens asserted themselves only with a great deal of difficulty: Khent-kaus vied with the men by building a pyramid of equal proportions to theirs; the queen mother of Pepi II ruled the land during her son's infancy. Of course, the outstanding example of the assertion of rulership by a woman occurred in the Eighteenth Dynasty when Hatshepsut declared herself "king" and had her royal mortuary temple built in the Valley of the Kings rather than in the Valley of the Queens. Later during the same dynasty, in the Amarna period of the early part of the fourteenth century B.C.E., the royal wife of Akhenaton, Nefert-iti, and their six daughters (no sons) were displayed quite prominently in art as participants in public life. Indeed, not only royal persons but women in general had rights to own property, to buy and sell, and to testify in court. All in all, the situation in Egypt seems to have been somewhat better for women than for their counterparts in Canaan and Mesopotamia, although it must be admitted that here too women of power were exceptional cases.

5

The Nature of Yahweh and Human Sex

The question of the sexuality and sexual role of Yahweh, the God of Israel, seems at first to be a moot point, simply because the biblical texts nowhere speak of a sexual partner. Such a possibility might have existed in the somewhat heretical community of Jews living on Elephantine Island in the middle of the Nile River during the sixth and fifth centuries B.C.E. However, the Hebrew Bible itself never speaks of such a relationship with a member of the opposite sex.

One can only wonder whether the institution of cult prostitution within the Jerusalem Temple (see 2 Kings 23:7) necessarily led the people to the view that Yahweh enjoyed such pleasures celestially. Indeed, by the understanding of correspondence between the heavenly and earthly worlds, such cultic activity would seem to have had a necessary correlation with Yahweh's sexuality. On the other hand, the Bible is full of examples of architecture, festivals, objects, and practices which have been so transformed in Israel's cult that they no longer have the same meaning as elsewhere.

What is certain is that Yahweh was very much related to fertility. It was Yahweh who established the regular course of the seasons with seedtime and harvest as times of paramount importance (Gen. 8:22). It was Yahweh who caused droughts as punishment on the people because of the actions of kings (2 Samuel 21; 1 Kings 17). Indeed Yahweh was the God who received the offering of first fruits of the harvest, presumably because the deity who fertilized the ground was its proper owner (Deut. 26:1ff.). Praises addressed to Yahweh as fertility deity include these:

> You make springs reach out into the valleys:
>   they flow between the mountains,
> they give drink to every creature of the field;
>   the wild asses quench their thirst. . . .

You cause grass to sprout for the cattle,
   and plants for humans to cultivate,
that they might bring forth food from the earth
   and wine which gladdens the human heart, . . .

(Ps.104:10–11, 14–15a)

Yahweh's role as Provider is not only a present reality but an eschatological hope. Whereas in the Canaanite myths Baal was swallowed up annually by the god of Death and Sterility, in apocalyptic expectations of the Hebrew Bible Yahweh will devour Mot. This reversal of roles between diner and menu will occur when Yahweh throws his eschatological banquet for all peoples (Isa. 25:6–8). In addition to several other benefits for humankind, Yahweh will once for all end the precarious cycle of rain and drought: "He will swallow up Mot forever." Now, however, the destruction of Mot involves not only the end of a fertility cycle but of human demise as well. That the author of this Isaiah Apocalypse was aware of Ugaritic materials is supported by the quotation concerning "Lotan" at Isa. 27:1 (see above, pp. 52–53).

Besides bearing responsibility for fertilizing plants and providing food for animals, Yahweh is likewise involved in the conception and birth of humans. Indeed it is Yahweh who closes wombs to make women infertile, as in the story of Abraham's and Sarah's plot against Abimelech (Gen. 20:1–18) and in the case of Hannah before she finally conceived and bore Samuel (1 Sam. 1:5–6). The means by which the infertile one approached Yahweh was not a magical practice connected with the sex act (as in Mesopotamia) or ritual repetition and sacrifice (as in Ugarit) but persistent prayer (1 Sam. 1:9–18). Only by this means did Yahweh open the womb to conceive, as he did for Hannah (1 Sam. 1:19–20), for Leah and Rachel (Gen. 29:31–35; 30:22), and as he will do in the future (Isa. 66:9). Even more intimate, in the womb itself Yahweh forms individuals and there commissions future leaders of the people (Jer. 1:5; Isa. 49:1).

Necessarily involved in and responsible for fertility, Yahweh is never explicitly described as having a sexual partner. It remains now to examine what analogies and metaphors of a sexual nature are used in relation to Yahweh and to determine what meaning they had in the faith of ancient Israel. Further, we need to consider whether the notion of correspondence plays a role in the relationship between Yahweh's sexuality and human sex.

YAHWEH AS THE HUSBAND OF A WIFE

It is the prophet Hosea in the eighth century B.C.E. who first uses marriage as a metaphor for the relationship between Yahweh and Israel. Indeed, so basic is the marriage motif to the prophet's entire proclamation that the very first words of Yahweh to Hosea explicate the prophet's mission in terms of marital infidelity.

> When Yahweh first spoke through Hosea, Yahweh said to Hosea, "Go, marry a woman of 'harlotry' and have children of 'harlotry,' for the land commits great 'harlotry' by forsaking Yahweh." So he went and married Gomer, the daughter of Diblaim, and she conceived and bore him a son. (Hos. 1:3–4)

Often understood to be a prostitute or at best a cult prostitute, the woman is more likely an up-to-date Israelite who had taken part in the bridal rite of initiation common among the Canaanites.[18] Thus, in an explicit way the woman represents the people of Israel who had kept "limping with two different opinions" (1 Kings 18:21), that is, constantly moving back and forth in belief and practice between Yahweh and Baal.

If this woman represents Israel in her attempt to have both worlds, Hosea represents the faithful husband Yahweh. Thus the Hosea-Gomer marriage is analogous to the relationship which Yahweh made with Israel. It is striking that Hosea's contemporary, Amos, speaking to that same general audience of northern Israel, uses intimate terminology to describe her exclusive relationship to Yahweh: "You only have I known out of all families of the earth" (Amos 3:2). Yet Hosea himself, and surely Amos too, in no way imagines genital activity between God and a people. It is the intimacy and exclusivity of the relationship which is communicated by the analogy. Later, or in other circles, this relationship between Yahweh and Israel would be labelled technically a "covenant" (*běrît*).

The use of the marriage analogy in Hosea takes on powerful and even shocking vibrations when Yahweh commands a second time that Hosea should love an adulteress, presumably Gomer (3:1ff.). While it is not explicit that the same woman is meant here, the context of the speech leads the reader to think that Gomer, having been married to Hosea and having borne children, has run off with another man. Hosea—obedient to Yahweh's command—purchases her from her lover, takes her home, and pledges mutual fidelity. What is shocking about this text is its offense against the law prescribed at

Deut. 24:1–4. A man is forbidden to take back a wife after she has been defiled by another. Indeed such an action is considered an abomination before Yahweh. When Hosea is commanded to perform precisely that act as analogous to the action of Yahweh in taking back unfaithful Israel, it is not only Hosea but Yahweh as well who risks the curse of "abomination." Yet these are the lengths to which God will go in order to restore the broken marriage.

Hosea's use of the marriage analogy clearly must be understood in light of the society in which he lived and preached. The northern kingdom of Israel consisted of those fertile hills and valleys where the indigenous religion of Canaan ran rampant. One needed only to look at the luscious growth and taste its fruit to know that there the god of fertility reigned supreme. That deity was Baal—and even the people of Israel came to believe in him, as we know also from an earlier prophet to that area, Elijah.

Preaching in this fertile land, Hosea set out to remind the people of their marriage to Yahweh, a relationship which was founded not in the fertile valleys of Canaan but in the sands of Egypt and in the limestone desert (12:9; 13:4–5; 2:14–15). It is not in nature but in history, not in a cyclical pattern but in a unique time- and space-bound event, the exodus, that Yahweh became Israel's God, and Israel Yahweh's people.

At the same time, Hosea was fully aware that past events could not compare in popular thinking with present benefits, and so the prophet portrayed Yahweh by means of numerous images taken from the animal and vegetable world. Yahweh is like a shepherd, fowler, lion, leopard, she-bear. Astonishingly, Yahweh is also like the "dew" which causes Israel to blossom and grow (14:5–7) and like the "tree" which gives both shade and fruit to the people (14:7, 8). Both these images derive from Canaanite religion: dew is the gift of Baal, and tree is the symbol of the female deity Asherah. Moreover, Hosea states explicitly that it was Yahweh and not Baal who "gave her the grain, the wine, and the oil" (2:8).

Having forgotten her true provider, Israel is now the defendant in a divorce case: Yahweh sues on the basis of adultery (2:2–13). The case against the people is clear. Ever since the brief honeymoon in the desert (Hos. 2:15), Israel had been whoring after other lovers. Even though Israel is the only family of the earth "known" by Yahweh, that is, with whom Yahweh has been intimate, Israel has no "knowledge of God," no faithfulness or loyalty in love, despite the fact that such knowledge is Yahweh's burning desire (6:6).

Following Hosea's lead, Jeremiah and Ezekiel described the relationship between Yahweh and Israel as a marriage in which Israel was unfaithful. For Jeremiah, the loving devotion of a bride described the people's attitude toward God during the wilderness period (2:2–3), but contact with the lures of Canaanite religion caused the bride to become an insatiable harlot (2:20–25; 3:1–5, 6–10). Ezekiel's portrayal of the relationship is the most sensuous of all; yet even that most intimate affair which resulted in a covenant of marriage came to ruin because of Israel's insistence on playing the harlot with any passerby. Addressing those exiles who were already experiencing a painful separation, Ezekiel proclaimed Yahweh's promise of forgiveness and reconciliation (Ezek. 20).

It was Second Isaiah who explicitly cited the marriage of Yahweh and Israel as the motive for deliverance from exile in Babylon. Although Yahweh has forsaken Israel for a moment, leaving her like an abandoned wife, nevertheless the role of Yahweh as her faithful husband will cause the shame of her youth to be forgotten (Isa. 54:5–8). Thus Yahweh is the husband of a wife named Israel. Not another deity but a people is Yahweh's marriage partner. Thus, the intimacy once known in the desert and still desired by Yahweh can in no way be depicted or described in genital terms. Intimacy without sex was probably as difficult for the Canaanites as it is for many today, but clearly the emphasis of this love affair is on loyalty rather than on the magical or mythological role of sex.

Nevertheless, the Hebrew Bible is not without the image of Yahweh's offspring.

YAHWEH AS THE PARENT OF A SON

In several announcements to various audiences Yahweh speaks of Israel as a son. The first of these—canonically—occurs in the speech which Moses was instructed to pass on to the pharaoh.

> Thus says Yahweh: "Israel is my first-born son, and I say to you: 'Let my son go that he may serve me'; if you refuse to let him go, behold, I will slay your first-born son" (Exod. 4:22–23).

The Parent-son relationship between Yahweh and Israel had thus been established in connection with or even prior to the deliverance from Egypt. Quite similarly, Hosea—who had made such profound use of the husband-wife analogy—interprets the exodus event as the deliverance of Yahweh's son: "When Israel was a child, I loved him, and out of Egypt I called my son" (Hos. 11:1).

In these passages the sexuality of the child is clear, but not that of
Yahweh. It is said neither that Yahweh is male or female nor that
Yahweh is mother or father. Likewise, there is no explanation regarding the means by which the parent-son relationship developed—whether by begetting, conceiving, or adopting. The issue is a
single one: the relationship of Israel to Yahweh, which is either the
motive for deliverance or its result.

It is left for other texts to speak of this relationship between God
and people in images pertaining to father and mother roles.

Yahweh as Father of a Son Named Israel

It is Jeremiah who uses the word *Father* explicitly to describe Yahweh in relationship with Israel. Steeped in the northern traditions
like Hosea, Jeremiah interpreted the downfall of the north a century
before his call, as well as the imminent destruction of Judah, as God's
judgment on the people's infidelity. Both Israel and Judah broke the
marriage vows by playing the harlot with many lovers (2:2–3, then
2:20–3:4, 9, 20). At the same time, however, Yahweh's heartbreak
over Israel is that of a Father who had hopes for his son.

> "I thought
> how I would set you among my children
> and give you a pleasant land,
> an inheritance most beauteous of all nations.
> And I thought
> you would call me Father,
> and would not turn from following me."
>
> (3:19)

Alas, the people did turn away from their Father as faithless children.

Yet that Father-son relationship cannot be dissolved, even by disobedience. That relationship itself serves as the motive for Yahweh's
deliverance of Israel from exile, just as the Parent-son analogy once
provided the basis for the exodus from Egypt.

> " . . . Behold I will bring them back from the north
>   country,
>   and gather them from the remotest parts of the
>   earth, . . .
>   because I am a father to Israel,
>   and Ephraim is my first-born.
>
> (Jer. 31:7–9)

Elsewhere too Yahweh is portrayed as acting like a father to Israel,
particularly as one who disciplines his son in order to refine him. In

the wilderness period, Yahweh tested and humbled Israel. "Know then in your heart that as a man disciplines his son, the Lord your God disciplines you" (Deut. 8:5). In this capacity Yahweh functioned like a teacher of wisdom, a father instructing his children.

> "My son, do not despise Yahweh's discipline
>   or be weary of his reproof,
> for Yahweh reproves him whom he loves,
>   as a father the son in whom he delights."
>
> (Prov. 3:11–12)

Thus, Yahweh is compared to a father when he performs the function of a wisdom teacher, and Yahweh is called Father when he performs as the King who delivers his people from bondage. In either case, the role which God plays, rather than divine gender, determines the use of the analogy.

Yahweh as Father of the Davidic King

On the basis of Nathan's oracle reported in 2 Samuel 7, David's successors to the throne in Jerusalem stood in a special relationship to Yahweh. Along with the divine promise that Yahweh would make David's dynasty endure forever—indeed, as an essential ingredient of the promise—God says of Solomon and the others to follow, "I will be his father, and he shall be my son" (v.14).

This mythical relationship of king to God is realized in ritual. Psalm 2, a royal coronation psalm, describes the action of the ceremony in Jerusalem when each succeeding Davidic king was crowned. Among the several stereotyped images is the announcement from Yahweh (through the priest?),

> " . . . You are my son,
>   Today I have begotten you."
>
> (v. 7)

This temporal note, "today", indicates that the relationship with God was not established at birth; rather on coronation day Yahweh adopted the king by the use of a legal formula, "You are my son." Jerusalem's rulers were not, therefore, divine beings, even though the right of primogeniture determined royal succession. They were adopted by God on the basis of the office and dynasty which Yahweh had established with David himself.

In Psalm 89, where the mythological victory of Yahweh over the sea provides a theological foundation for the Davidic covenant, Yahweh promises that just as he stilled the raging sea, so he will set the hand of his anointed one (his messiah) on the sea (vv. 9–10, 25). This transfer of primordial power to the king who faces various enemies will enable the king to cry, "Thou art my Father, my God, and the Rock of my salvation" (v. 26). As for Yahweh, he will elevate this king beyond all others: "I will make him the first-born, the highest of the kings of the earth" (v. 27). It is in connection with deliverance and power over enemies that the Davidic ruler uses the title "Father," and thus the role of warrior, so vital to the throne of Jerusalem, and the "Father" image go hand in hand.

The promise of Yahweh to make the Davidic king "firstborn" presents an interesting dilemma. Earlier we had seen that the "firstborn" son of Yahweh was Israel. Indeed it was that relationship which provided the motive for delivering the people from Egypt (Exod. 4:22–23) and from exile (Jer. 31:9). How can Yahweh have two firstborn sons when even in the birth of twins one must determine which was delivered first from the womb (Gen. 25:22–26)? The simplest solution to the problem is, of course, to recognize that different traditions are involved. It is indeed even likely that since "Ephraim" is the firstborn of Yahweh at Jeremiah 31:9, the northern kingdom with its emphasis on old tribal traditions considered itself to be the community which Yahweh brought out of Egypt. By contrast, the exodus tradition seems not to have occupied center stage in the south; there the Davidic and Jerusalem traditions prevailed. Thus, while the old northern tradition, used by Jeremiah to speak of a new exodus, asserted the firstborn status of the people, in Jerusalem that same position of honor was accorded Davidic kings.

Yet, insofar as the two traditions occur in the Hebrew Bible, it might be in order to suggest that there are not two firstborn sons but one. The Davidic king is the representative of the people as God's son. Thus, while the Son of God title is bestowed on a king on coronation day, the honor does not separate him from the rest of the people of Israel but identifies him with his subjects as together they relate to Yahweh. This understanding is far removed from the sexual role of the Egyptian god Min-Horus who engendered himself as each succeeding king. It is the role of protection and deliverance rather than sex and procreation which defines Yahweh as Father in regard to king and people.

Yahweh as Mother of a Son

If the traditional male roles of protection and pedagogy led the ancient Israelites to speak of Yahweh as Father, then the divine roles of compassion and mercy were conveyed by various images related to mother. One aspect of the female image is related to the belief that various emotions were founded in specific organs of the human body. The liver was the seat of joy; when it was poured out, the person was sad (Lam. 2:11). The kidneys were the seat of conscience (Ps. 16:7), and the heart was the center of the intellect, the mind (Prov. 16:9). Thus, in a society where internal organs were of more interest psychologically than physiologically, it is consistent that "mercy" is related to the Hebrew term for the female anatomical part: "womb" (*reḥem*).

In the same chapter in Jeremiah in which Yahweh based deliverance from exile on his being "Father" to Ephraim (Jer. 31:9), the prophet used the female image to support the loving, intimate relationship between the two of them.

> "Is Ephraim my dear son?
>   Is he my darling child?
> For as oft as I speak against him,
>   I still remember him.
> Therefore my heart yearns for him;
>   I surely will have mercy (*rāḥam*) on him,"
>   says Yahweh.
>
> (Jer. 31:20)

During the Babylonian Exile in the sixth century B.C.E., Second Isaiah compared Yahweh to a mother. In response to Israel's painful sense of abandonment, Yahweh assured: "Can a woman forget her suckling child, that she should have no compassion on the son of her womb?" (Isa. 49:15). Earlier, the same prophet related Yahweh's sudden change in behavior regarding Israel's exile to the pains of a woman giving birth. Just as the long waiting of pregnancy suddenly erupts in the travail of labor, so Yahweh changed from silence at Israel's plight to the action of deliverance and restoration (Isa. 42:14).

In a series of rhetorical questions by which God demonstrates to Job unfathomable power in contrast to human limitation, God appears as father and mother over nature.

> "Has the rain a father,
>   or who has begotten the drops of dew?
> From whose womb was the ice delivered,
>   and who gave birth to the hoarfrost of heaven?"
>
> (Job 38:28–29)

That God is portrayed as giving birth to dew, ice, and frost, depicts the divine one as Mother Nature. Yet the same explicit female activity portrays Yahweh as Israel's mother. Addressing Israel (Jeshurun), the author of Moses' Song describes the people's apostasy: "You were unmindful of the Rock which bore you, and you forgot the God who suffered travail at your birth" (Deut. 32:18).

Indeed, burdened by his responsibilities for the people in the wilderness, Moses boldly defended himself against Yahweh's anger. "Did I conceive all this people? Did I bring them forth, that you should say to me, 'Carry them in your bosom, as a nurse carries the suckling child, . . . ?'" (Num. 11:12). The implication is that not Moses but Yahweh conceived Israel and brought them forth. It is, therefore, Yahweh who should take the responsibility for feeding the people meat.

Since Yahweh was portrayed as Father to Israel and also to the Davidic king, one should not be surprised that in addition to Yahweh's bearing and giving birth to Israel, the Divine Mother gives birth to the ruling messiah on coronation day. In the announcement to the king at Ps. 2:7, Yahweh adopts the king by the legal formula, "You are my son," and then immediately proceeds to speak as a mother: "Today I have given you birth!" Addressed to an adult male, this formula can in no way be taken literally. It is, like the analogies cited above, one means by which the relationship of Yahweh to the Davidic king is described. Even though the act of giving birth by a man is incomprehensible (see Jer. 30:6), it is the function of the relationship rather than the sexuality of God which is important to observe here.

The parental analogies and images cited above, like a multitude of images from the plant and animal worlds, describe the ways in which God relates to the world and to people. God is neither male nor female, but Yahweh functions in various roles which the ancient society of Israel assigned to male and female, to father and mother. That in the same society, even in the same pieces of literature in that society, God is described both as father and mother leads us now to consider further "the image of God" as it relates to humans.

THE RELATIONSHIP OF YAHWEH
TO HUMAN SEX

In Israel's environment the sexuality and the sexual activity of the gods were related directly to human sexual behavior. The Mesopotamian king performed the sexual role on the part of the god; the Egyptian god was incarnate in the sexual act of the pharaoh; in Canaan sacred prostitution, corresponding to heavenly ecstasy, was the means by which fertility of land and humans was ensured. Now if Yahweh is intimate but not genital with Israel, if Israel's God has no sexual partner but merely sexual metaphors, what can be said of human sex?

The Role of Procreation: Genesis 1:27–28

The much-discussed poem in the Priest's creation account affirms both the asexuality of God and human sexual activity. By synonymous parallelism the relationships among the various components are deepened.

> So God created humankind in his own image,
>   in the image of God he created him;
>   male and female he created them.
>
>   (Gen. 1:27)

The verb "created" appears in all three lines. The synonyms for the subject "God" in lines two and three are "he" and "he." "Humankind" is parallel to "him" and "them" as objects of the verb. That structure leaves as synonyms "in his own image," "in the image of God," and "male and female." That the Priest should describe God's image as bisexual is completely consistent with the father and mother analogies discussed above. While God is neither male nor female, God is understood and described by humans in terms of the sexual roles of both sexes. God's role as creator of the world is communicated humanly speaking by roles assigned to male and female alike: to bear fruit and thus create human life throughout the earth (v. 28). In addition, this divine image in terms of male and female is to exercise dominion over the rest of creation: as kings and queens ruling all other living things. By this function, too, something about God is known and communicated on a human level.

The creation account at Genesis 1:1–2:4a was written as it is not to affirm human sexuality but to address exiles in Babylon during the sixth century B.C.E. with the creation blessing of God: do not decrease but increase there and so give testimony to a living God who rules over the universe (see Jer. 29:6). Yet it is precisely in this proclamation of hope that the Hebrew theologian asserts the place of sex and sexual roles. The blessing of progeny could not be achieved apart from sexual intercourse of male and female, and so the sex act was ordained and blessed by God at creation itself when the Creator assigned roles to every created phenomenon. When God examined his work, even the sexual nature of male and female, he pronounced the mark of approval: *tôb*!

The God of the Hebrew Bible needs no sex of his own. Completely without a sexual partner and encompassing in the divine self both male and female roles, God bestows the gift of sex upon human and animal creatures. As humans responsibly cooperate in the creative act and rule the world as stewards, the image of God is presented to the world for human comprehension.

The Mutuality of Male and Female:
Genesis 2:18–25

The simultaneous creation of male and female, as well as the responsibilities assigned to both sexes in Genesis 1, attests to the equality of male and female as part of God's ordering of the universe. That partnership seems at first glance to have been unknown to the author of Genesis 2, and so the Yahwist has often been labeled a male chauvinist. In the first place, he describes the creation of the sexes sequentially, with the male appearing first. In the second place, the Yahwist describes the woman as "a helper fit for" the male (so *RSV*).

As regards the sequence of male then female, the interpreter should recall that in the preceding account (Genesis 1), the higher forms of life were created toward the end of the week, on the sixth day. Thus, one cannot assume male superiority on the basis of the Yahwist's sequence. Indeed, upon examining the lone male in the garden, Yahweh determined it was "not good" (*lō' ṭôb*) for the man to be without female, and so the primary human relationship established at the beginning was heterosexual companionship.

The description of the woman should be translated more literally "help as his counterpart" (Gen. 2:18, 20). *Kĕnegdô* simply means "as opposite him" and in no way implies that the woman is inferior to or even subordinate to the man. As for the "help" designation, one cannot but emphasize that elsewhere in the Hebrew Bible, the word *'ēzer* is used only in reference to Yahweh. Either Yahweh is the source of help (Ps. 20:2; 121:1–2; 124:8) or Yahweh himself is help (Exod. 18:4; Deut. 33:7; Ps. 33: 20; 70:5; 115:9–11). Far from indicating assistanceship, the word might be related to the Ugaritic *ġzr*, which connotes strength. Thus, the woman in Genesis 2 is at least the equal of the man out of whose rib she was formed.

When the male awoke from his "deep sleep," he marveled at the creature whom Yahweh introduced to him. Following the joyous poem celebrating the man's relief at having a partner, the narrator concludes the event by expressing the physical and mutual attraction the two had for each other. In their relationship as male and female, indeed in their sexual activity and in their complete partnership, "they become one flesh." Essential to their union is exclusivity: the man shall forsake all other human, even parental, relationships in order to "cleave to his woman" as Israel is constantly instructed to cleave to Yahweh. Their physical naked splendor is completely natural, for they have not yet developed mistrust, deception, incriminating accusation, and arrogance. Male and female were naked and not ashamed.

If Genesis 1 portrayed human sex solely in terms of progeny, Genesis 2 depicts sex as pleasure and beauty in commitment. The Yahwist's paradise account is not alone, however, in such an affirmation of the joys of human sex.

The Mutuality of Male and Female:
The Song of Solomon

The traditional interpretation of the Song of Solomon as an allegory of the relationship between Christ and the church must give way to its original function as a love song, or a collection of love songs, which portrays vividly the romance of a man and a woman. The love epitomized here is *eros*—sexual love which takes pleasure in the anatomical parts of the partner and which extols the beautiful physical affection a man and a woman can share. Similar to many such love songs in the literature of Israel's neighbors, this Song is particularly interesting for our purposes.

    (1) Sexual love is not an embarrassment but unequivocally good. Indeed, the entire love relationship between the male and female brings *shalom*, completeness and wholeness, by participation in life's joys (Song of Sol. 8:10; *RSV* "peace").

    (2) The love affair is by no means designed for the production of progeny. The pleasure of the bedroom rather than the results for the nursery occupies the poet's concern here. Moreover, it is not even clear in the Song that the man and the woman are married to each other.

    (3) The woman is by no means a passive agent serving as the instrument for the man's pleasures. Rather she takes at least as much initiative in the lovemaking as the man and enjoys its pleasures equally. Thus she is his partner in sex, "the one opposite him."

Taken together, Genesis 2 and the Song of Solomon attest to the equality of male and female and to the natural beauty of human sex. Without the need for correspondence with heavenly activity, human sex is God's gift to male and female alike. Knowing full well what it is to be in love (Hosea 1–3), Yahweh extends its pleasures even beyond his own experience to include sexual activity.

The Partnership Gone Awry

According to the Yahwist, the beautiful relationships established by Yahweh were radically distorted by the first human decision. As long as Yahweh was the actor, *shalom* prevailed in the garden. However, as soon as the male and female made the conscious decision to eat the forbidden fruit, everything changed. The quest for absolute freedom, to experience all things, to become like gods, overturned God's created equality and naturalness in sex.

On the basis of her deed at the fruit tree, the woman would experience pain in childbirth, and in her relationship with her husband she would be sublimated to his rule and authority. Moreover, while she would desire her husband, nothing is said about his desire for her (Gen. 3:16). Thus, the hierarchy of the sexes—so evident to the Yahwist in his own day—is founded upon the rebellion by the first humans in the paradise prepared by God. The man suffers brokenness in his relationship to the ground. No longer will he till and keep the ground and thereby eat its produce; now such work will be performed in vain (3:17–19). Only the woman, therefore, suffers punishment in the heterosexual scheme, but in her loss of equality the male has lost the *shalom* which that partnership was intended to create.

The consequences of this distorted relationship are many indeed. Even in the prescriptions for making vows to Yahweh, the inequality is blatant: a man is responsible for what he vows, but a woman's vows are subject to a man's discretion (Num. 30:1–16). Such laws imply that a woman cannot be held responsible for what she says. She is, however, held completely accountable for what she does in matters of sex, while the attitude toward males is "boys will be boys." The evil advances of women must always be avoided by impressionable young men (Prov. 5:3–8; 6:24–26). Moreover, while the wisdom teachers promised dishonor and disgrace for the man who commits adultery with his neighbor's wife (Prov. 6:29–35), the law codes prescribe the death penalty for an unfaithful wife (Num. 5:11–31). The premarital state of virginity is literally vital for the woman, while nothing is said of the same condition in a male (Deut.

22:13–21; see also Gen. 19:8). To be sure, there are cases in which a man and woman caught in adultery are punished equally (Deut. 22:22–24), but generally it is the woman who is held responsible for sexual offenses and punished accordingly.

The entire legal and cultural situation derives theologically—in the present context of the Scriptures—from that act in the garden when humans made their first decision. The sexual equality established by God had been changed to inequality by the actions of humans, and so even the gracious gift of sex from the asexual God was thrown into the realm of lust instead of love, manipulation in place of sharing, shame instead of mutual and natural attraction.

6

God, the Son of God, and the Restoration of Sexual Equality

Perhaps no other issue in our day raises such emotion as that concerning the Incarnation of God's Child as a male and the related questions of the sexuality of God and of humans. There are those who argue that Jesus *is* God, and since God made Jesus in his image, then the male child must represent a male deity. Furthermore, since Jesus himself called God "Father," our deity must be portrayed as masculine. Spokespersons for the feminist movement have argued that this type of argumentation over the centuries has led to an affirmation of maleness rather than of humanness. To counteract such effects, it is suggested, one should speak of Jesus as Child and of God as Parent. In this way some of the misinterpretations of key passages, particularly in Pauline writings, might be corrected, and sexual equality between male and female might be realized.

These issues in the New Testament need to be examined in light of our study of sex and sexuality in the myths of the ancient Near East and in the Hebrew Bible. It is the concern of the present writer, however, that the particularity of the historical person Jesus and the proclamation concerning Jesus' identity not be made ambiguous in order to settle a different issue which can be treated on its own ground.

THE SEXUALITY OF GOD IN THE NEW TESTAMENT

The witnesses of the New Testament do not emphasize as strongly as those of the Hebrew Bible the creative role of God and the related activity of fertility. One might argue that since the "Old Testament" was the Bible of Jesus and the early church, there was no need to re-

peat such emphases, particularly when the new concern was to proclaim the identity of Jesus and the results which God accomplished in
his life, death, and resurrection.

Nevertheless, the New Testament is not lacking in attesting to
God's concern for nature and fertility. In Jesus' parables of the kingdom, God is frequently portrayed as a sower of seed, the owner of a
vineyard, or a landowner. More pertinent, the Q saying about God's
feeding the birds of the air and clothing the grass of the field is intended to alleviate human anxiety (Matt. 6:25–33; Luke 12:22–31).
Here God's role in providing sustenance continues a tradition which
we traced from the third millennium B.C.E. down through the Hebrew Bible.

Furthermore, just as the gods controlled conception in humans and
thus needed to be persuaded in various ways—by magic, by sacrifice, or by prayer—so too does God open the womb in the New
Testament. As he did for Sarah and Abraham when they were beyond the point of human ability (Gen. 17:17; 18:11), so did God enable Zechariah and Elizabeth in a similar state to experience the joys
of childbirth (Luke 1:5–25).

Yet most astonishing of all is God's role in the birth of Jesus. According to Mark's Gospel, Jesus was acclaimed to be Son of God at
his baptism (Mark 1:11). That announcement, much like that of God
to the Davidic king on coronation day (Ps. 2:7), seemed to relate Jesus' divine sonship to an adoption formula. For Matthew and Luke,
however, that adoptive sense was not sufficient to explain Jesus'
identity, and so those evangelists pushed Jesus' divinity back to the
conception in Mary. Since her husband-to-be, Joseph, was not cred-
ited with the pregnancy (Matt. 1:18–25; Luke 1:34), the question of
God's sexuality in regard to Mary's conception must be raised.

According to Matthew's account, Mary was "found to be with
child of the Holy Spirit" (1:18; cf. v. 20). Her betrothed, Joseph, was
prepared to divorce her quietly, but Mary's state of virginity was
confirmed to Joseph in a dream by an angel of the Lord. To this account the author adds one of his many fulfillment passages, citing
Isa. 7:14 as the prophecy of a virgin birth which was now taking
place. (The historical reference to the pregnant young woman in 735
B.C.E. need not concern us here.) Thus the divine origin of the human
Jesus is set forth at the beginning of Matthew's Gospel. Jesus' conception was not the result of human action but of that of the Holy
Spirit.

Luke spells out the conception of Jesus in a quite different form. Here exists the possibility that God is sexually involved, and such a possibility would indicate clearly that God is indeed male. When the angel Gabriel announced to Mary that she would conceive and bear a son Jesus, she pleaded her bewilderment and her virginity. "How can this be, since I have not known a man?" (Luke 1:34). At first glance the angel's response might suggest divine sexual activity. "The Holy Spirit will come upon you, and the power of the Most High will cover you . . ." (v. 35a). The terms used here are particularly important to examine, because Luke is fond of Septuagint terminology, especially in the infancy narratives. If the verbs "come upon" (*eperchesthai*) or "cover" (*episkiazein*) appear in the Septuagint for sexual relations, then for the first time in the Bible would God be involved genitally with a sexual partner. The common word for sexual intercourse in the Septuagint is *eiserchesthai* (Hebrew *bō'* = to enter), but the related term *eperchesthai* is never so used. Interestingly, however, the Lucan term does appear in connection with the Spirit in Isa. 32:15 where the effect is fertility on the land. As for the verb *episkiazein*, there is likewise no sexual context for the term in the Septuagint. The most interesting case is Exod. 40:35 where "the cloud *covered* the tent of meeting," indicating God's presence with the people of Israel as they journeyed from Mount Sinai. Both Greek verbs convey some impact—fertility and divine presence—but God is no more involved sexually in Luke's account of Jesus' conception than Yahweh is in the Hebrew Bible.

The use of the Holy Spirit to impregnate Mary removes the accounts in Matthew and Luke from mythological tendencies. In mythology—as we have seen in the ancient Near Eastern stories—either the god takes human form or a human takes divine form in the conception of offspring. Yet in the case of Jesus, the human partner remains human, and the divine partner remains spirit. The result is a child who is both human and divine.

Furthermore, unlike the parallels from the Hebrew Bible where God's intimate partner is a whole people, here in the infancy narratives about Jesus the partner is an individual woman. The result of this particularity is that God's child will not be a people—even Israel—but a son who shall be called Jesus. Such a result from a human woman and the Holy Spirit makes this tradition unique.

In the Manual of Discipline from the Qumran caves there exists a statement which—if restored correctly—might have some relationship to the account of Jesus' conception by God's Spirit. The sen-

tence speaks of the call to assembly of the community's council
"when [God] begets the Messiah among them" (1QSa 2:11–12). Interestingly, however, the verb represents precisely the same divine
action in the Hebrew Bible when God "begat" (*yālad*) Israel (Deut.
32:18) and each succeeding Davidic king (Ps. 2:7). That action, we
have seen, is never performed genitally by a father; it is a mother's
act or a parental declaration of adoption. The Qumran quote is interesting nevertheless because it projects that role of Divine Parent into
the eschatological scene and applies it to the *expected* Messiah.

For Luke the reason for relating the story and in particular for describing the conception in Mary as due to the Holy Spirit is clear
from the continuation of Gabriel's response to Mary:

> "Therefore the child to be born (of you)
>   will be called holy,
> the Son of God."

> (1:35b)

It is, therefore, not the sexuality of God but the identity of Jesus as
God's Son in a unique way which is the purpose of the narrative in
Luke.

It cannot be denied, of course, that according to the New Testament witnesses, Jesus called God "Father." Indeed, it is likely that Jesus did in fact use this title, particularly because it would have been
presumptuous for anyone else to initiate the familiar form *Abba*. For
some people today this usage settles the issue of God's sexuality once
for all: if Jesus called his Parent "Father," God must be male. However, the issue is not so simple. Even though Jesus' knowledge of
God was much clearer and more intimate than anyone else's and
even though *Abba* was not commonly used in Judaism for God, Jesus
was nevertheless a man of his times. What Jesus actually knew about
God is impossible to determine. All that we have available are the
human words and analogies which Jesus and the Gospel writers used
in order to communicate to their first-century Jewish and Gentile audiences. If Jesus had spoken words which lay outside the religious
traditions of his contemporaries, such as calling God "Mother," with
whom among his own Jewish people would Jesus have been credi-
ble? Though motherly imagery is used for Yahweh quite frequently
(see above, pp. 96–98), never is the title "Mother" employed. Indeed,
in order to communicate his profound knowledge of God, even Jesus
had to restrict himself to the limits of human language and understanding: "The kingdom of God is like. . . ."

THE SEXUALITY OF JESUS
The Maleness of God's Child

When God made the decision to make the Word flesh, it seems God had little choice but to make a male. This limited choice was based not on the gender of God (we have already seen that God is portrayed for human comprehension both as Father and Mother) but on the necessity for communication. Born of Jewish descent for whom the "Old Testament" was the Scripture, the child of God could be proclaimed as such only if the child were male. To be sure, certain concepts of God such as "spirit" and "wisdom" are feminine, but the words and images which convey the impact of that child's relationship to God are almost exclusively masculine. In other words, it was the historicality, the given culture of the times and of the specific people, which determined the gender of God's child. As "daughter of God" the child's relationship and ultimate origin would have been difficult to communicate in first-century Judaism even though the phrase "daughter of" cities, land, and people is used frequently to personify its inhabitants (e.g., "daughter of Zion," "daughter of my people," etc.). The expression "daughter of . . . God" occurs only to describe Israel's idolatry (see Mal. 2:11). As "son of God," however, the child's identity—while unique—could be approximated in such a way that continuity with the former traditions was possible.

We have seen that "Son of God" had essentially two identities in the Hebrew Bible: the people of Israel and the Davidic king. Passages and images related to both these "sons" are used to communicate the identity of Jesus as Son of God, though the latter "son" is much more explicit and frequent as a source than the former.

The people of Israel as Son of God provides Matthew with an interesting opportunity to announce Jesus' identity. At 2:15 this evangelist quotes Hosea 11:1 as a prophecy which is fulfilled when Joseph and Mary fled to Egypt and returned at Herod's death. The prophet Hosea used the statement "Out of Egypt have I called my son" to describe the past historical deliverance of Israel, but in Matthew's scheme that past reference took on future expectations and was applied to Jesus.

In addition to Matthew's own application of this imagery, there are, in material common to Matthew and Luke (so-called "Q"), references to Israel as God's Son which are used for the purpose of identifying Jesus. The "Q" version of the temptation of Jesus (Matt.

4:1ff.; Luke 4:1ff.) begins with the test of hunger in the wilderness. Jesus could have proved to the devil that he was "the Son of God" by changing stones to bread, but instead he quoted the saying of Deut. 8:3 that "man shall not live by bread alone, . . ." This eighth chapter of Deuteronomy described Yahweh's testing of Israel in the wilderness—a test of hunger in which Yahweh himself sustained the people with manna. Indeed, Israel's entire experience of the wilderness testing was a matter of Yahweh's discipline, "as a man disciplines his son" (v. 5). Thus, Jesus seems to appear as God's Son, Israel.

The image of the Davidic king as the Son of God is used much more widely in the New Testament. We have seen previously that Mark's scheme of the rebuking authority, transferred from Yahweh to Jesus, demonstrates Jesus' identity as God's Son, particularly on the basis of the transfer of Yahweh's power over the Sea to the Davidic king (see above, pp. 31, 58–61). Furthermore, we shall see below (pp. 175–76) that the adoption formula from the Davidic coronation ceremony (Ps. 2:7) is cited at Jesus' baptism and at his transfiguration in order to proclaim Jesus as Messiah.

While the logic is difficult to follow, Matthew begins his Gospel with a genealogy which consists of three groups of fourteen generations each: from Abraham to David, from David to the exile, and from the exile to Christ. The role of David in the scheme is perhaps even more enhanced if one interprets the "fourteen" in terms of gematria: the numerical value of the Hebrew letters for "David" totals fourteen. To establish Davidic lineage for Jesus by this genealogy, Matthew has traced the line through Joseph. Yet immediately following the genealogy (1:1–17), the evangelist reports that Mary was pregnant with child not through Joseph but "of the Holy Spirit." While maintaining that divine initiative in the conception of Jesus, Matthew continues by citing Isa. 7:14, a sign which was addressed to the "house of David," that is, King Ahaz, and Mic. 5:2, the beginning of a "messianic" prophecy which speaks more of Davidic lineage than of a birthplace. In other words, Matthew combines in his opening chapters the Davidic descent and the miraculous conception of the Holy Spirit.

Luke likewise holds together both these ideas. In his introduction of the characters involved, the author describes Joseph as belonging to "the house of David" (1:27). Further, in Gabriel's speech to Mary concerning her conception and the birth of Jesus, Luke includes four lines of poetry which combine sonship and the Davidic throne.

> "He will be great, and will be called Son of the Most High;
>   and the Lord God will give to him the throne of his father David,
> and he will reign over the house of Jacob for ever;
>   and of his kingdom there will be no end."
>
> (Luke 1:32–33)

The lines sound as though they are quotations out of royal psalms from Israel's cult or out of royal oracles (cf. Ps. 21:5–7; 89:25–29; Isa. 9:7; 2 Sam. 7:9–16; yet for more general usage see Sirach 4:10; Wisd. of Sol. 2:18). To have stopped here the conversation between Mary and Gabriel would have led some readers to the conclusion that Jesus was the Son of God in the same way as the kings of the Davidic dynasty. Yet in response to Mary's immediate and traditional question about the logistics of this improbable conception, Luke quotes Gabriel's speech about the Holy Spirit coming upon and covering her: "therefore the child to be born will be called holy, the Son of God" (1:35). Thus, Jesus would be God's Son not simply like the earlier dynastic succession of Davidic kings but in a new way: by the action of the Holy Spirit from the moment of conception. On the basis of this clarification in his infancy story, Luke can use interchangeably "the Son of God" and "the Christ" (4:41) without leaving the impression that Jesus is simply one more member, even the last member, of David's dynasty.

The interpretation of the origin of Jesus' divine sonship by Matthew and Luke settles an issue which was already raised in Mark but never really answered. As Jesus was teaching in the temple, he challenged the statement of the scribes that the Christ was the son of David. Against such a teaching Jesus quoted Ps. 110:1 in which "David himself calls him Lord," and so he must be more than David's son. Yet Mark had not clearly demonstrated *how* Jesus is more than a Davidic king. In fact, in the announcement at Jesus' baptism (Mark 1:11) the adoption formula used for crowning Zion's rulers was directed to Jesus. Even though Mark (or his sources) has Yahweh-ized Jesus in several ways (as one example, see the rebuking privilege discussed above, pp. 58–67), that evangelist could be interpreted as explaining the origin of Jesus' sonship to God in Davidic terms alone.

Some scholars object to the use of the Davidic king background to establish Jesus' identity as Son of God. They note—correctly—that "Son of God" does not appear in prophetic passages which anticipate the expected eschatological Messiah, but only in passages such as 2 Sam. 7:14; Ps. 2:7; 89:26–27 which deal with the present kings of the Davidic dynasty. While the observation is accurate, the conclusion is not completely justified for two reasons: (1) in the classical Messianic prophecies (Isa. 9:27; 11:1–9; Jer. 23:5–6; Mic. 5:2–4; Zech. 9:9–10) the word "Messiah" does not appear either (Heb. *māšîaḥ* = anointed one), yet those passages are cited in the New Testament to "prove" that Jesus is the expected Messiah/Christ; (2) the New Testament writers did not limit themselves to *future* Messianic texts in order to demonstrate Jesus as Messiah; Ps. 2:7 and 2 Sam. 7:14, both describing Davidic royalty in Israel's history, are indeed used to identify Jesus. It seems, therefore, that the Davidic ideology did provide an important—though not exclusive—means to announce that Jesus was the Son of God.

Whatever the origin for explaining Jesus as Son of God, the emphasis on Jesus' sonship clearly indicates that the child of God was male. Yet it is not his maleness which is the issue. The concern of the early church was to announce the good news of the reign of God; its first task was to continue Jesus' own kerygma that the time was fulfilled and that the awaited kingdom was at hand. On the basis of the resurrection of Jesus, the church proclaimed not only the message which Jesus preached but also the good news about Jesus himself. The reign of God had broken into human history in the life, ministry, death, and resurrection of the man Jesus. According to some expectations in the Hebrew Bible, when God would establish the coming kingdom, there would be set over it the eschatological ruler of Davidic descent. An essential part of the church's proclamation was that the kingdom and the appearance of the Messiah coincided, and the Messiah was Jesus. Indeed, the Messiah in this case was the agent God used in establishing the new reign. Such a role was a new interpretation by the church, and so certain liberties were taken with royal texts from the Hebrew Bible.

Among those liberties was the use of the messianic title "Son of God" to describe the eschatological Messiah rather than simply the historical kings in Zion. That Jesus was the Son of God emphasizes not his maleness but his messiahship, and the reason for that identification was to proclaim the kingdom of God as the new reality. In the historical-cultural setting of first-century Judaism, with its heritage of the Hebrew Scriptures, the maleness of God's eschatological child was simply assumed, and the child-parent relationship could be communicated only if that child was male. Yet as the prologue to John's Gospel so powerfully proclaims, the Word became not male, not female, not man, not woman but *flesh*, and so it is humanness rather than a particular sex which is affirmed by the Incarnation.

The Question of Jesus' Sexual Expression

Since Jesus was truly human, he had to have been one sex or the other, and he was male. That traditional assertion of his humanity has raised various questions about his sexuality, and more precisely about his sexual activity. Generally, Jesus is regarded as being "above that." Perhaps the stories of his own virginal conception have led to the conclusion that he himself remained a virgin. Yet it should be stressed again that Matthew and Luke reported conception in Mary by the Holy Spirit in order to assert the identity of Jesus as God's Son in a unique way. Their purpose was not to denigrate normal sexual expression but to demonstrate Jesus' divine origin.

Nevertheless, the New Testament is completely silent on the question of Jesus' celibacy, and this silence has produced a flood of books on the subject. Studies based on the sociological status of marriage in first-century Judaism have led some to conclude that Jesus was probably married and had children, while conjectures about his thirty "hidden years" have led others to suggest homosexual tendencies. Nikos Kazantzakis in his well-known *The Last Temptation of Christ* portrays Jesus as successful in his attempt to control lustful desires for Mary Magdalene, while four and one-half centuries ago Luther suggested that Jesus had enjoyed sexual relations with Magdalene and with other women.

The question of Jesus' sexual expression presents a no-win situation. If one argues against such a possibility, then it is probable that cultural values other than those of first-century Palestine are being imposed. If, on the other hand, one argues for Jesus' sexual involvement—either within marriage or without—then one must recognize that no New Testament writings are even remotely supportive of such a view, not even the disciples' question at seeing Jesus talking with the woman at the well: "What are you after?" (John 4:27).

It is possible that the New Testament's silence about Jesus' sexual expression is due not to piety but to identity. Whether or not Jesus experienced sexual desire or pleasure is of little significance in comparison with the questions about his identity which would have arisen if such activity had been recorded. The early church—and the Gospel writers in particular—had built-in difficulties proving that Jesus was the eschatological Davidic ruler. For one thing, there was no tradition in the Hebrew Bible that such a Messiah would suffer and die, to say nothing of hanging on a tree (see Deut. 21:22–23). Yet because of the theological significance of that event, and because of historical memory itself, such a report could not be silenced. However, to identify Jesus as the eschatological Messiah and simultaneously to suggest that he had had sexual relationships, possibly producing children, would have contradicted the entire tradition unnecessarily. In the Hebrew prophecies regarding the future "Messiah" there is no expectation that he would produce children to succeed him. Such prophecies speak not of David's line of descendants, but of "a shoot," "one who is to be ruler," "a righteous branch." The rule of the "Messiah" in the eschatological kingdom of God does not continue but ends the dynastic succession of Davidic kings.

Finally, however, it must be admitted that Jesus has a bride. He is wedded to his disciples who should not worry about fasting until that day when Jesus, the bridegroom, is taken away from them (Matt. 9:14–16; Mark 2:18–20; Luke 5:33–35). The marriage of which Jesus speaks, of course, is an analogy for the relationship which exists between himself and his followers. The analogy is used to answer a question about the non-fasting nature of Jesus' disciples in contrast to the behavior of John's followers and of the Pharisees.

The same imagery of bride and bridegroom is used by other New Testament writers to describe the relationship between the church and Christ. Paul speaks of his role in arranging the wedding of the Christians in Corinth to Christ so that he might present the church as a "chaste virgin" (*The Jerusalem Bible*) to her husband on the day of matrimony (2 Cor. 11:2). Elsewhere the apostle interprets the marriage formula of Genesis 2:24 to mean the relationship between Christ and the church (Eph. 5:31–32). Above all, it is John the Seer who looks forward to the last day when the marriage between the Lamb and his Bride will be consummated (Rev. 19:7; 21:2, 9; cf. 22:17).

This sexual image thus serves a particular function in the New Testament: to describe the relationship between Christ and the church in a way which was quite similar to the marriage between Yahweh and Israel in the Hebrew Bible. However, while the prophets of Israel spoke of the wedding as having occurred in the past historical events of the exodus and wilderness wanderings, Paul and John the Seer look to the eschaton when the engaged couple will finally be wed.

THE RESTORATION OF
SEXUAL EQUALITY

In our discussion of the early chapters of Genesis, we observed how the equality between male and female established by God at creation was shattered by the human rebellion described in Genesis 3. It is now our concern to investigate the effects on this male-female relationship caused by the ministry, death and resurrection of God's male child Jesus.

The Role of Men and Women in the
Infancy Narratives

We have already observed that in the accounts of the conception of Jesus recorded by Matthew and Luke, the male role is completely subsumed under that of the female. The "virgin birth" renders Joseph obsolete! The female role played by Mary, on the other hand, is essential to the Incarnation; without her the child of God could not have become human.

The reader does not get the same impression when reading Luke's account of the conception and birth of John the Baptist. Of the two parents involved, the father Zechariah seems to occupy more of the narrator's attention. The announcement of the improbable birth was delivered by the angel Gabriel to Zechariah, not to Elizabeth. When the baby was delivered and about to be named, both mother and father joined in the insistence that he be called John. Yet at that same moment when Zechariah's voice returned to him, it was he who blessed the Lord in song, the so-called Benedictus.

Thus in the conception and birth of John the Baptist, Zechariah performs the roles which belong to Mary in the conception and birth of Jesus: hearing the announcement, expressing human incomprehension, singing praises. Could this device be one means by which Luke announces that in Jesus began a new age? Could it be that the roles surrounding John's birth were the traditional ones, because John belonged to the period prior to the kingdom of God (see 7:28)?

As the infancy story continues in Luke, Joseph plays an important role since he belonged to the lineage of David. Yet after the shepherds' visit to the manger scene and their report of the heavenly announcement, it was Mary who is portrayed as the reflective parent, pondering these things in her heart (2:17–18).

When the couple took the infant Jesus to Jerusalem for purification, they were met by two persons who confirmed the uniqueness of this child. One was the man Simeon who blessed God and the new parents; the other was the prophetess Anna who gave thanks to God (2:22–38).

The next trip to Jerusalem recorded by Luke took place when Jesus was twelve years old. The family "went up" for the Passover festival, but on their return trip the parents realized that their son was not with them. Both mother and father returned to Jerusalem where they found him in the temple, sitting among the teachers. Yet it was Mary who held the dialogue with their son about the incident. Again, Luke reports, "his mother kept all these things in her heart" (2:51).

The Place of Men and Women in
Jesus' Ministry

Throughout Jesus' ministry, both men and women are cared for equally. While all the evangelists report Jesus' concern for male and female alike, it is Luke above all who deliberately balances stories of men and women in order to stress sexual equality. For example, at Luke 7:1–10 the evangelist tells of Jesus' healing of the centurion's son; the following paragraph reports his raising from death the widow's son. At 7:36–50 Jesus instructs the man Simon while he forgives the sins of a woman. The healing of the woman with the flow of blood (8:43–48) is surrounded by Jesus' raising from death the daughter of Jairus (8:40–42, 49–56). The instruction of the lawyer by means of the parable of the Good Samaritan is followed immediately by the instruction of Mary in her sister's home (10:25–42).

Even in his records of Jesus' teaching Luke balances male and female imagery. "The kingdom of God . . . is like a grain of mustard seed which a man took . . . like leaven which a woman took . . ." (13:18–21). Further, in response to complaints that Jesus received and ate with sinners, he answered, "What man of you, having a hundred sheep . . ." and "What woman, having ten silver coins . . ." (15:3–10).

Furthermore, Luke expands the allusion made in the other synoptics to the women from Galilee who were present at the crucifixion. The third evangelist mentions early in his Gospel that along with the twelve (men) who accompanied Jesus during his preaching in Galilee were "some women who had been healed of evil spirits and infirmities": among the many who provided out of their means were Mary Magdalene, Joanna, and Suzanna (8:1–3).

In all four Gospels Mary Magdalene is consistently portrayed as one of the women to whom the news of Jesus' resurrection was announced on Easter morning. However, in Luke the reference is particularly striking, for just as the Incarnation was announced first to a woman named Mary, so the Resurrection was proclaimed to women, two of whom were named Mary (24:1–11).

The Role of Men and Women in
the Early Church

The Pentecost experience was interpreted by Peter as the fulfillment of the prophecy by Joel:

> And in the last days, it shall be, God declares,
>   that I will pour out my Spirit upon all flesh,
> and your sons and your daughters shall prophesy,
> and your young men shall see visions,
>   and your old men shall dream dreams;
> yea, and on my menservants and my maidservants in those days
> I will pour out my Spirit; and they shall prophesy.
>   (Acts 2:17–18, quoting Joel 2:28–29)

This hope for the future would be realized on the day of the Lord
when the reign of God would be established. From the New Testament perspective the reign of God began in the ministry, death, and
resurrection of Jesus Christ, and so the "last days" experiences have
begun, too. That men and women prophesy together is one of the
signs of this new age.

Throughout the Book of Acts, as the gospel spreads to various
lands, both men and women play important roles. Jews and Greeks,
men "and not a few of the leading women" joined Paul and Silas as a
result of preaching in Thessalonica (Acts 17:4). The couple Aquila
and Priscilla hosted Paul in Corinth while he preached in the syna-
gogue there (18:1–4), as did Lydia of Thyatira, whom Paul persuaded and baptized in Philippi (16:11–15).

In Paul's correspondence to the churches he founded and in some
letters claimed to be Pauline, some key passages regarding male and
female appear. Clearly Paul and/or those writing in his name were
not completely outside the prevailing cultural understanding of male
domination. Most explicit is the charge that women should be silent
in church and acquire whatever information they need from their
husbands—at home (1 Cor. 14:33b–36). Elsewhere, the same silence
and general subordination of women is based on the sequence of creation day: Adam first, then Eve, and the transgression of the first
woman (1 Tim. 2:8–15).

Less explicit about charging women to be silent but still assuming
male domination are two key passages: Eph. 5:21–23 and 1 Cor.
11:2–16. Eph. 5:22 admonishes wives to be "subject to your husbands," because "the husband is the head of the wife as Christ is the

head of the church, his body, and is himself its Savior" (v. 23). Surely no one could argue that the church was equal to Christ, and so the argument seems to subject the wife to her husband's discretion. Yet the responsibility of wife to husband is by no means unilateral, for the apostle continues by laying a mutual charge on the husband: " . . . love your wives, as Christ loved the church and gave himself up for her . . ." (v. 25). The model for husbands to love their wives is the love which Christ demonstrated on the cross. It is, therefore, not the husband's discretion by which he exercises authority but the example of Christ's sacrifice. Far from unilateral control, moreover, the passage concludes with mutual responsibilities of husband and wife: ". . . let each of you love his wife as himself, and let the wife see that she respects her husband" (v. 33).

The extremely complicated argument of Paul at 1 Cor. 11:2–16 "reflects the to and fro of a school discussion" (Conzelmann, *1 Corinthians*,[19] p. 182) in which Paul's esoteric wisdom teaching and Hellenistic Jewish expectations are evident. The entire discussion centers on the common ritual practice (which Paul defends) of women covering their heads during worship. On the one hand, Paul lists the lines of authority as follows: God over Christ, Christ over man, man over woman. As for the final link in the chain, proof is cited from the creation story of Genesis 2: "For man was not made from woman, but woman from man. Neither was man created for woman, but woman for man" (1 Cor. 11:8–9). Somehow this sequence explains why women should cover their heads. On the other hand, as soon as Paul comes to that conclusion, he seems to reverse himself: "Nevertheless, in the Lord woman is not independent of man nor man of woman; for as woman was made from man, so man is now born of woman. And all things are from God" (vv. 11–12). Thus the established tradition in Corinth required that a woman cover her head in worship because of the male-female sequence at creation; "nevertheless in the Lord" (probably a reference to baptism) the creation sequence is rendered obsolete. The ritual practice of women covering their heads is thus based not on a distinctively Christian understanding of sexuality but on a custom, the precise origin of which is unknown.

In two other passages Paul is more clear about the equality—or at least the mutuality—of male and female within the Christian community. In his discussion of sexual asceticism in 1 Cor. 7, Paul argues that it is better to refrain. However, in light of human temptation, "each man should have his own wife and each woman her own husband. The husband should give to his wife her conjugal rights, and likewise the wife to her husband. For the wife does not rule over her own body, but the husband does; likewise the husband does not rule over his own body, but the wife does" (7:2–4). This expression of mutuality in sexual relations overcomes that pronouncement by God to the woman following the first act of disobedience in the garden: "and he shall rule over you" (Gen. 3:16). The redemptive act of God in Christ restores the partnership which God established in Genesis 1–2.

More commonly known is the key passage from Galatians 3. Here Paul describes the new situation which has resulted "now that faith has come": "for in Christ you are all children of God, through faith. For as many of you as were baptized into Christ have put on Christ. There is neither Jew nor Greek, there is neither slave nor free, there is neither male nor female; for you are all one in Christ Jesus" (Gal. 3:26–28). Certainly such ethnic, social, and sexual distinctions remain in the world, but they have no significance in Christ, that is, in the redeemed community called the church. The salvation event accomplished in Christ restores the equality which God intended from the time of creation but which was destroyed by human sin.

Discussion of these passages from Paul's writings forces us to return to his charge that women should be silent in church (1 Cor. 14:33b–36). Certainly it is possible that here Paul is reflecting his cultural heritage rather than his new understanding of sexuality "in the Lord" or "in Christ." We have seen that in 1 Corinthians 11 he wavers back and forth in the same discussion. However, it is likely that this passage is not original with Paul but rather a later insertion by someone of like mind with the author of 1 Timothy. Not only does the paragraph intrude into the thought between verse 33a and verse 37, but it also seems to contradict some of the arguments Paul advances in the same book. Furthermore, that women should be silent in church is not consistent with Paul's frequent greetings in his letters to men and women who are leaders in the various congregations.

Thus, far from being the male chauvinist Paul is often claimed to be, this prolific apostle makes his position clear in several key passages: "in Christ" sexual distinctions are abrogated. Whether in the marriage of Christians or in the Christian community in general, the hierarchy of the sexes initiated by human sin is demolished in favor of the equality and mutuality of male and female. The redemptive event thus restores the creation promise given to those made in the image of God.

SUMMARY OF SEXUALITY IN LIGHT OF THE NEW TESTAMENT

The New Testament writers only rarely used mythological allusions pertaining to sexuality and fertility. The avoidance of this motif is consistent with the radical demythologization already evident in the Hebrew Scriptures where Israel's prophets in particular combatted the lures of Canaan. In addition, the announcement that God had sent his Son into the world challenged the writers of the New Testament to express that Father-Son relationship while simultaneously avoiding certain mythological tendencies within their own Graeco-Roman culture.

Nevertheless, various issues which we have examined from ancient Near Eastern mythology are worth considering here in order to observe the retransformation made necessary by the new theological reality in Christ. The major issues which we have treated are the role of God in fertility, the sexuality and sexual expression of Jesus, and the effect of the Christ-event on the equality of the sexes.

The Role of God in Fertility

References to God as Creator of the world and Granter of fertility are few in the New Testament. Perhaps this scarcity is due to the fact that the proclamation of God's role in creation and nature was simply assumed from the use of the Old Testament in the early church. Apart from a few nature-type references in the teaching of Jesus, New Testament writers seem concerned with creation primarily when they intend to demonstrate the role which Christ played in creative action (see particularly 1 Cor. 8:6 and Col. 1:15–20).

Nevertheless, the special role of God in the procreation of humans is continued from ancient times but in a different way. The reader will recall that in Mesopotamia the means by which humans overcame sterility was the practice of various forms of magic. Several legendary texts from Canaan describe human kings using petition and sacrifice to the gods in order to attain children, particularly a male heir to the throne. In addition, we noted how young Canaanite women of marriageable age participated in the rites of initiation in order to ensure a potential husband of offspring. In both Canaan and Mesopotamia the role of fertility had something to do with the correspondence between the sexual actions and fate of certain deities and the ritual activities of humans. To some extent the same was true of Egypt.

In contrast to this magical and mythological correspondence the writers of the Hebrew Scriptures used the marriage of Yahweh only as an analogy to describe in powerful terms the relationship between Yahweh and the people of Israel. Without a celestial sexual partner Yahweh's role in changing human sterility to fertility was accomplished solely by a gracious response to persistent prayer.

In the infancy narratives of Luke's Gospel God took responsibility for the birth of humans. Similar to the role of God in the ancient story of Abraham and Sarah, God caused the aged couple Zechariah and Elizabeth to conceive and give birth to John. The announcement of this unlikely event came to Zechariah as a response to his prayer (Luke 1:13), although Zechariah's bewilderment seems to imply that he had long ago given up hope (v. 18). If this interpretation is correct, then God had not merely responded to persistent prayer as in the earlier case of Hannah (1 Samuel 1) but had in fact taken the initiative in reviving an old dream. This initiating action, of course, is more explicit in the announcement of Gabriel to Mary regarding the birth of Jesus. Far from responding to prayer, God placed the unmarried woman in a precarious position by causing her to become pregnant. This role which God plays is strikingly different from any story we have examined. Furthermore, the means by which Mary conceives is far removed from any mythological speculation, for pregnancy without sex was not part of those other religious systems.

The Sexuality and Sexual Expression of Jesus

The earlier discussion of the Egyptian pharaoh as the incarnation of the god Horus and as the son of Re leads one to consider the comparison and the contrast with Jesus, the Son of God and the Incarnate Word. While some conceptual and terminological relationships appear obvious, more striking is the uniqueness of Jesus over against the dynastic succession to Egypt's throne. Essentially the difference lies in the self-procreation system which was so much a part of Egyptian mythology: the pharaoh as god caused the conception of a god (his successor) by intercourse with a woman who represented his own mother. By contrast, Jesus was conceived as Son of God not through intercourse at all but through the Holy Spirit acting upon a virgin. Thus Jesus' origin as Son of God is described quite differently from that of the Egyptian pharaoh. Furthermore, the New Testament is completely silent about Jesus' sexual activity, and so he can in no way be considered as reproducing himself or his own kind for all eternity. This silence in the New Testament, we have suggested, seems related to the notion that the expected eschatological "messiah" was the end, not the continuation of the dynastic succession of David. Thus Jesus' Bride is not a fertile woman but the community of believers called the church, just as Yahweh's bride in the Hebrew Scriptures was the covenant community of Israel.

In Egyptian religion the self-perpetuation of the pharaoh was a primary means of denying death and sterility in favor of a static immortality. The New Testament portrayal of Jesus, by contrast, affirms human mortality as a consequence of sin but also announces the dynamic victory of resurrection from the dead.

The Effect of the Christ-event on Male-female Equality

In Mesopotamia and Egypt (and probably also in Canaan) the status of women was by no means equal to that of men. Exceptional cases of women as power figures in Mesopotamia and as objects of art and affection in Egypt's Amarna Period have been discussed. However, the ancient Near East was clearly a man's world.

The Yahwistic writer of Genesis 2–3 treated the cultural inequality between the sexes as a theological matter. He explained the situation of his own day, the tenth century B.C.E., as due to the experience in Eden's garden. Although God had created man and woman to be counterparts for each other, the disobedience at the fruit tree threw that relationship—as well as others—into a distorted state. As a result of sin the man rules over his wife.

The ministry of Jesus, particularly as Luke reports it, was characterized by equal treatment of men and women. In his caring work, as well as in his teaching, male and female received like treatment and concern. The effects of his ministry of reconciliation, furthermore, were experienced by everyone, regardless of their sex.

Certainly some vestiges of the cultural inequality are evident in the New Testament, particularly at 1 Timothy 2 and 1 Corinthians 11 where the male-female sequence in Genesis 2 is interpreted as determinative for male priority. In our study of Genesis 2 we have suggested that this sequence is not as important as the terminology "help as his counterpart" which establishes equality. Nevertheless, in spite of these and other passages which assume the priority of the male,

Paul's letters assert strongly an anti-cultural position as well: in Christ the equality intended by God at the time of creation is restored.

FERTILITY AND RESURRECTION

While the fertility/sexual imagery is rare in the New Testament, the powerful and unique sequence of Jesus' death and resurrection in history is described by analogies which are natural and cyclical. In John's Gospel such imagery about seeds and sowing—frequent in the synoptics—is used by Jesus to speak of the necessity of his death: ". . . unless a grain of wheat falls into the earth and dies, it remains alone; but if it dies, it bears much fruit" (John 12:24, *RSV*). Likewise Paul uses the same kind of analogy to answer the (rhetorical?) question concerning how the dead are raised. He begins his explanation of the nature of the resurrection body by the example from nature: "What you sow does not come to life unless it dies" (1 Cor. 15:36, *RSV*). Thus Jesus' own resurrection (John) and the general resurrection from the dead (Paul)—both eschatological events of a once-and-for-all kind—are described by means of the cyclical pattern of sterility and fertility.

Clearly the mythological pattern is transformed here by the new theological reality of Christ's resurrection. While one can point to the probability that such imagery in John and in Paul derives from fertility religions of the Hellenistic world, nevertheless the similarity of their cyclical patterns and those of the ancient Near East makes the analogy pertinent to our discussion.

No less pertinent is the use of an Old Testament quotation—already a transformation of a mythological motif—to conclude the discussion of resurrection in 1 Corinthians 15. In our discussion of the Canaanite story of Baal we noted that following his defeat of Yamm, Baal was invited to the netherworld by Mot where that deity "Death" swallowed him like the vegetation of the earth. The story of the descent of Baal corresponded to the annual drought and dying of crops in the hot Middle Eastern summers. In the apocalyptic section of the Book of Isaiah there is expressed the eschatological hope that Yahweh will reverse the roles of diner and menu, for "he will swallow up death (*môt*) forever" (Isa. 25:8). Already in the Isaiah passage the destruction of Mot will eliminate not only the annual cycle of fertility and sterility but also the human cycle of death and life. It is this eschatological hope which Paul cites (from Greek Old Testament versions) in order to speak of the coming resurrection of the dead: "Death is swallowed up in victory" (1 Cor. 15:34, *RSV*).

Finally, John the Seer pulls together many of the images and motifs we have discussed here. In his final vision of the last day he reports

> Then I saw a new heaven and a new earth; for the first heaven and the first earth had passed away, and the sea was no more. And I saw the holy city, new Jerusalem, coming down out of heaven from God, prepared as a bride adorned for her husband; and I heard a voice from the throne saying, "Behold, the swelling of God is with people. He will dwell with them, and they shall be his people, and God himself will be with them; he will wipe away every tear from their eyes, and death shall be no more, . . ." (Rev. 21:1–4).

Part Three

THE QUALITY OF THE
SACRED MOUNTAIN

7

The Mountain as Holiness Absolute

Essential to an understanding of the sacred mountain in mythology is a realization of space quite different from our quantitative perspective. In our world space is evaluated in terms of proportions and location. In mythological thinking space is more a matter of quality than quantity. That is to say, space is not valued relatively but absolutely. Whatever an individual or community experiences in a place determines its value. The experiences might be pleasurable, disturbing, awe-inspiring, or mysterious, but if a deity is encountered there in any way, then that space acquires the quality of holiness.

This type of thinking is not completely outside our realm of understanding, for we too experience space in more than one way. A mountain climber's response to a slope is not determined simply by the height and shape of the hill; it arises also from the confrontation with that which defies conquest. Similarly, the need for many people to "have space" indicates a desire not simply for distance from other people but for privacy of feelings, thoughts, and emotions even within the company of others.

It is the purpose of the present chapter to probe the nature of this spatial quality of various mountains in the mythology and theology of the religions in our study. Our basic questions here involve the characteristics and functions of holy mountains and, above all, the means by which these various mountains came to be experienced as holy.

Before examining the particulars of this or that holy mountain, however, it is important to observe a rather general tendency in regard to holy places. Mythologically speaking, there is at the center of the world a sacred mountain—not quantitatively a single mountain but qualitatively that mount in each religious community where the encounter with the holy occurred. This hill marked the spot where

126

heaven, earth, and the netherworld merged to form the *axis mundi*.[20] Since there was particular power in such space, sanctuaries of various sorts were constructed so that the earthly and human community might be nurtured by communication with the heavenly and divine assembly of the gods. Because such essential nourishment was found here, such space was often referred to as "the navel of the earth," the umbilical cord through which the mother feeds the infant. Moreover, since in mythology the actions of the deities correspond to phenomena on earth, the sanctuaries constructed on such holy mountains likewise corresponded to the model of the gods' home in the heavens.

EGYPT: THE PRIMEVAL HILL
OF CREATION

While there exist several creation myths from ancient Egypt, the customary one describes the precreation state of things as a watery chaos. By correspondence in time, this original condition occurs annually in the flooding of the Nile River. Furthermore, just as the Nile recedes and causes little hills or islands to appear in the midst of the river, so at the beginning of time did a hill emerge as earth out of the primeval deep. In *illo tempore* there stood on that hill the creator god Atum, who as the All within himself did not need to be created but who created everything that is. Thus the hill which emerged at the time of the creation and on which the god stood was a holy place where worshipers could come into contact with creative power. At such a holy place a community built a temple for communion with its god; thus were constructed the sanctuaries and sanctuary cities of Heliopolis, Hermonthis, Memphis, Thebes, and Ramses. Each temple priesthood claimed that its sanctuary was the point at which the primeval hill had emerged.

The god Atum was the deity worshiped particularly at Heliopolis, near modern day Cairo. Up the Nile was the famous temple to Amon-Re at Thebes.

> Thebes is *normal* beyond every (other) city. The water and land were in her from the first times. (Then) (ii II) sand came to *delimit* the fields and to create her ground on the hillock; (thus) earth came into being.
> (*ANET*, p. 8)

Still further up river, Elephantine Island emerges from that point in the Nile where ancient divers could not find the bottom and believed, therefore, they had discovered the point at which the river gushes forth from the caverns of the deep. Built on the southern end of that island is the temple of Khnum, an ancient creator deity who was visited through the ages by such personages as Ramses II in the thirteenth century and Cleopatra in the second century B.C.E. Apparently by contact with creative power, Egypt's rulers could increase their own might and influence.

The temples built upon the primeval hill were regarded as the gods' homes. Since, however, the gods were of such cosmic nature as air, sun, horizon, storm, and so forth, the temple-home was depicted as the microcosm of the world. The pylons through which one entered the sacred precincts were believed to reach to heaven. The ceilings in the temples were often painted blue and studded with stars. The Sacred Lake, still visible at the temples of Karnak and Denderah, might indeed have served as the primeval deep. The floor was usually portrayed as the ground from which the lotus and papyrus grow as pillars, and the innermost holy of holies where the god's image was kept was regarded as the primeval hill.

While the Egyptians did not feel that the god was confined to the dwelling, he was represented there by his image, a statue bearing his particular symbols. Through some sort of manipulation of this statue, various decrees were issued concerning the erection of buildings, campaigns of war, judgments of guilt or innocence, and so forth. In other words, the deity was present in a particular way in that holy place and would answer questions about his will for this or that aspect of the community's life.

That many temples claimed to be built upon the primeval hill presents a problem in quantitative terms. Our logic insists that we ask how it is possible for several places to represent *the* hill which emerged at the time of creation. One can, of course, explain the diverse claims as being polemical, one priesthood vying with the others for the position of supremacy among sanctuaries. Such internal fighting is by no means unknown in the history of Egyptian religion. For example, during the fourteenth century B.C.E. the Pharaoh Akhenaton removed from temples all references to the god Amon in order to extol the worship of the solar disk, the Aton. (The change of his own name from Amenophis IV to Akhenaton is evidence of the revolution.) Immediately after his death his religious movement ended when his successor, at first named Tutankhaton, changed his name to Tutankhamon, and followed suit throughout the temples in the land. However, it might not be polemics so much as qualitative thinking that allows a number of locations to claim the status of primeval hill. If the worshiping community experiences creative power at a sanctuary and since its deity itself shares in the creative power of Atum, then that community can claim appropriately that it is not *a* but *the* primeval hill.

Related to the life-giving force of creation is the understanding that new life too would result on the primeval hill. At several temples, built of course on the original hill, there existed the tradition that Osiris's grave was located in the basement. Yet this temple-hill was not simply the place of his burial; it was also the space where Osiris rose from death and was enthroned as king. On the basis of that tradition, one can understand that earlier the pyramids themselves were constructed to represent the primeval hill. In the dedication ritual of the royal pyramids of Mer-ne-Re and Pepi II (twenty-fourth century B.C.E.), the creation of the universe was recalled as the god Atum was invoked to bless this analogue of the holy hill (see *ANET*, p. 3).

While it is difficult to determine the precise relationship between the primeval hill from creation and the so-called "mountain of Bakhu upon which heaven rests," it is at least important to note that "a serpent is on the brow of that mountain, . . ." whose name is "He Who is on the Mountain That He may Overthrow" (*ANET*, p. 12). The serpent seems to be the same as Apophis who attempts to swallow the sun god in his nocturnal journey through the netherworld. If so, the text indicates that heaven and the netherworld converge at this mountain.

The basis for the sacralization of the hill in Egyptian mythology was its role in creation. The participation of the hill in that primordial event made each place of worship cosmically sacred. Its quality continued century after century even as new temples were built upon the same sites, even into Ptolemaic and Roman times when the old pharaonic designs were copied. Thus was the holiness of certain sites made absolute in ancient Egypt.

MESOPOTAMIA: THE GATE OF THE GODS

While in Mesopotamia, as in Egypt, mountains do not abound or play a major role in the life of the people, the temple itself or a precinct in the temple area could represent the cosmic mountain where the earthly and heavenly worlds converge. Mythologically the origin of such a mountain-temple is most fully described in the *Enuma elish*.

After Marduk had vanquished Tiamat and had cut her in half to form the sky, the victorious new king surveyed the heavens to find a site for a temple. Discovering the spot directly over Ea's abode built on Apsu, he duplicated the palace of his father, his own birthplace, and called it Esharra. Then, following his organization of the heavenly luminaries and the divine responsibilities on earth and in heaven, Marduk was offered "a throne, a recess for his abode." It was to be "like that of *lofty* Babylon." In fact, the temple built for Marduk was located in Babylon, "the place that is your home." Named Esagila, "house of the lofty head," the temple on the earth corresponded to the Esharra which Marduk had made in heaven. Thus, on the sacred axis were built the temples of heaven, of earth, and of the netherworld.

As soon as the temple was constructed, the gods held a banquet

> "The great gods took their seats,
> They set up festive drink, sat down to a banquet,"

> (*ANET*, p. 69)

just as they had done earlier when they met in Anu's temple to commission Marduk as their representative in battle. Thus, on the basis of his victory and his arrangement of the cosmos into its present order, Marduk's home at Esharra and its earthly counterpart in Babylon became the new location of the divine assembly.

In addition to serving as Marduk's place of enthronement, the new palace would function as the spot where the gods could stop for nightly rest as they journeyed back and forth between the palace in the Apsu and that in the heavens. By this understanding of the city's temple, the city itself was appropriately named Babylon, *Bab-ilī* or *Bab-ilāni,* "the gate of the gods."

While this view of the temple as the meeting place of the divine assembly and as the point of contact between the earthly and heavenly worlds was new to Marduk and Babylon in the second millennium B.C.E., it was not new to Mesopotamia. As we have seen in our discussion of the primordial conflict, the present form of the *Enuma elish* is a Mardukized or Babylonized version of earlier concepts and stories. Before the building of Marduk's temple in Babylon, the sanctuary where the assembly of the gods met was the temple in the city of Nippur. According to the political structure of Sumer, the gods convened in a corner of the forecourt of Ekur (which can be translated "house of the mountain"). The entire temple area was called Dur-an-ki, meaning "bond of heaven and earth." Thus the assembly of the gods took place not on a mountain but in a courtyard in rather flat terrain. Nevertheless, that a temple precinct was considered to be the counterpart of the cosmic mountain is attested to at the Phoenician city of Sidon where such an area is called "the high heav-

ens" (*šāmēm rômîm*). Thus, although in a flat land, the temple or parts
thereof represented that cosmic height where the divine and the human worlds connect.

When the gods assembled in Nippur, their functions were not unlike those which Marduk assumed later. However, in a political system quite different from that under which Marduk operated, their
decisions were more of an ad hoc nature. Basically, those decisions
fell into one of two categories: the election and disposition of human
and divine leaders, including kings; and the judging and sentencing
of wrongdoers, human and divine, in a law-court setting. Under
Marduk's reign the establishment of an enduring dynasty in Babylon
changed the first function of the assembly, while the second fell under the jurisdiction of those gods assigned to govern the heavens and
the earth. In either case, when the gods did assemble, an essential ingredient was food: the temple was the place for the divine banquets.

So closely intertwined were the divine power at the temple and the
god of the temple that it was customary to refer to some gods by the
epithet "mountain." Enlil was called "the great mountain," perhaps
in the geographical world a reference to the eastern mountains from
which the tributaries originate. Later, the national god of Assyria,
Ashur, was referred to repeatedly as "the great mountain" (*šadû
rabû*), and the temple of Asshur was called *E.hursag.gal*, "house of
the great mountain."

As in Egypt, the temple in Mesopotamia was the god's home.
When the construction of a temple was completed, the image of the
god was carried in with joyful procession. In the Babylonian temple
the deity was displayed in a shallow room and gazed at by awestruck
worshipers who stood on the opposite side of a monumental door
some distance from their god. In Assyrian temples worshipers entered into the same room with the deity in a quite intimate relationship. In any case, the structure of the temple of the god was quite
similar to the architectural plan of the royal residence, the palace;
moreover, the daily schedule of the god's activities was similar to
that of the king. Thus the temple was indeed a royal residence for a
reigning god, even though his permanent abode was in heaven.

On top of the tower which stood in the temple precinct, the deity
could sojourn. This tower, called by the Babylonians a *ziqqurrat*
("mountain peak"), reached toward heaven and served the function
of a landing site for the deity in his descent from heaven and his ascent from the Apsu. Such perhaps is the meaning of the place of re-
pose for the gods, as the *Enuma elish* describes a function of Marduk's Esagila. Unfortunately, neither literary nor archaeological

evidence is available to learn more about the sacred place on top of the temple-towers. There are indications, however, of a stairway leading to the top and of blue-colored bricks facing the uppermost area. The stairway would have been essential for the priest(s) in ritual to ascend and descend the tower, but it is possible that mythologically the deity himself traversed these steps. As for the blue coloring on top, it is likely that the intention was to represent the sky (as in the Egyptian temples), thus indicating that the top reached into the heavens where the gods lived.

Thus, while the topography of Mesopotamia did not provide a natural "navel of the earth," the temples and the accompanying temple-towers did represent cosmic mountains which reached from the netherworld (Apsu) through the earth to heaven and which functioned as the holy space of convergence for the three worlds. There the gods met to dine and decide, issuing edicts which affected life in the heavens and on the earth, raising up kings and destroying cities, passing verdicts and executing punishment. And there too worshipers could be received by the god as though they were guests in a royal palace.

The means by which the various sites became holy is not unlike the motive for sacralizing places in Egypt. While evidence is not available to determine the precise origin of every sanctuary, that which can be determined from a few might indeed provide a general answer. According to the *Enuma elish*, the origin of Marduk's temple in Babylon goes back in *illo tempore* when that deity defeated the onslaught of chaos and immediately thereafter created and organized the present structure of the universe. Thus the space was made sacred in an absolute sense by participation in that cosmogonic act.

The temple of Inanna in Nippur likewise was made sacred on the basis of creation, for a Sumerian myth called "The Creation of the Pickaxe"[21] tells that the temple was the "place where flesh sprouted forth," that is, where humankind came into existence. Thus established in the primeval time, the temple area in Nippur possessed that quality of holiness which enabled the city to play an important, indeed leading, role in the life of ancient Sumer.

CANAAN: A TALE OF TWO MOUNTAINS

In the Ugaritic texts there are several mountains which are clearly regarded as the homes of the gods. In particular, the head of the pantheon, El, located his mountain home at Mount Lala (questionable reading; perhaps an error for Mount of El). Likewise, the victor over the chaos waters, Baal, acquired through his victory the right to a palace which was constructed on Mt. Zaphon. Each of these sacred mountains requires special attention, for the functions performed at each one were fundamentally different.

The Home of El

El's mountain abode is mentioned for the first time when Yamm's messengers appeared before the divine assembly in order to relay Yamm's request that Baal become his slave. The journey is described as follows:

> The lads depart, they delay not.
> [There, they are off] on their way
>   To the midst of the Mount of Lala,
>   Towards the Assembled Body.
>
>   (*ANET*, p. 130)

This brief reference, whether correctly read as Lala or not, indicates that the location of the divine assembly over which El presides is a mountain.

More pronounced in the texts is the description of the location of El's mountain dwelling. While various deities depart their own homes and arrive at El's house, the visit by the goddess Asherah suffices to present the stereotyped formula.

> There, she is off on her way
>   at the springs of the two rivers,
>   in the midst of the channels of the two deeps.

In his study *El in the Ugaritic Texts* Marvin Pope came to the conclusion that on the basis of this watery description El lived in the netherworld, having been cast down from heaven.[22] While Pope provides some interesting arguments to support the case, it must be remembered that descriptions of the heavens and the netherworld and also of the heavens and the earth tend to correspond to each other, particularly in regard to divine houses. Marduk made his temple in heaven to correspond in every way to Ea's home over the Apsu, and Marduk's earthly temple in Babylon was constructed after the pattern of his heavenly Esharra. That El's home was located in aqueous environs does not necessarily mean it was subterranean. Indeed, since the descriptions of El's home include consistently the dual form "two rivers"/"two deeps," one can conclude that his abode was located at the cosmic mountain which, as the *axis mundi*, provided entrance to both the heavenly and abysmal worlds. According to the understanding of the cosmos in ancient times, an ocean or deep existed over the firmament as well as beneath the earth. Both could water or flood the earth: by rain pouring through windows in the firmament, and by the gushing of subterranean springs (see Gen. 7:11; 8:2). The sources or springs of these rivers/deeps would then be the center of the universe, the holy mount which had its base in the netherworld and its top in the heavens.

As for the mountain's earthly point of contact, Pope suggests the modern Khirbet Afqa, which in ancient times was Aphaca, the site of shrines to Astarte, Aphrodite, and Venus. Located in Syria, northeast of Beirut, Khirbet Afqa lies at the source of the ancient river of Adonis now named Nahr Ibrahim. Though once associated with orgiastic rites, like the source of the Jordan at Banyas where the Roman fertility deity Pan had her sanctuary, the location's natural gifts make it a likely home for El. The river emerges from a cavern and plunges into a deep gorge, while above the cavern the cliffs rise over a thousand feet.[23] The relationship between the description in the Ugaritic texts and the site at Khirbet Afqa is established on the basis of the term *apq*, translated above (and often in Hebrew) as "channels." The connection of *apq* with "two deeps" is approximated at Ps. 18:16 (identical to 2 Sam. 22:16): "The foundations of the world were laid bare, And the channels of Yamm were seen." In any case, the geographical setting for the earthly counterpart of El's abode might indeed be located at the mountain of Khirbet Afqa. If not, some similar site would be necessary to serve the purpose of locating El's presence in such a way that worshipers had access to the deity at the axis of the world. Whatever the precise location on terra firma, the description of El's home indicates that it lies at the source of water which brings fertility to the land.

That the assembly of the gods met at El's abode indicates that one of the major functions of this space was the making of decisions and the issuing of edicts. In the Baal-Anath cycle the major decisions seem to center around the issue of building permits. El, apparently speaking for the assembly, first gave permission for a palace to be built for Yamm and later, after the defeat of Yamm and due to pleading by Lady Asherah, for a home to be constructed for Baal. In addition to these similar decisions, the divine assembly with El as spokesman granted Yamm's request that Baal become his slave. Behind all these issues is one pervading question: who has mastery over the land and the other deities? The edicts of the divine assembly determine the ruler of the world and that decision corresponds to the quality of life on earth: either order or chaos will prevail in the cosmos. Thus the decisions on the holy mount at the center of the world affect the entire cosmos in a totally qualitative way.

Furthermore, like the deities in the assembly of Mesopotamia, those in Canaan feasted together at the holy space. Perhaps it is in this eating together that the gods reestablished their fellowship and their responsibilities to one another in an intimate way. The use of such meals among humans is attested to frequently in the Bible (see Josh. 9:11–15; Gen. 26:28–31). Whatever the actual purpose of the dining, the sacred mountain of El was the place for divine banquets, during or after which decisions were made and edicts issued.

The Home of Baal

The other major mountain in the Ugaritic texts is that of the god Baal: Mount Zaphon. This height served as the home of Baal even before his palace was built, for at this location Baal received messages of various kinds, including the news that El had finally given permission for a palace to be constructed there.

The descriptions of Zaphon are particularly instructive. Following his victory over Yamm and the permission by El to build, Baal commissioned the master craftsman god Kothar wa-Khasis to begin the project.

> "Quickly build the house
>   Quickly raise up the palace
>   In the midst of the recesses of Zaphon.
> A thousand fields the house shall encompass
>   A myriad of acres the palace."

That Zaphon is a mountain is clear from the references to "Zaphon's summit" and to the "recesses" of Zaphon where the palace was built.

> Come quickly, for I will truly reveal it
> In the midst of my mountain, divine Zaphon,
> in the sanctuary, on the hill which I possess,
> in a pleasant place, on the hill which displays my power.

When the construction of the palace on Zaphon was completed, Baal dedicated his new home by holding a banquet for the gods.

> He summons his siblings to his house,
>   (His ki[nd]dred to his palace:
>   Summons Asherah's seventy children. . . .
> He satisfies the gods with jars of wine,
>   He satisfies the goddesses with pitchers.
> So eat the gods and drink.

Just as Marduk held a banquet at the completion of his palace construction in Babylon, so did Baal invite the divine assembly of gods and goddesses for a festive occasion at his new palace on Zaphon. There are no decisions made here, nor are edicts issued. The banquet is simply a party of seventy deities for the purpose of dedicating the palace.

That some chaos forces had attempted periodically to drive Baal from his holy place is attested to in a speech by his sister Anath who vows to continue her warlike pursuit on any such enemies. She will fight anyone

> who would drive Baal from the summits of Zaphon,
> who would seize his ears like a bird,
> who would drive him from the throne of his kingdom,
> from the dais, the seat of his rule.

Thus Baal's supremacy seems always open to challenge by those who seek his lordship, but Anath defends the holy mountain in order to protect Baal's reign. The mountain remains sacred to Baal, it seems, on the basis of such victories over chaos, and so in two passages at least the mountain is called "the mount of victory" (*ǵr tliyt*).

The presence of Baal on his holy mountain terrifies his enemies, for Zaphon is the place of his awesome theophany. Although Baal had serious reservations about windows in his new palace, the craftsman god dispelled his fears, and Baal tried out the new-fangled contraptions (pictured as rifts in the clouds).

> He opens a casement in the house,
>   A window within the pa[lace].
> Baal op[ens] *rifts in* [the cloud]s.
> Ba[al gives] forth his holy voice,
>   Baal discharges the *ut[terance of his li]ps.*
> His h[oly] voice [convulses] the earth,. . . the
>   mountains quake,
>   A-tremble are . . .
> East and west, earth's high places reel.
> Baal's enemies take to the woods,
>   Hadd's foes to the sides of the mountain.

> (*ANET*, p. 135)

The signs of the presence of Baal are most appropriate for the appearance of a storm-god, for his voice is expressed in thunder which roars through the clouds near the summit of his mountain.

As one would expect, that mountain had its counterpart on the earth. Zaphon in the heavens is probably identified on earth as Jebel el Aqra in northern Syria. This elevation of almost a mile captures the clouds and storms in a dramatic way. When the summit is encompassed in cloud and when thunder roars into the valley below, then the worshipers know the presence of Baal in their midst. Since Zaphon is directly north of Ugarit, the ancients used the term to designate that particular compass point, just as Negeb became "south," and Yamm (the Mediterranean Sea) was "west." In other words, since the heavenly Zaphon was concretized in the experience of the Canaanites as Jebel el Aqra, that area thus became known as "north," and "Zaphon" itself became generally used for "north." Even more locally, in the city of Ugarit there has been found a temple to Baal which was in every way oriented to Mount Zaphon. Thus did the actions in the heavens become intimate for the people in the earthly city of Ugarit. One might even conjecture that the banqueting of the gods at the holy mount was experienced in the local temple by the gifts of food and drink brought by the people as sacrificial offerings to their favorite gods.

The Two Gods and Their Mountains

El and Baal possessed palaces on their respective holy mounts, each of which had its counterpart in the earthly experience of worshipers. The two hills were indeed cosmically sacred, for the occurrences at each spot were determinative for the life of the community. At El's abode decisions were made and edicts issued which determined rulership of the earth and heaven. On Baal's mountain battles were fought to maintain his lordship over chaos powers, and life-giving storms depicted the presence of the deity.

The means by which these mountains became sacred is easier to determine for Baal's home than for El's. The Ugaritic texts are rather explicit in setting the stage for the construction on Mount Zaphon: only after Baal demonstrated his superiority by victory over Yamm did he acquire the right to own a palace from which to rule. In our earlier discussion of the setting of that cosmic battle, we concluded that the "event" took place when the Sea was controlled in its raging, and the life-giving rains of late autumn and winter prevailed. Thus did Baal's kingship and his right to a place of enthronement have its basis in the natural cycle: Zaphon was sacred because of a seasonal victory of Baal.

On the other hand, the texts from Ugarit simply assume the leadership of El in the divine assembly and the sanctity of his mount at the springs of the two rivers/deeps. Is it possible that in an older tradition El likewise was victorious in a battle (annual or otherwise) which gave him the right to that position at the *axis mundi*? Patrick Miller has advanced some evidence to allow for this possibility. In an article "El the Warrior"[24] Miller has pointed out that: (1) the name El is derived from a root meaning "strength"; (2) the epithet "Bull" refers not only to his sexual prowess but also to strength in battle; (3) Sanchuniathon equates El with Kronos who engages in war and repels the usurper Uranos; (4) in other Ugaritic texts El is portrayed as strong and mighty; and (5) in the Keret Legend from Ugarit it is El who leads the king in battle. Miller suggests that the portrayal of El in Ugarit as old and weak might not have been true all over Canaan. Moreover, many of the features depicting El as a warrior might reflect traditions older than the fourteenth-century texts from Ugarit. While all this is probable, the basis for the sanctity of El's mountain is not at present available.

It is perhaps appropriate at this point to note the tension which existed between El and Baal in the stories we have been considering. Several times in the Baal-Anath cycle Yamm is called "the Beloved of El," and judging from the show of favoritism in the construction of Yamm's palace and in the gift of Baal as Yamm's slave, the title certainly seems appropriate. Baal, for his part, never takes a belligerent role against El, but his sister Anath threatens the assembly leader in rather shocking terms. Further, while Baal is sometimes called a son of El and himself speaks of "Bull El, his father," more frequently is Baal called "the son of Dagan" (grain), even by El himself when he hands over Baal to be Yamm's slave. Thus there is evident a conflict in the divine assembly between El and Baal-Anath which perhaps explains why Baal had a difficult time acquiring a home "like the gods." This conflict might, in fact, represent a diminishing influence of El in the religion of Canaan, or more precisely in northern Canaan, during the fourteenth century B.C.E.

8

The Relativity of Yahweh's Mountain

REFLECTIONS OF "NAVEL" IMAGERY
AT VARIOUS SHRINES

The classical passage for the presence of the sacred mountain from the culture of the ancient Near East is, of course, the story of the Tower of Babel at Gen. 11:1–9. This concluding story in the history of humankind, which began in Genesis 3, tells how humans living in the plain of Shinar determined among themselves to build a city "and a tower with its top in the heavens" (v. 4). While there is combined with this motif that of an original universal language, our concern here is merely to observe an awareness by the Hebrew writer (the Yahwist of the tenth century B.C.E.) of the significance of the Babylonian *ziqqurrat*s: the top reached to heaven and thus provided the point of contact between the divine and human worlds. The ironic twist in the story occurs when Yahweh, not the Babylonian deities, descends from heaven and, distraught at their aspirations, brings such judgment on the city that the inhabitants are scattered without achieving their purpose. By combining this motif with that of the universal language, the author reinterprets the meaning of the name Babel ("the gate of the gods"): it is here the place where the Lord "confused" (*bālal*) the language of all the earth.

In addition to this story of Babylonian allusion, the nocturnal vision by Jacob at Beth-El reflects similar notions from a Canaanite cult (Gen. 28:10–17). Fleeing from the wrath of his father and brother, Jacob spent the night at an unnamed sanctuary ("a certain place"). There Jacob dreamed of a "mound" which stood on the earth, "and the top of it reached to heaven" (v. 12). Moreover, that this was indeed the point of contact with the divine world is explained immediately: "and the angels of God were ascending and descending upon it." Further, when Jacob awoke from his sleep, he declared, "How awesome is this place! This is no other than the house of God, and this is the gate of heaven" (v. 17). Typically of such visions, most of the verbs describing his vision appear in the participial form which, in Hebrew, designates a continuing act. The human enjoyed a peek into eternity; he saw the cosmic mountain where from time immemorial earth, heaven, and netherworld converge. Thus the angels were ascending and descending as they traversed the cosmic realms. While the translation of *sullām* as "ladder" is tempting in light of the stairways on the *ziqqurrat*s, the term is related to words which mean "highway" or "seige ramp" and is best translated "mound of earth." In light of this similarity with the Babylonian temple-towers and of the description of Beth-El as the "gate of heaven," one is indeed led to think of the Mesopotamian tradition for understanding the passage. However, the interpreter must bear in mind that the sanctuary is located in Canaan and is basically an El-temple. The name of the site, for which Jacob is here given credit, is Beth-El, "the house of El." This passage, therefore, demonstrates a similarity in the sacred mount imagery between Mesopotamia and Canaan. Further, on the basis of the story of Jacob's experience at the place, the story is Yahweh-ized, and Jacob erects a stone pillar to represent the cosmic home of God which he had seen in his vision (v. 22). That a stone, capable of being moved by human hands, is the earthly counterpart of God's heavenly home indicates that it is not the proportions of the rock but the quality of the space which determines sanctity.

Almost hidden in most English translations is the precise reference to "the navel of the earth" attested to in the Bible. In Judges 9 the story of the siege of Shechem by Abimelech and his army is told. Inside the city, Gaal, who had earlier spoken of refusal to serve Abimelech, stood in the gateway at sunrise. There he saw the warriors rising up in ambush, and so he turned to Zebul, ruler of the city who had planned the entire attack, "Look, men are coming down from the mountain tops." When Zebul paid no attention to his claim, Gaal repeated, "Look, men are coming down from the navel of the earth, and one company is coming from the direction of the Diviner's Oak" (v. 37). The translation in most English versions of the Bible is "the center of the land," as though it were a reference to a geographical location. Only *The Jerusalem Bible* retains the literal and mythological rendering "Navel of the Land." (The Hebrew *ṭabbûr hā'āreṣ* appears in the Septuagint as *omphalos tēs gēs*, thus "navel of the earth.") Moreover, the context of the story in Judges 9 supports this interpretation, for standing at the gate of Shechem, Gaal would have been looking at Mount Gerizim, an important Canaanite sanctuary which later became Hebraized and eventually became the center of Samaritan worship, as it remains to this day.

In this connection one might allow the possibility that Mount Tabor in Galilee received its name from the belief that it was the *ṭabbûr hā'āreṣ*. It must be admitted, however, that as the word appears in the Hebrew Bible itself (Jer. 46:18; Hos. 5:1; Ps. 89:12), the spelling differs from the word for "navel." The mountain name consists of a *taw* rather than *tet* and a single *bêt* in place of the double *bêt*.

Baal's mountain home Zaphon appears in the Hebrew Bible in a highly mythological passage, the precise background of which is difficult to determine.

> How you have fallen from heaven, Helel son of Shahar!
> How you have been cut down to the netherworld,
> You said to yourself,
> I will ascend on high,
>   on (among?) the stars of El I will raise my throne.
> And I will sit enthroned in the mount of assembly,
>   in the recesses of Zaphon.
> I will ascend upon the high places of cloud(s),
>   I will make myself like Elyon.
> However, to Sheol you are brought down,
>   to the recesses of the pit. . . .
>
>   (Isa. 14:12ff)

This taunt is directed to a historical person, the king of Babylon, but the mythological background from the culture of Canaan is obvious by the references to El, Elyon, and Zaphon. Moreover, the identity of the mythological character who aspires to the "recesses of Zaphon" but is thrown down to "the recesses of the pit" likewise has Canaanite characteristics. His name, Helel, means "the morning star," and he is identified as "the son of Shahar," that is, "dawn" or more precisely the brief moment before dawn. There are several possible parallels in the Ugaritic literature to the attempt of a young god (or prince) to take over the throne from the older ruling god (king); however, a cosmic battle between Helel and Elyon is not yet attested. In any case, the background is some sort of nature myth in which such a battle for enthronement on Zaphon (interestingly Baal's mount) takes place, but the entire story is transformed in order to address the vain illusions of the historical king of Babylon.

Mount Sinai

The nature of this study does not permit a detailed treatment of the location of Mount Sinai or of the relationship of Sinai to Horeb or the mountain of God. Scholars have wrestled with the location problem from various viewpoints, with varying results. Weighty arguments are given for pinpointing Sinai in areas other than the traditional one in the southern Sinai peninsula. For some, the evidence falls in an area east of the Gulf of Aqabah, and for others, in the area of Kadesh. Further, there are those who suggest that the mountain of God (mentioned without specific name) was the one at Kadesh, and that Mount Sinai was another hill with which the former's traditions were merged. The possibility of Horeb as either one of these, or yet a third mountain, remains a problem that might not be explained simply on the basis of different sources in the Tetrateuch and Deuteronomy. To complicate matters even more, the necessity of determining cult leaders for these various mountains causes Moses and Aaron in particular to be very mobile indeed. The many studies dealing with these problems are important for understanding the merging of traditions and of the texts pertaining thereto. Moreover, if some agreement could be reached regarding these traditions, the separateness of the mountains and their respective characteristics might provide valuable information for this study. However, as it is, the present writer would need to base too much on conjecture, and so perhaps we must be satisfied with the present tradition in which the mountains are merged or at least identified one with the other.

SINAI AS THE NAVEL OF THE EARTH

While the precise expression *ṭabbûr hā'āreṣ* does not appear in the Sinai traditions in the Tetrateuch (Exodus 19–Numbers 10) or in the poetic traditions about Mount Sinai, there is one passage in particular which indicates that Sinai was the place where the heavens and the earth met.

> And to Moses he said, "Come up to Yahweh, you and Aaron, Nadab and Abihu, and seventy from the elders of Israel, and you shall worship from afar. But Moses alone shall draw near to Yahweh, but they shall not draw near, and the people shall not come up with him. . . . And Moses and Aaron and Nadab and Abihu, and seventy from the elders went up, and they saw the God of Israel, and under his feet was like the work of sapphire stone, like the substance of heaven for purity. And to the chiefs of the children of Israel he did not stretch out his hand. And they envisioned God, and they ate and drank (Exod. 24:1–2, 9–11).

The passage describes an invitation which has been edited in such a

way that Moses alone should go all the way to the top while everyone else would go only part way. Such editing was necessary for the
addition of the tradition at verses 12–18 in which Moses alone was to
receive the two tablets and to experience the instructions which follow. In any case, that the whole troop went to the top originally
is indicated by their experience there. "They saw God," at least his
soles, as his feet rested on a slab of lapis lazuli (*sappîr*). Later, in Ezekiel's vision of the heavenly court, the firmament is described as
awesome crystal, and the throne on which God sat was like *sappîr*
(see Ezek. 1:22–26). Perhaps indeed it was the footstool before his
throne on which God's feet rested. In any case, the human leaders of
Israel, high up on the mountain, found themselves standing under
the firmament at the point of God's presence, indeed where God's
throne and his palace were located.

The number of human leaders involved in this invitation to the
mountain is of significance in interpreting the passage. According to
his traditio-historical studies of the Moses stories, Martin Noth[25]
came to the conclusion that the seventy elders were the original persons in the passage, and that Moses and the three others were added
later. While the reasons he gives for this conclusion might be debata-
ble, it is significant that there is no reason why the number seventy
should have been selected at this point in the story. In chapter 18 of
the Book of Exodus, Moses had selected God-fearing men to help
him in the administration of justice for the people, but no mention is
made of seventy. Later in the story, at Num. 11:16–30 (J), seventy
of the elders were commissioned for the purpose of alleviating Moses's burden (cf. Exod. 18:22 [E]).

Here in Exodus 24, it seems, it is not the context of the passage
but the mythological background of the holy mountain that provides
the reason why seventy are selected. When Baal's palace was finished, the fertility god invited to his new home seventy gods and
goddesses, all the children of Asherah, for a festive banquet, where
the gods "ate and drank." Since at the feast of Marduk, when his palace was erected, fifty of the great Babylonian gods were invited, it
seems that the Canaanite version of the myth has been taken over by
the Hebrew storytellers and transformed to the human sphere: it is
no longer seventy deities but seventy human leaders of his delivered
people whom God invites to his palatial banquet. Thus, the myth is
here historicized: the celestial banquet for the seventy guests is
brought down to earth. Furthermore, in the present context of the
passage, the meal can now be understood as the eating and drinking

which seals the covenant between Yahweh and the people of Israel that had just been made with blood at the foot of the mountain (vv. 3–8).

SINAI AS THE PLACE OF THEOPHANY
AND COMMISSIONING

In addition to the banquet marking the point where the heavens and earth converge, Sinai qualifies as the sacred mountain because awesome theophanies occurred there. At the very beginning of the Sinai tradition, in the nineteenth chapter of Exodus, the sequence of events is as follows: the people arrive at the foot of the mountain (vv. 1–2), Yahweh invites Moses up the mountain where the first elements of a covenant ceremony appear (vv. 3–8; the remainder occur at 24:3–8), Yahweh promises that he will come in a cloud so that the people might hear the conversation, and then Moses makes the necessary preparations—completely cultic in nature—for the theophany three days hence. In verses 16–19 the theophany is described by the intertwining of two different sources: the Yahwist and the Elohist.

Yahwist	Elohist
And Mount Sinai was wrapped in smoke, because the Lord descended upon it in fire; and the smoke of it ascended like the smoke of a kiln, and the whole mountain quaked greatly. . . . And the Lord came down upon Mount Sinai, to the top of the mountain; and the Lord called Moses to the top of the mountain, and Moses went up.	On the morning of the third day there were thunders and lightnings, and a thick cloud upon the mountain, and a very loud trumpet blast, so that all the people who were in the camp trembled. Then Moses brought the people out of the camp to meet God; and they took their stand at the foot of the mountain. And as the sound of the trumpet grew louder and louder, Moses spoke and God answered him in thunder.

While any such division must remain somewhat conjectural, the different uses of the name of the deity—God (Elohim) and Yahweh—happen to coincide with different types of theophanic descriptions: that of the Yahwist portrays a volcanic eruption, while that of the Elohist, a storm. One should not, however, look for the site of Sinai in an area of volcanoes active during the second millennium B.C.E., because the Yahwist's account represents typical imagery, as does that of the Elohist. However, each one has its own emphasis and perhaps intends to convey a particular impact. The Elohist's home, it seems, was centered in the northern kingdom of Israel during the ninth century B.C.E. Like his contemporary Elijah, the major problem he faced was the identification of Yahweh and Baal. Thus it has been argued by Hans Walter Wolff[26] that the kerygmatic formula for the Elohist was "fear God" and obey him in the midst of the claims of the Canaanites to worship Baal. The Elohist's portrayal of God in this passage appears quite similar to that of the storm-god Baal when that deity opened the windows of his palace and convulsed the earth with his holy voice of thunder (see above, p. 136). Just as Elijah had Yahweh beat the prophets of Baal at their own game of storm phenomena (1 Kings 18:20–40), so the Elohist describes the appearance of God on his holy mountain in similar terms. The effect is polemical while at the same time the home of God is clearly marked: such storm appearances occur at the abode of God.

The description by the Yahwist in volcanic terms clearly presumes a mountain ablaze with fire, but the more interesting connection with mythology is the notion that Yahweh must "come down" from his heavenly home in order to alight on the mountain, the counterpart of his abode on the earth. The Babylonian *ziqqurrat*s served precisely this purpose, as we discussed above in relation to the Tower of Babel story. It was the Yahwist indeed who preserved for us that story in Genesis 11, and so he was quite well aware of the significance of the sacred mount in Babylon.

Whether a volcanic eruption or a storm, either of these theophany forms could be duplicated in the cult at a local sanctuary. The fire and smoke of the Yahwist can be accomplished by the burning of incense; the clue to the thunder duplication appears in the Elohist's own text: trumpet blasts. Thus, whether or not a community lived near Mount Sinai, the Sinai experience of the presence of God in his home could be shared at any sanctuary. The physical distance from Sinai—wherever it was located—was of no concern as long as the quality of the experience could be realized in ritual.

In the next narrative complex of Sinai material, namely Exodus 24, the Priestly writer offers a description of a theophany on the mountain which seems to be a combination of the two in chapter 19. (Indeed, by the time of the Priest's work, the Yahwist and Elohist sources were already combined.) The theophany here occurs shortly after the festive meal discussed above. Moses and Joshua left the elders and climbed the rest of the way to the summit in order to receive the two tablets of law and commandment. Then occurs the theophany:

Then Moses went up on the mountain, and the cloud covered the mountain. The glory of the Lord settled on Mount Sinai, and the cloud covered it six days; and on the seventh day he called to Moses out of the midst of the cloud. Now the appearance of the glory of the Lord was like a devouring fire on the top of the mountain in the sight of the people of Israel. And Moses entered the cloud and went up on the mountain. And Moses was on the mountain forty days and forty nights (24:15–18).

Here the Priest describes a theophany which includes both cloud and fire, that is, storm and volcano imagery, but the difference in his portrayal centers on this key term: glory (*kābôd*). The glory of the Lord expresses itself visibly so that the people of Israel, far below the summit, might know that God is present on his mountain. Using a characteristic literary device from West Semitic literature, the author tells that Moses waited on the mountain "six days; and on the seventh day" the Lord summoned Moses to enter into the cloud itself, much like a chief priest in the temple would enter the holy of holies.

Apart from these narrative theophanic descriptions, such awesome appearances of God on his mountain occur also in the ancient poems of Deut. 33:1–2; Judg. 5:4–5; and Ps. 68:7–10. The relationship between Yahweh and Mount Sinai, his abode, was so close that in two of the poems cited, Yahweh is called specifically "the One of Sinai" (*zeh sînay*; Judg. 5:5; Ps. 68:8; the translation "yon Sinai" is both gramatically impossible and inconsistent with the use of the demonstrative pronoun in Semitic inscriptions to designate the deity of a given place).

Before leaving the important theophany passages, there is one more to consider, indeed the first encounter with Sinai/Horeb which the reader of the Bible experiences: that of the burning bush in Exod. 3:1–15. Placed immediately after Moses's marriage into the Midianite family of the priest Jethro/Reuel, the theophany is set within grazing distance of the Midianite home. It was while tending the flocks of his father-in-law that Moses was attracted to a strange sight on "Horeb, the mountain of God" (v. 1). The angel of Yahweh appeared to Moses as fire in the midst of a bush, and yet the bush was not consumed by the fire. Clearly in this story the theophanic form of fire which we have seen in connection with the appearance of God in Exodus 19 is merely an attention-getting device. It serves the purpose of drawing the observer near to the sacred place: "the place . . . is the ground of holiness." There is nothing about the dirt which is holy in itself, thus not "holy ground," but the space on which Moses was standing had the quality of holiness because Yahweh was present there, taking the visible form of fire, and speaking through his messenger, that is, his angel (*mal'āk*).

If the theophany itself serves to gain Moses's attention, then the purpose for the entire encounter appears in a twofold way in what follows. First, God reveals to Moses his identity as "the God of your father, the God of Abraham, the God of Isaac, and the God of Jacob" (v. 6). To the reader of the Bible, this self-introduction combines the traditions of the patriarchs in the Book of Genesis with what is to follow. Second, what does follow is the purpose of God to free the people of Israel from their bondage in Egypt, so that the gift of the land promised to the patriarchs might be realized (vv. 7–10). Moreover, God himself will deliver (vv. 7–8) or will send Moses to deliver (vv. 9–10) the people, because he has heard the cry of the people for help, has seen their affliction/oppression, and knows their sufferings. Obviously, by the unnecessary duplications here two sources are involved (Yahwist and Elohist), and the respective roles of Yahweh/God and Moses are not entirely consistent. For the Yahwist, Yahweh will deliver, and Moses will serve as the spokesman for Yahweh before the people (vv. 7–8, 16–17). According to the Elohist, God sends Moses to deliver the people (vv. 9–10). Apart from these duplications and inconsistencies, however, the passage must be treated as a whole.

It is in connection with this saving commission of Moses that the Elohist described the origin of the name Yahweh (vv. 13–15). Until this point in his story which began at Genesis 15, that writer used for the deity the name Elohim, "God." Now in the revelation of the will and purpose of God, the name Yahweh was given to Moses for cultic use by the people of Israel. When one considers the intimate relationship between a person and his or her name, the impact of this self-revelation becomes extraordinarily profound: God risks overfamiliarity and even attempted manipulation by those who know the Name, but God takes that risk because the salvation of the people and the divine plan for the land are at stake. This powerful connection between the name-giving and the holy mountain in the Elohistic tradition is not apparent in the work of the Yahwist who has used the name Yahweh ever since Gen. 4:26. Further, the mountain connection is later dissolved by the Priest who placed the name-giving in the land of Egypt (Exod. 6:1–2).

The use of the theophany in Exodus 3 as an attention-getting device leading up to the revelation of the Name and will of Yahweh

forces us to return to the function of theophanies which occur later at
the mountain before the people. What follows the theophanies in Exodus 19 and 24 is of profound importance in the development of the
tradition.

SINAI AS THE PLACE FOR THE
GIFT OF TORAH

The arrangement of the material in chapters 19 through 34 in the
Book of Exodus is quite peculiar and obviously the result of a complicated process of editing. Immediately after the theophany of chapter 19 Moses was instructed to warn the people against climbing the
mountain. The chapter ends with the statement that he descended
and talked with the people. Then chapter 20 begins "And God spoke
all these words," upon which follows the traditional Decalogue.
Since Moses had already left the mountain, one must ask about the
identity of the audience to whom God spoke these Ten Commandments. The answer appears in verses 18–21 which describe the fear
and trembling of all the people as they saw and heard what was
occurring on the mountain. In other words, all the people comprised
the audience for the speech of God. (The whole situation is expli-
cated more clearly in Deuteronomy 5.) Then the people, having
heard God speak, decided that once was enough, and so they instructed Moses to go by himself for any further instructions and to
come back with a verbatim report. (At Deut. 5:28–29 Yahweh com-
mends the people for their wisdom in this decision to use mediators.)
Returning into the presence of God, Moses received the Book of the
Covenant (20:22–23:22) which he read before the people in connection with the covenant ceremony at the foot of the mountain
(24:3–8). Immediately thereafter is the meal on the mountain top
(vv. 9–11), the (further?) trip to the top by Moses accompanied by
Joshua (vv. 12–14), and the Priestly theophany of the glory of the
Lord (vv. 15–18). Then follow seven chapters of instructions by
Yahweh to Moses, all of which have to do with the means by which
Yahweh will be present for the people when they leave Mount Sinai
on their trek toward Canaan: the construction of the ark and the tabernacle as well as the establishment of the priesthood which will me-
diate between Yahweh and the people (chapters 25–31).

It is thus striking that immediately after the theophany of Exodus
19 is reported the gift of the *tôrāh* by which God gives directives for
the redeemed people to live holistically, that is, in regard to himself,
to the sacred realm, to family members, to community members,

and to the property of others (Exod. 20:1–17). Further, as soon as this Decalogue is set forth, there appears in short order the Book of the Covenant by which Yahweh quite specifically lays down rules and punishments for life in an agricultural society, thus in Canaan.

Moreover, following the theophanies in Exodus 24 occur the Priestly instructions concerning the relationship which Yahweh will have with the people after they leave Sinai. Indeed, it is more appropriate to speak of the relationship after Yahweh leaves Sinai, for the Book of Exodus ends with a description of the function of the tabernacle which demonstrates the portability of Yahweh and his glory: "Then the cloud covered the tent of meeting, and the glory of the Lord filled the tabernacle. . . . For throughout all their journeys the cloud of the Lord was upon the tabernacle by day, and fire was in it by night, in the sight of all the house of Israel" (Exod. 40:34–38).

In other words, each theophany on the mountain is followed by Yahweh's instructions (the meaning of *tôrāh*) for life elsewhere. While it is impossible to know the precise origins of the several law codes contained in this material or the dates at which they were woven into the Sinai narrative, the sequence of the present arrangement is striking. Ironically, in the midst of various passages which demonstrate the sanctity of the space in mythological terms, the arrangement of the law codes and their content as well tend to remove Yahweh from Sinai by his own plan and provision. That this God gives up his own palatial residence in order to become a wanderer with the people expresses a theological reality quite unusual—if not unique—in the ancient world.

Mount Zion

FROM THE REED SEA TO THE
PROMISED LAND

The Song of Moses, or Song of the Sea (Exod. 15:1–18), consists of two parts: the first describes the victory of Yahweh over the Egyptians at the Reed Sea; the second celebrates the tradition of the conquest of Canaan. The primary concern of the latter section is the "abode" of Yahweh.

> In your covenant loyalty you have led a people whom you had redeemed,
> In your strength you have guided (them) to the abode of your holiness. . . .
> You will bring them in and plant them on the mount of your heritage,
> the site for your abode (which) you established, O Yahweh.
>
> (Exod. 15:13, 17)

The words which describe Yahweh's abode are strikingly similar to those terms which, in the Ugaritic texts, designate the home of Baal on Mount Zaphon (see above, pp. 135–37). Such terminology, as well as orthographic evidence, has led to the conclusion by some scholars that the poem dates from an early period, perhaps the eleventh century B.C.E. While the words describe Baal's home, they do not necessarily point to Jebel el Aqra for the abode of Yahweh in Canaan. In the course of time, perhaps with the building of the Jerusalem Temple itself, that terminology was taken over by the Mount Zion cult.

Indeed, the highly polemical Psalm 78 sets forth a development by speaking first of the land of Canaan itself as "the mountain," then the rejection of the Shiloh sanctuary, and finally the election of Judah/Mount Zion where Yahweh built his sanctuary:

> And he brought them in to the territory of his holiness,
>   the mount which your right hand acquired.
> And he assigned them a portion of (his) heritage
>   and settled the tribes of Israel in their tents.
>
> (Ps. 78:55)

Immediately it is reported that the people of Israel (northern kingdom) rebelled against God, provoking him to anger with their "high places" of worship. "And he forsook the dwelling of Shiloh, the tent where he dwelled among people" (v. 60). That rejection of the tribe of Ephraim led to the election of a new tribe and sanctuary:

> And he chose the tribe of Judah,
>   Mount Zion which he loves.
> He built his sanctuary like the high heavens (rāmîm),
>   like the earth which he established forever.
>
> (vv. 68–69)

The last verse cited indicates that the temple on Mount Zion was built on the model of the heavenly home of God, a feature we have seen in Mesopotamia and in Canaan.

FROM MOUNT SINAI TO MOUNT ZION

A more direct march from the old holy mountain to the new is described in Psalm 68, but likewise from a biased point of view. When Yahweh left his holy mountain (Sinai), a theophany of storm marked the departure (vv. 7–10); this portrayal is followed by a generalized account of holy war (vv. 11–14), his rejection of Samaria's mount (vv. 15–16), and a series of terms which describe the new holy mount. At Zion is "the mount which God desired for his abode where Yahweh will dwell forever" (v. 16). Amidst his armies "Yahweh came from Sinai into the sanctuary." Further, Yahweh ascended "the high mount" (*mārôm*: v. 18) where processions of Israelites (vv. 24–27) and of earthly kingdoms (vv. 32–34) were summoned to sing his praises.

The psalm is striking in its portrayal of Yahweh. On the one hand, Yahweh is described in terms which are typical of Baal. The theophany at the departure from Sinai results in rain and thus nourishment for the earth, the benefits of a fertility deity. Near the end of the psalm Yahweh is said to be the one "who rides in the heavens, the primordial heavens. Behold, he gives forth his voice, the voice of power" (that is, thunder; v. 33). Consistently in the Ugaritic texts Baal is called "the rider of the clouds," an appropriate designation for a storm god.

On the other hand, used rather casually as the term for God is the Hebrew word *'el*.

> Blessed is the Lord, who day by day strengthens us.
> El is our victory.
> El is for us an El of victories.
>
> (vv. 19–20)

The final verse clearly connects the name of the God with the name of the people: Awesome is God in your (his!) sanctuary, El of Isra-el . . . (v. 35).

Thus in this psalm about the transition of God's abode from Sinai to Jerusalem/Zion, Yahweh is characterized by terms and images characteristic of Baal and is simultaneously identified with that chief god of the Canaanite assembly, El. It remains now to observe if and how these relationships are made elsewhere in connection with the holy mount Zion.

ZION AS ZAPHON, MOUNTAIN OF DEFENSE

Particularly striking is the location of Mount Zion "in the far north," a peculiar geographical designation for a hill on which the community stood to sing Psalm 48.

> Great is Yahweh, and praised greatly
>   in the city of our God, the mount of his holiness.
> Beautiful of elevation is the joy of all the earth,
>   Mount Zion (of) the recesses of Zaphon,
>   city of a great king.
>
> (vv. 1–2)

It is clear here that Zaphon is not a compass point relative to some other place but rather a place of absolute quality: it is the home of God. As such, Zaphon's recesses have been transferred from Baal to Yahweh, and so the heavenly home now has its counterpart not in northern Syria at Jebel el Aqra but in Jerusalem at Mount Zion. Further, the psalm moves on to describe a mythological defense of the mountain—portrayed in typical holy-war terms—and thus recalls the tradition that Baal and Anath repeatedly defended Zaphon against the attack of Chaos.

Even without using the name Zaphon, other Zion psalms tell of this defense of the mountain from attack by anonymous enemies (Pss. 46, 76), a tradition which Isaiah the prophet historicized to proclaim hope to the city under siege by the Assyrian armies in 701 B.C.E.

> ". . . so Yahweh Sabaoth will come down
>   to fight upon Mount Zion and its hill.
> Like hovering birds, so Yahweh Sabaoth will protect Jerusalem,
>   protect and deliver, spare and rescue."
>
> (Isa. 31:4–5)

Further, in the narrative material about the siege of Jerusalem in Isaiah 36–39 (almost identical to 2 Kings 18:13–20:19) the arrogant claims of the Assyrian king are thwarted by Yahweh's nocturnal attack on the invading camp. That defense led to the withdrawal of Sennacherib and to the account of his subsequent death (Isa. 37:36–39). Immediately thereafter, when Hezekiah of Judah became ill and petitioned Yahweh for help, Yahweh promised him a sign that he would deliver the king from his illness and the city from Assyria. That sign was the turning back of the sun dial, that is, of the sun itself (38:5–8). In any case this tradition, moreover, is attested to quite early in David's occupation of Jerusalem. On two occasions David's former allies, the Philistines, tried to overtake him in the Valley of Rephaim to the south of Jerusalem. On the first attempt David drove them back, but the second victory belonged to Yahweh who went out to smite the army of the Philistines (2 Sam. 5:17–22). This battle marked the first defense of Jerusalem by Yahweh.

ZION AS THE PLACE OF THEOPHANY
AND COMMISSIONING

As Yahweh's divine home, one would expect his presence there to be represented by theophanies. Indeed, as soon as the priests carried the ark of the covenant into the Holy of Holies of Solomon's brand new Temple—on dedication day itself—a theophany occurred.

> And when the priests came out of the holy place a cloud filled the house
> of Yahweh, so that the priests were not able to stand for ministering be-
> fore the cloud, because the glory of Yahweh filled the house of Yahweh
> (1 Kings 8:10–11).

Thus was completed the movement of the glory of the Lord from
Sinai through the entire wandering of the people to the new mount
of holiness where Yahweh's own house was built.

From the time of Solomon, Mount Zion's God appeared in theophany forms for various purposes. Several psalms continue to portray the divine presence, some in terms of clouds, fire, and light-
nings, to defeat the enemies of Zion (Ps. 97:1–9), some in terms of
fire and tempest to deliver the oppressed and to judge the wicked
whom God rebukes (Ps. 50:21). In connection with the historical defense of Jerusalem/Zion from Assyrian attack, Isaiah speaks of Yahweh as one "whose fire is in Zion, whose kiln is in Jerusalem" (Isa.
31:9), precisely terms used to describe Yahweh's presence on Mount
Sinai.

Further, just as Yahweh appeared in a fiery theophany on Mount
Sinai to call Moses to the task of deliverance, so Yahweh called Isaiah
to be a prophet of judgment in the midst of a fiery theophany in the
temple on Mount Zion. "And the foundations of the threshold shook
at the voice of him who called, and the house was filled with smoke"
(Isa. 6:4). The theophany of Sinai is represented in the ritual of the
temple on Zion by the burning of incense on the altar (see v. 6). In
both cases, that of Moses and that of Isaiah, the theophany serves to
attract the attention of the human to whom Yahweh then reveals his
will and whom he commissions to execute that will.

ZION AS THE PLACE OF THE
DIVINE ASSEMBLY

The account of the call of Isaiah leads us to consider another characteristic of the home of Yahweh: it is the place where God is enthroned over an assembly of divine beings.

> In the year of the death of King Uzziah, I saw Yahweh sitting upon a
> high and raised throne, and his entourage was filling the temple. Sera-
> phim were standing above him, six wings for each one. With two
> (wings) he covered his face, with two he covered his feet, and with two
> he flew (Isa. 6:1–2).

These attendant creatures at the throne of Yahweh sang his praises:

> Holy, holy, holy is Yahweh Sabaoth!
> The fullness of the whole earth is his glory.
>
> (v. 3)

As in the vision of Jacob at the sanctuary at Beth-El, this vision of
Isaiah describes the action in participial forms. The prophet-soon-
to-be has his glimpse of the enduring situation as he is at worship in
the earthly counterpart of Yahweh's home, the Jerusalem Temple.
That vision of heavenly reality depicts Yahweh, enthroned over the
ark of the covenant, as King of the assembly of divine creatures, just
as El was so portrayed in the Canaanite texts, and Marduk in the
Enuma elish. Moreover, as occurs regularly in the assemblies of those
two deities, here also an edict is issued, the content of which is the
inevitable judgment of Yahweh on his own people. One might compare here also the decision of the Sumerian divine assembly at Nippur to destroy the city of Ur, historically caused by Elamites and the
Sun people but cosmically by Enlil's own destructive force.

Isaiah's vision of the King over the divine assembly is quite like
that of Micaiah ben Imlah, who—likewise in action described by
participles—saw Yahweh enthroned amidst "all the host of heaven"
(1 Kings 22:19). Moreover, in this case also came an edict from the
assembly: judgment upon King Ahab. The agent here who volun-
teered (like Isaiah) to accomplish the will of the assembly was "the
spirit" (v. 21), who would become "a spirit of deception in the
mouth of all his prophets" (v. 22), and thus lead to Ahab's downfall.
When this passage is considered alongside the call of Isaiah, it is
striking that in both cases the King in the heavenly assembly seeks
some particular agent to carry out the edict, much like the role given
to Marduk in the *Enuma elish* and, even more pertinent, that assigned
to the storm god Enlil in the earlier Sumerian pantheon (see above,
p. 12). While this agent is likewise a divine being in Micaiah's vision
of the assembly, in Isaiah's vision the agent is the human prophet
himself, thus a transformation of the familiar motif.

The portrayal of Yahweh as King over the divine assembly is attested also in several psalms. For example, Psalm 29, the Canaanite
background for which has long been recognized, begins

> Ascribe to Yahweh, O sons of El,
>   Ascribe to Yahweh glory and strength.
>
> (vv. 1–2)

while the psalm goes on to speak of the theophany of the storm god
and culminates in his enthronement as King.

> Yahweh sits enthroned over the primeval abyss,
>   Yahweh sits enthroned as King forever.

While the psalm probably originated outside Jerusalem traditions, the later use in the Jerusalem cult would have been completely in order, for there Yahweh was enthroned on the ark of the covenant, situated in the Holy of Holies.

ZION AS THE PLACE FOR THE
CORONATION OF KINGS

While Solomon himself was anointed and acclaimed king at the bottom of Mount Zion, that is, at the Gihon spring, his successors in the Davidic line seem to have enjoyed a ritual coronation which included the summit of the mountain as well. Though it is difficult to reconstruct the coronation ceremony in detail, most scholars agree that the ingredients are included in Psalms 2 and 110. The former psalm describes the situation which exists at the accession of each new king: the surrounding nations get testy and plot to overthrow the inexperienced ruler (2:1–3). Such plotting against Yahweh and his anointed (his messiah) is only a laughing matter, however, for Yahweh will drive them away, and his anointed will break them in pieces. The terror of his fury (v. 5) is reminiscent of the fear which Baal causes when he thunders from Zaphon (see p. 136). In the midst of these allusions to the motif of the protection of Zion, Yahweh declares (through a priest?): "I have set my king on Zion, the hill of my holiness" (v. 6). Furthermore, on coronation day itself Yahweh makes the king his son by announcing a traditional adoption formula: "You are my son, today I have given you birth" (v. 7). This magnificent adoption occurs on the holy mount with each succeeding Davidic king.

In the other coronation hymn, Psalm 110, there are so many textual problems that very little can be determined with any degree of certainty. Zion is mentioned as the place of the royal scepter (v. 3), and there might be a reference to "holy mountain(s)" in a parallel line (v. 4). Moreover, the Parent-child relationship explicit in Psalm 2 might be expressed here quite mythologically. The rendering of the Septuagint for the difficult Hebrew text of verse 3b is as follows: "From the womb before (of?) Morning Star (*šaḥar*) I begat you." In the highly mythological story at Isa. 14:12ff. (see p. 141), the king of Babylon is taunted as "Helel, son of Shahar," who has fallen into the recesses of the netherworld because he presumed to ascend to the recesses of the north (Zaphon). Moreover, in an Ugaritic text called "The Birth of the Gracious Gods," the two children born to El are named Shahar and Salem, sometimes translated as "Dawn and

Dusk." It would seem, if the Septuagint is correct, that the sonship of the Davidic king to Yahweh is described in terms of a mythological birth rather than as a legal adoption.

In any case, that such extra-Israelite notions could have affected the coronation/royal imagery is completely understandable when one realizes that since kingship was a new institution for Israel, existing forms and images were necessarily utilized. That process is undeniable, in fact, in the immediately following verse: "you are a priest forever after the order of Melchizedek." That a Canaanite priest-king of pre-Israelite Jerusalem serves as the prototype for all ensuing Davidic kings relates directly to our discussion of the holiness of Zion.

YAHWEH, EL, AND BAAL: THE TRADITIONS OF THEIR HOMES

Apart from the reference in Ps. 110:4, the name Melchizedek appears elsewhere in the Hebrew Bible only at Gen. 14:18. There the returning victor Abraham is served food and drink by Melchizedek who is described as "king of Salem" and "priest of El Elyon." Startlingly, this man pronounced a blessing on Abraham in the name of El Elyon, "maker of heaven and earth," who was given blessing and credit for delivering the enemies into Abraham's hand (vv. 19–20). Further, Abraham's response to the blessing and to the gift of victory was a tithe to the king (or the god). Then Abraham swore an oath to "Yahweh El Elyon" regarding the disposition of booty (vv. 22–23).

According to Psalm 76, a Zion psalm in which the divine defense of the city is explicit, Salem and Zion appear as synonymous words in parallelism, both designating the place as the abode of God (v. 2). Thus, Salem is the same as Jeru-salem, the city occupied by the Jebusites before David's conquest, and Melchizedek was one of its kings (perhaps the first).

As for El Elyon, the god for whom the king was also a priest, space here permits only limited, and perhaps oversimplified, discussion. The god El is well-known from the Ugaritic texts and from several other sources of Canaanite religion. Moreover, on the basis of the biblical material it seems clear that El was the deity worshiped by the patriarchs. He was *El Roi*, "El who sees," at a spring between Kadesh and Bered (Gen. 16:13). At Beersheba he was *El 'Olam*, "El the Eternal One" (Gen. 21:33), and at Jerusalem, as we have seen, he was *El Elyon*, "El the High One" (Gen. 14:18–22). Apart from a specific location, *El Shaddai*, "El the Mountain (or Mountaineer)," was the name of the deity for the entire patriarchal period until the name

Yahweh was given to Moses (Exod. 6:2), as the Priestly writer describes the situation (see above, p. 147).

The epithet Elyon appears as the name for a separate Phoenician deity alongside El in a treaty text from Sefire, but in the Hebrew Bible, while Elyon does indeed appear by itself, the term is an epithet which usually accompanies either El or Yahweh. In some of the Zion psalms we have examined previously, Elyon appears in close relationship with the city of Jerusalem and Zion. Indeed that city is the dwelling which Elyon had sanctified (Ps. 46:4), which Elyon had established (Ps. 87:5). Elyon appears in synonymous parallelism with Elohim (46:4), with Yahweh (91:9; 92:1), and with Shaddai (91:1), to name just a few cases. Moreover, the combination Yahweh Elyon appears at Ps. 47:2, and the fuller form Yahweh El Elyon occurs in the Melchizedek story at Gen. 14:22. (Yahweh does not appear, however, in the Septuagint at this point.)

All these titles lead the present interpreter to conclude that in Jerusalem Yahweh was merged with the reigning Canaanite deity El, known there by his epithet Elyon, when David and his people settled side by side with the Jebusites. Indeed, the story about Abraham and Melchizedek might have been told precisely at that time, in order to demonstrate to both sides that their living together peacefully was prefigured by the revered patriarchs of both parties. Moreover, that the patriarchs of Israel did worship El is well attested to by the traditions preserved in the Book of Genesis. Thus Zion was originally the holy mountain of El, and recognition of El's authority over the divine assembly of which Yahweh was one member is still attested to at Deut. 32:8.

> When Elyon gave inheritance (to) nations,
>   When he separated (the) children of humanity,
> He established boundaries of (the) peoples
>   according to the numbering of the sons of El
>   (Septuagint).
> For the portion of Yahweh is his people,
>   Jacob is the allotment of his inheritance.

When Yahweh eventually became identified with El ("Yahweh is great El," Ps. 95:3), then Mount Zion became the space where Yahweh was enthroned as King (Ps. 95:3; 99:1–4, 9; 97:1, 8–9; 48:2, and often). Thus Yahweh became the head of the divine assembly, a characteristic of El's mountain, and the one who issues edicts for the governance of the land.

At the same time, the holy mount of Yahweh on Zion retained many of the characteristics of Baal's mountain: defense from the attack of chaos forces, theophany forms, and the name Zaphon. However, while these characteristics of the mountain as well as various descriptions of Baal (storm deity, rider of the clouds, etc.) were transferred to Yahweh, Yahweh and Baal were not merged, even though some of the Israelites could not keep them apart (see Elijah's mission and complaint at 1 Kings 18:20ff.).

ZION AS THE PLACE OF ESCHATOLOGICAL FULFILLMENT

Just as the ancient myth of the defense of the holy mountain took historical form in the preaching of the prophet Isaiah during the eighth century B.C.E., so that myth became the hope for the "day of Yahweh." The destruction of Jerusalem/Zion by the Babylonians under Nebuchadnezzar (586 B.C.E.) caused the traditional motif of the mountain's defense to be pushed into the future. In a "day of Yahweh" passage, in the preaching of Deutero-Zechariah, Yahweh promises he will gather nations to attack and plunder Jerusalem and its inhabitants, just as he sent the Assyrian armies to distress it in the eighth century B.C.E. (see Isaiah 29). Some Jerusalemites will be carried away to exile, and others will be left in the city. Standing on the Mount of Olives opposite the sacred hill, Yahweh will split the terrain. Causing people to flee (the holy war characteristic), he will come with his holy ones (that is, his army). The result will be life and bliss for Jerusalem, but plague on all who wage war against the city (Zechariah 14).

Earlier in the Book of Zechariah, in the writings of the prophet himself (chapters 1–9), the portrayal of salvation and *shalom* on the holy mountain is even more pronounced. In chapter 8 Yahweh promises that he will return to Zion from the exile. His dwelling in Jerusalem will be the reason that the city will be called "the faithful city, and the mountain of Yahweh of hosts, the holy mountain" (8:3). Old and young alike will experience joy and peace in Jerusalem.

In the terrible day of Yahweh described by the prophet Joel, hope is held out for those who call upon the name of Yahweh, "for in Mount Zion and in Jerusalem there shall be those who escape, as Yahweh has said, and among the survivors shall be those whom Yahweh calls" (Joel 2:32). This note of calling is reminiscent of the invitation issued from the holy mounts in Mesopotamia, Canaan, and elsewhere in the Hebrew Bible itself (Sinai in particular).

Typical of his concern for the poor and the needy, the prophet Micah, a contemporary of Isaiah in Jerusalem, looks forward to the day of Yahweh when the remnant to be saved will consist of the lame and the outcasts, and Yahweh will reign over them on Mount Zion from this time forth and forever (Mic. 4:7). This passage demonstrates that the eschatological hope for Mount Zion existed even before the city was destroyed in 587/586 B.C.E.

While these passages speak of the benefits for Israel (or for a remnant of Israel) on Mount Zion in the future, others are much broader in scope as they portray the mountain as the space where all people will come to enjoy the benefits of Yahweh. The old cosmological notion of the divine banquet, already historicized on Mount Sinai when the seventy elders of Israel ate and drank (Exod. 24:9–11), was transferred to Mount Zion as an eschatological banquet for all humanity.

> On this mountain Yahweh Sabaoth will make for all peoples a feast of fat things, a feast of wine on the lees, . . . And he will destroy on this mountain the covering that is cast over all peoples, the veil that is spread over all nations. And he will swallow up death forever. . . .
>
> (Isa. 25:6–8)

It is enlightening to compare the descent of Baal into the Netherworld, a major motif in the Ugaritic texts. After having constructed his palace on Mount Zaphon, Baal seems to have attempted to control Mot ("Death"), the god of sterility. In a complete turn of events Mot ordered Baal to descend to his realm, and Baal complied. This descent, on the one hand, is described as Baal entering Mot's mouth where, of course, he was chewed up and swallowed. On the other hand, Mot or one of his messengers instructed Baal on the logistics of entering the Netherworld: Baal must lift up the mountain which covers the hole leading to the underworld and descend at that point. In other words, the mountain (called Kankaniya) lies directly over the home of Death, who waits to swallow up the god of fertility. According to Isa. 25:6–8, Yahweh will reverse the procedure in the last days: Yahweh, who has just provided the lush and fertile gifts for the mountain-top banquet, will swallow Death (*māwet*). This reversal will bring to an end the annual cycle of the seasons, for Yahweh's meal of Death will settle the issue "forever."

Furthermore, just as the *tôrāh* of God was given to Israel on Mount Sinai following the theophanies (Exodus 19, 24) and just as the will of God was issued from Mount Zion (Isaiah 6), so on the day of Yahweh to come "in the latter days" all peoples will respond to the sudden and majestic elevation of Mount Zion as "the highest of the hills" with the desire to learn the *tôrāh* of Yahweh.

> "Come, let us go up to the mount of Yahweh,
>   to the house of the God of Jacob,
> that he may teach us his ways
>   and that we may walk in his paths."
> For out of Zion shall go forth the *tôrāh*,
>   and the word of Yahweh from Jerusalem.
>
> (Isa. 2:3 = Mic. 4:2)

As the passage continues, this mountain shall be the place at which Yahweh will lead people to give up war in favor of *shalom*, just as elsewhere nature itself will live in harmony and *shalom* "on the holy mountain" (Isa. 11:9).

SACRALIZATION AND DESACRALIZATION IN THE HEBREW BIBLE

The original means by which Sinai and Zion became holy mountains is difficult to determine, but it is likely that both were considered sacred by some peoples before Yahweh was related to them. Only on the basis of conjecture can one suggest that Sinai was the sacred mount of the Midianites when Moses experienced the presence of God there. To be sure, there is some textual evidence to support such a claim, but the interpretation of that evidence is disputed. The evidence regarding Zion is more clear, but even there the reconstruction of the development from El to Yahweh suggested above is by no means the only way to resolve the problem.

Our concern, however, is to determine what made the mountains sacred for Israel, at least according to the inspired writers whose testimony is preserved in the Hebrew Bible. Such literary evidence, after all, is our only basis for understanding the situations in Egypt, Mesopotamia, and Canaan. While some psalms suggest that Yahweh (as El/Elyon) became king (on Zion) on the basis of his creation of the world (see especially Psalms 95, 96), the narratives about Israel's first contacts with the mountains deal not with creation but with historical events in the life of the people. In other words, while the concept of the holy mountain is shared by many peoples and while most of the characteristics of the sacred mounts in the Hebrew Bible might

even be borrowed from elsewhere, especially from Canaanite religion, the basis for sacralization is different. We have seen that for
Egypt and for Mesopotamia, the sanctity of the places was based
upon the creation event and the creative power of the gods. For
Canaan the mountain of Baal was sacred because of that god's victory over the natural forces which would bring chaos on the land/
earth. However, for Israel the mountains did not have such an absolute quality from the primordial time or from the perpetual cycle of
nature. In the Hebrew Bible the mountains were holy because of the
functions they served in Yahweh's history with Israel.

At Mount Sinai, Yahweh first revealed to Moses his plan for the
deliverance of the people from Egypt and for the gift of the land of
Canaan. Moreover, it was at the same time and place that God revealed his name to Moses: Yahweh, the God of the fathers. Then,
having saved the people, Yahweh gave his *tôrāh* for the benefit of the
redeemed community and made preparations to leave the mount
along with the people. In other words, when Yahweh's historical
purposes for Mount Sinai were accomplished, he moved. The result
was that Sinai was no longer a special space with the quality of God's
presence, for when Elijah fled there for sanctuary, he discovered that
Yahweh was not present in the usual theophanic forms. Yahweh was
present as he spoke, just as his speaking presence was known elsewhere by Elijah (1 Kings 19:19ff.).

Mount Zion itself, while sacred for the Jebusites as a home of El
Elyon, arrived at its position of sanctity for the Hebrews at a date in
history. It occurred during the reign of David about 1000 B.C.E., that
is, *after* he had become king. In order to provide Jerusalem with a
sacral basis for the Israelites, David brought into the city the traditional ark of the covenant which for years had been kept at the house
of Abinadab in Kireathjearim "on the hill" (1 Sam. 7:1). The ark was
brought into Jerusalem with processional celebration and set within a
tent, a home to which Yahweh had been accustomed since leaving
Mount Sinai.

Recognizing that his reign and security were gifts from Yahweh,
David suggested to his prophet Nathan that it did not seem appropriate for Yahweh to live in a tent while the king had a beautiful cedar home. At first the desire of David to build a temple for Yahweh
seemed good, but during the night Yahweh told Nathan that he had
been perfectly content with the tent for many years and had no desire
to move into a house (that is, temple). On the contrary, Yahweh
promised, he would make a house (that is, dynasty) of an enduring

nature for David, whose son and successor would build the temple for Yahweh.

Through the years which followed, King David experienced "the peaks and the pits" of human experience. He had made his kingdom strong, but rebellion by one of his own sons caused incredible grief. Then near the end of his prestigious reign, David committed the sin of taking a census of the people—actually instigated by Yahweh in order to bring judgment on Israel. David could choose one of three punishments. He opted for a divine plague which was brought by Yahweh's angel as far as Dan in the north to Beersheba in the south. When the angel was about to strike Jerusalem from the hill above, that is, from the rock which served as a threshing floor for Araunah the Jebusite, Yahweh prevented it. Instructed by his prophet Gad, David ascended the mountain, purchased the threshing floor from Araunah, and built there an altar to Yahweh to whom David offered burnt offerings and peace offerings. Thus "the plague was averted from Israel" (2 Sam. 24:15–25).

The erection of the altar and the sacrifices offered there marked that spot as a high place for Israel. Indeed, centuries later Ezekiel called the top of the altar with four horns "the *har'ēl,*" that is, "the mountain of El" (43:15); such a four-horned top was characteristic of the Babylonian temple-tower, the *ziqqurrat* ("mountain peak"). Thus David's altar to Yahweh built on the threshing floor on Mount Zion might serve as the space at which the heavens and the earth converge. It is no wonder that Ezekiel elsewhere speaks of Jerusalem as "the navel of the earth" (*ṭabbûr hā'āreṣ;* 38:12); moreover, it is also completely understandable why the Temple beside this altar is named "the house of Yahweh" in which he sits enthroned as King over all the earth (Ps. 47:2).

Even with all the mythological freight which became attached to the hill after the building of the Temple, other Yahweh sanctuaries persisted in the land, one of them as close as Arad. It was only in connection with the reforms of Hezekiah and Josiah, with their emphasis on centralization of the cult in Jerusalem, that Mount Zion became for some people the confine of Yahweh rather than a convenient counterpart to his universal heavenly abode.

Whether such a confinement of Yahweh in a sacred place was intended by the official circles or was the popular interpretation of the centralization is difficult to determine. In any case, it was necessary for Jeremiah to preach against such distortions (see especially chapters 7 and 26) and for the Deuteronomic–Deuteronomistic school to offer theological alternatives to such a notion. Indeed, if the corrective were not already present in the work of this school from the beginning, it became imperative after the destruction of the temple in 586 B.C.E. If Yahweh had been localized in the Temple and enthroned upon the ark, then the God of Israel was dead, and the people should have found other gods—and indeed some did precisely that in Babylon.

The alternative proclaimed by the Deuteronomists took several forms. Yahweh placed his name in the Temple (Deut. 12:5, 7 and often) where he caused it to dwell (pitch a tent), but his actual abode (permanent dwelling) is in heaven (Deut. 26:15). As for the ark of the covenant, it was for this school a container for the tablets of the law and not a throne for Yahweh (Deut. 10:1–5; 1 Kings 8:9).

Indeed, the Deuteronomistic redaction of the prayer of Solomon virtually desacralizes the Temple on dedication day itself: "But will God indeed dwell on the earth? Lo, heaven and the highest heaven cannot contain you! How much less this house which I have built!" (1 Kings 8:27). As the prayer continues, eight times does Solomon plead that Yahweh hear the prayers of the people "in heaven" (vv. 30, 32, 34, 36, 39, 43, 45, 49). Located thus in heaven, Yahweh would be experienced among the people, wherever they were—even in exile—through the mediating word proclaimed by the prophets (see, e.g., Deut. 18:15–22). Thus the Temple served its purpose as the space at which the people of Israel could experience for centuries the presence of Yahweh and know his benefits. However, unconfined as he was, Yahweh could become present to the people in the flatlands of Babylon even though they could not come to him at the now un-holy mount. The restoration of Zion as the space which would provide *shalom* for Israel and for all the peoples would wait for that day of Yahweh when he would reign decisively and unambiguously over all the world.

9

The Mount of God and His Son

In the Hebrew Bible the sacred mountains served several functions in Yahweh's relationship with his people. The mountain—particularly Sinai and Zion—represented Yahweh's abode; it was the space on which Yahweh descended from heaven. This descent on the *axis mundi* provided the means by which Yahweh revealed his personal name and identity to Moses, proclaimed his will in terms of *tôrāh* and judgment or salvation, and commissioned leaders and kings to carry out his purposes.

New Testament writers continued the understanding of the sacred mount but transformed its use and function in such a way that the identity of Jesus was the major concern. Not only did the specific announcement about his identity as God's Son occur on a mountain, but the functions which Jesus performed on "the mountain" are the same as those attributed to Yahweh on the sacred mounts of the Hebrew Bible.

Some translations of the Greek New Testament cause the reader to miss the impact of "the mountain" simply because the Greek *to oros* is generalized by such renderings as "the hills," "the hill country," or simply "a mountain" or "a hill." Yet because of the actions which Jesus performed on *to oros*, the expression refers not to any mountain but to the cosmic hill.

Apart from Jesus' functions on "the mountain," however, it is beneficial to note at the outset an awareness in the New Testament of a cosmic mountain. Perhaps the best example is the apparently innocent reference to "a very high mountain" in the Matthean version of the Temptation story. After the devil had challenged Jesus' identity as the Son of God in the wilderness and on the pinnacle of the Temple in "the holy city," "the devil took him to *a very high mountain* and

showed him all the kingdoms of the world and the glory of them"
(Matt. 4:8). The Greek words which describe the mount, *oros hypsēlon lian* are used in the Septuagint *only* for holy mountains. The
precise combination *oros hypsēlon* describes Canaanite "high places"
(Deut. 12:2; Isa. 57:7; Jer. 3:6), the home of the gods in Zaphon (Isa.
14:13), the height of Jerusalem from which good tidings are to be
proclaimed (Isa. 40:9), the mountain of Zion where the little sprig
becomes a great tree (Ezek. 17:22), and the place of Ezekiel's vision
of the Temple (Ezek. 40:2). With the possible exception of Ps. 104:18
where the plural form of the combination appears, *oros hypsēlon* sig-
nifies only that space for a believing community which served as the
cosmic hill.

Interestingly Luke omits any reference to a mountain in his account of the Temptation: "And the devil took him up and showed
him . . ." (Luke 4:5). The reason for omitting the mountain at this
point will become clear when we examine the specific function of
"the mountain" in Luke's gospel. In any case, that Matthew speaks
of "a very high mountain" from which Jesus could see all the kingdoms of the world seems to indicate not a topographical but the cosmological mountain.

THE MOUNTAIN AS THE SPACE OF
JESUS' SOLITUDE AND VICTORY

Among the synoptic Gospels there is some variance concerning the
role of "the mountain." Yet while certain events in the life of Jesus—and indeed his teachings as well—are interpreted differently, all
three attest in some way that *to oros* is the space where Jesus sought
solitude.

Immediately after the feeding of the five thousand, both Mark and
Matthew report that Jesus sent his disciples across the sea in a boat
while he remained to dismiss the crowd. When he had achieved that
purpose, Jesus "ascended the mountain to pray" (Mark 6:46). Matthew emphasizes the solitude of the scene by adding "by himself. . . .
When evening came, he was alone there" (Matt. 14:23).

That Jesus ascended "the mountain" by himself seems at first
glance to relate him to Moses and Elijah, the only two humans with
whom Yahweh conversed on Mount Sinai. Yet the context of this
account of Jesus' ascent identifies Jesus more with Yahweh than with
those heroes of old. Both in Mark and in Matthew (see also John
6:15ff.) Jesus descended the mountain in order to calm the sea which
threatened his disciples. By treading upon the raging waters, Jesus

brought under his control this representative of Chaos (see above, pp. 60–61). It was at Mount Zaphon that Baal and Anath drove off the attack of watery chaos, and at Mount Zion (located in Zaphon) Yahweh drove back a naval (!) attack on Jerusalem (Psalm 48) or those enemies who acted like raging waters (Isa. 17:12–14). Thus the context of Jesus' ascent and descent seems to point to the cosmic significance of the mountain and to identification with Yahweh.

If this event in any way indicates that Jesus, like Yahweh in the Hebrew Bible, has exclusive rights to the solitude of "the mountain" and that others are included only by invitation, then perhaps the story of the exorcism of Legion belongs in the discussion (see above, pp. 151–52). In Mark's version the possessed man lived among the tombs on the east bank of "the sea" (Mark 5:1ff.). When the unclean spirit begged Jesus to send him into the swineherd "on the mountain" rather than expelling him from the country, Jesus obliged. Then the herd rushed down the steep bank and drowned "in the sea." The cosmological impact of the story is more pronounced in Luke's version: the plea by the unclean spirit is no longer to avoid expulsion from the country but to prevent Jesus from casting him "into the abyss" (Luke 8:31). That this version likewise concludes with the drowning of the swineherd might indicate that unclean spirits had no rightful place on "the mountain," and so they were driven from the top of the axis to its base in the deep (cf. Isa. 14:12ff.).

While Luke does not report the mountain-sea sequence following the feeding miracle, the evangelist consistently presents "the mountain" as the space of Jesus' solitude, particularly for the purpose of prayer. Moreover, this solitary experience on the mountain occurs at night, while during the day—at this and other locations—Jesus relates to others. At Luke 6:12–13 the daytime sociality includes the disciples whom he invites to join him on the mountain. At 21:37–38 the author indicates that when Jesus was in the Jerusalem area, he spent his days teaching in the Temple, but at night—apparently alone—he lodged "on the mount called Olivet." This reference seems to indicate that the Temple site, Mount Zion, was not the space at which Jesus sought mountain solitude. Rather it was the Mount of Olives which served such a purpose. Indeed for Luke that mountain seems to function as the point of contact between earth and heaven: it is from the Mount of Olives that the resurrected Jesus ascended on a cloud into heaven (Acts 1:9–10, 12).

Thus "the mountain" serves each of the synoptists in somewhat different ways as that space which belongs to Jesus alone. The mount possesses the quality which allows Jesus solitude to pray, and simultaneously it is the space which is defended from the presence of Chaos and from which Chaos is subdued. The Incarnation necessitates a modification in the traditional imagery precisely at this point. In the Hebrew Bible Yahweh "comes down" upon holy mounts in order to accomplish his various purposes (Gen. 11:5, 7; Exod. 3:8; 19:20), even to defend and deliver Mount Zion from attack (Isa. 31:4–5). Since Yahweh lives in heaven, he must descend upon the earthly counterpart of his abode in order to accomplish his will. In the New Testament, since the Son of God is already earthly, that is, incarnate, Jesus descends "the mountain" itself in order to effect God's will, even to control chaos below.

Yet, while simultaneously defending Jesus' exclusive rights to the mountain, the synoptists allow the presence of others in the company of Jesus. Such a possibility for Mark and Luke, however, depends completely upon his invitation.

THE MOUNTAIN AS THE SPACE OF INVITATION AND COMMISSION

According to Mark 3:13–17 Jesus ascended the mountain in order to commission twelve to be his apostles. On this occasion Jesus did not remain alone on the mountain but invited others to join him. Whether there were more than twelve on the guest list from which Jesus selected a dozen is difficult to determine in Mark's account. In any case, the parallels with sacred mounts in the Hebrew Bible are clear. God invited Moses to Mount Horeb by attracting his attention with the burning bush and later called the seventy elders plus four leaders to "come up" to the summit of Mount Sinai (Exod. 3:1ff.; 24:1, 9–11). It is likely that in both cases some sort of commissioning was involved (see above, pp. 144–48). On the Temple mount in Jerusalem an invitation to "go" for Yahweh was issued, and Isaiah was commissioned on the basis of his willingness to be "sent out" to preach (Isa. 6:1–13). Consistent with that tradition, "the mountain" serves the author of Mark as that qualitative space at which an invitation precedes a commissioning of some (or all) of those invited.

The functions to which the twelve are commissioned indicate a continuation of the ministry of Jesus which Mark introduced in chapter 1. The twelve are "sent out to preach and have authority to cast out demons" (v. 14). The content of the preaching must be the same as that of Jesus' kerygma: the Day of Yahweh and of the ensuing kingdom is imminent. Furthermore, the authority to exorcise demons likewise indicates that the apocalyptic battle is occurring in the ministry of Jesus and his disciples (see above, pp. 62–63). Thus "the mountain" serves as the space where Jesus commissions his proclaimers of the kingdom, perhaps where he forms the nucleus of a new people for the eschaton. Luke emphasizes in a way not so explicit in Mark that Jesus went up on the mountain "to pray" all night long, and that from the top he invited disciples from whom he chose twelve (Luke 6:12–13). Thus, more like God than any human persons in the Hebrew Bible, Jesus issued the invitation *from* the mountain where he would select from those invited to the summit.

Matthew records two separate commissionings corresponding to the two functions of Mark's account. The first one gives authority to the twelve to cast out unclean spirits and to heal various infirmities (Matt. 10:1). This commissioning occurs, however, not on a mountain. The second commission, that of teaching and baptizing among the nations, continues the mountaintop motif. However, this experience is transferred to the very end of Matthew's Gospel (28:16–20). Having traveled to Galilee because of the angel's instructions to Mary Magdalene and the other Mary on Easter morning, the disciples went "to the mountain to which Jesus had directed them." Interestingly, nothing was said in the angel's instructions about a mountain in Galilee. However, this passage is Matthew's version of the commissioning of the twelve which took place, according to Mark and Luke, by invitation to "the mountain" early in Jesus' ministry. Thus Matthew finally makes his reference to "the mountain to which Jesus had directed them" for the commission. The speech by Jesus on this mountain points to the divine authority which has been given him, an authority clearly related to cosmic mountains in the ancient Near East and in the Hebrew Bible. On the basis of this authority, Jesus takes over the divine function of commissioning those invited to the mountain in order that they might have universal effect on all nations.

THE MOUNTAIN AS THE SPACE FOR GIVING THE TORAH

The passage in Matthew which corresponds not to the function but to the position of the commissioning on the mountain is the Sermon on the Mount. In other words, following initial acclaim by the people of Jesus' teaching and healing ministry, Matthew records the Sermon on the Mount rather than the commissioning of the twelve, as do Mark and Luke. The account begins by reference to Jesus and his disciples "on the mountain" (5:1). The content of the instruction there is quite varied, apparently representing different kinds of teaching/preaching materials. First appear the Beatitudes, then some pointed teachings about the disciples' role as the salt and the light of the world (5:1–11, 12–16). From 5:17–48 is a section which clearly alludes to the Sinai law given by Yahweh to Moses.

The teachings here show that Jesus' mission was not to destroy the law and the prophets but to fulfill the will and purpose of God to which the law and the prophets bore witness. Yet what follows is a series of antitheses which Matthew alone reports. In these antitheses Jesus contrasts the words of the Sinai law with his deeper understanding of God's will. Six times, in fact, appears the formula "You have heard that it was said" (5:22, 27, 31, 33, 38, 43) or something similar, and what follows that saying from of old is a reference to a statute given by Yahweh to Moses on Mount Sinai. In each case Jesus' own authoritative claim follows, "But I say unto you, . . ." "On the mountain" Jesus establishes himself as the ultimate interpreter of God's will for Judaism.

There were many renowned rabbis in Jesus' day who were authorities on the *tôrāh*. They studied it night and day, and like the blessed one in Psalm 1, they delighted in its meditation. Yet those who heard the Sermon on the Mount were astonished, because Jesus taught not merely as one who *was* an authority but as one who *had* authority. In the Hebrew Bible the only one who had the authority to speak on the mountain was Yahweh; now that divine authority on the mountain is transferred to Jesus.

While tradition has located this mountain at the edge of the Sea of Galilee and has marked the place with a church building, the information in the Gospel does not enable precise identification of the mountain. Yet, in light of the new *tôrāh* given there by Jesus and because of the repeated reference to the Sinai laws, this mountain in Galilee has the same quality as Mount Sinai of the Hebrew Bible. In other words, Sinai and the Mount of the Beatitudes occupy the same quality of space, and in that sense they are identified. Simultaneously, Jesus is revealed as the Son of God who speaks with the authority of Yahweh on the mountain.

Significantly, the author of Matthew's Gospel completely alters the notion of Mark and Luke that the mountain at this point of Jesus' ministry is the place of invitation. For this evangelist the mountain "went public." While the introduction to the Sermon at Matthew 5:1–2 seems to limit the audience of Jesus' teaching to the disciples, the conclusion indicates that "the crowds" had heard his authoritative words (7:28–29). Perhaps this reinterpretation of the mount in Matthew is due to a deliberate attempt to follow a different Sinai tradition: that when Yahweh spoke the Decalogue from Mount Sinai, he addressed not an invited few but the whole people of Israel (Exod. 20:18–21; Deut. 5:4a, 22). On the other hand, Matthew might have in mind a totally different motif: that the mountain is the space where the eschatological community is to be revealed (see above, pp. 158–60). In Matthew's sermon itself there exists a clue for this interpretation: "A city set on a mountain cannot be hidden" (5:14). Apparently Matthew has in mind the revealing of the church as the community of the eschaton; far from representing an exclusive club, the new community is open for all, with no invitation necessary.

Where Jesus ascended "the mountain" on another occasion in Matthew's Gospel, the crowds brought to him all sorts of people in need of healing. To the amazement of the crowds, he did in fact heal all their infirmities, and so "they glorified the God of Israel" (Matt. 15:29–31). These instances of the amazement of multitudes "on the mountain" is peculiar to Matthew among the other Gospels. However, his use of the theme in connection with the "fulfillment" of the *tôrāh* and the prophets (Matt. 5:17), his comment about the city on the hill (5:14), and his reference to the healing of the infirmed (Matt. 15:29–31)—all these relate the mountain to the coming of the kingdom of God. Thus some eschatological expectations of the Hebrew Bible (see above, pp. 158–60) reach their goal in Matthew's "mountain."

THE MOUNTAIN AS THE SPACE FOR INVITATION TO REVEAL JESUS' IDENTITY

While the expression "the mountain" (*to oros*) appears in various places in the New Testament as a space of special quality, only in one instance is there attested the expression "the holy mountain." The words *en to hagio orei* appear at 2 Pet. 1:18 to describe the presence of Peter and the others with Jesus when the majestic voice from heaven announced "This is my Son the Beloved, with whom I am well pleased." Thus the "holy mountain" for the author of 2 Peter is the Mount of the Transfiguration. It remains to determine if and how that mountain is evaluated as holy in the accounts of the Synoptic Gospels and what quality it possesses on the basis of the narratives.

The account, reported at Mark 9:2–9 (parallels at Matt. 17:1–8 and Luke 9:28–36) might be summarized as follows: "After six days" Je-

sus ascended a high mountain along with Peter and the brothers
James and John, the sons of Zebedee. While they were on the mountaintop, Jesus' appearance was changed into dazzling white. In the
midst of this splendor, there appeared talking to Jesus both Elijah
and Moses. Peter suggested building booths for the three, but the author comments that Peter really did not know what to say due to
fear. Then a cloud enveloped the disciples (or the entire company?)
and a voice announced to the invited three the identity of Jesus. The
announcement accomplished, the disciples saw only Jesus.

Earlier we had examined two theophany accounts from the Sinai
tradition of Exodus 24 (pp. 142–46). The one described the entourage
of Moses, Aaron, and the brothers Nadab and Abihu, along with the
seventy elders who were invited to ascend the mountain; there they
saw the God of Israel and ate and drank the customary meal. As a
transition to the second theophany about the glory of Yahweh, Moses took Joshua and went to the summit (as though the others had
not already been on the top). The second theophany was then reported, according to which a cloud covered the mountain "for six
days; on the seventh day" the voice spoke out of the cloud, sum-
moning Moses to enter it. As the account continues, Moses received
there the instructions for building the tabernacle and the ark, for establishing the priesthood—all means by which Yahweh would continue his presence with the people when they and he left the mountain for Canaan. When the narrative action continues again in chapter
32, there is reported the story of the golden calf, Moses's angry
smashing of the two tablets from Yahweh, and further—in chapter
34—the reissuing of two tablets on the mountain. When Moses descended from this experience, his face was so transformed that it was
necessary for him to veil its shining when he spoke to the people
down in the camp.

When one compares the whole narrative and legal complex of this
Sinai tradition with the account of the Transfiguration in Mark's
Gospel, the following parallels appear:

1. In both cases the events occur on a mountain.
2. In each story a theophanic cloud overshadows the mountain
   and envelops the visitor(s).
3. The divine voice speaks out of the cloud.
4. A transforming glory affects the major visitor on the mountain.
5. The time element in each story is the same: "after six days" in

Mark 9:2 means the same as "on the seventh day" in Exod.
24:16 (cf. the parallelism at Hos. 6:2).

6. There is in each case a Jesus on the mountain: in Mark 9 it is he
   who invites the others, and in Exodus 24 the Septuagint reports that *Iesous* (Joshua) accompanied Moses to the summit.
7. Others are invited to experience the vision. The group consists of the spokesman who is forever getting into trouble
   (Aaron/Peter) and a pair of brothers.

Scholars and guides have debated, and continue to debate, the exact identity of the mountain—whether it is Tabor or Hermon or
some other high elevation. However, more important than the identity or proportions of the mountain is its quality. The parallels above
indicate that the mountain has the same quality as Mount Sinai. That
identification is made even clearer by the presence of Elijah and Moses on the mountain. In the Hebrew Bible those two individuals are
the only humans to whom Yahweh ever spoke on Sinai/Horeb, and
so they appear in this tradition in which Sinai is revisited.

The identification of the Transfiguration Mount as the holy mountain can be substantiated by the terminology itself. In our discussion
of the Temptation story we had indicated that the expression *oros
hypsēlon* ("a high mountain") occurs in the Septuagint exclusively for
holy mountains. That precise combination appears at Mark 9:2 to describe the mountain to which Jesus invited the three disciples. It is no
wonder that on the basis of this terminology, the author of 2 Peter
spoke of the Transfiguration as having occurred "on the holy
mount."

While the narratives about the Transfiguration Mount and Mount
Sinai employ the same temporal expression, it is particularly important to observe that "after six days"/"on the seventh day" fulfills different functions in the two passages. The expression itself is a Semitic literary device[27] which introduces a climax to some preceding
action. On Sinai that prior action was a cloud theophany which cul-
minated in the gift of *tôrāh* to Moses, a sequence which we have seen
to be common in Sinai theophanies. On the Transfiguration Mount
the cloud theophany was likewise followed by the revelation from
God, this one concerning the identity of Jesus. However, the temporal expression is used not for the lingering cloud on top of the mountain but as an introduction to the entire story. That new position
means that the activity for which the Transfiguration account was a
climax must be found in what precedes the story.

The prior action is a discussion about Christology (Mark 8:27–33). On the way to the villages of Caesarea Philippi, Jesus raised the issue of his own identity. He first asked the disciples, "Who do people say that I am?" Their answer indicated that the crowds regarded him as a prophet: John the Baptist, because his exorcisms and healing miracles, some felt, could be attributed only to the power of one raised from the dead (see 6:14); Elijah, apparently because some of his miracles were much like those of the Elijah/Elisha stories (the raising of the only son of a widow and the feeding of multitudes with a meager amount of food; see Luke 7:11–17; Mark 6:30–44 and especially John 6:1–14); one of the other prophets, perhaps because his preaching resembled that of those proclaimers of old.

Jesus then turned the question from the point of observation and report to that of confession: "Who do you say that I am?" Peter answered boldly, "You are the Christ/Messiah!" Such a confession meant that, for Peter, Jesus was the long-awaited ruler of the Davidic line whom God would set over his own kingdom to govern with justice and righteousness. The Dead Sea Scrolls amply attest to the expectation in the centuries just before and during Jesus' lifetime of a Messiah (in fact, of two Messiahs—Davidic and Aaronic). Perhaps because of nationalistic and militaristic notions attached to the Messiah expectation at this time, Jesus usually hedged on his willingness to use this title. Indeed, here at Mark 8:29–30 Jesus neither confirms nor rejects the confession; he merely commands silence about the matter. This ambiguity stands in contrast to Matthew's account of Peter's response, where Jesus completely affirms the confession.

Following that confession, Jesus answers an assumed question: "Who do I say that I am?" He speaks of the necessity of the Son of Man to suffer, be rejected, killed, and after three days rise again. This image and title connected with the *necessity (dei)* of suffering seems to call to mind the Maccabean martyrs to whom is given the kingdom of God (see Dan. 7:13–18). It might also call to mind the prophet Ezekiel who is called Son of Man more than seventy times; it is Ezekiel more than any other prophet who suffers vicariously for the people's sins (Ezek. 4:1–5:17). In either case, this description of Jesus as suffering Son of Man did not fit in Peter's mind with the confession the disciple had just made, and so—quite inappropriately—he rebuked Jesus, but in turn was rebuked— appropriately—by Jesus (see pp. 58–67). There follows a discussion by Jesus of the necessity of suffering on the part of his disciples, and of the immanence of the kingdom of God.

Finally, "after six days"/"on the seventh day" occurs the climax to the preceding christological discussion. The climax on the Transfiguration Mount is the answer to the assumed question "Who does God say that he is?" The definitive announcement from the cloud which is addressed to the invited representatives of the disciples is powerful indeed:

> This   is   my son   the Beloved (Mark 9:7)
> *houtos   estin   ho huios mou   ho agapētos*

The impact of these words on a first-century audience familiar with the Greek Old Testament now needs to be determined. The initial words "This is my Son" would surely call to mind the adoption formula used on Mount Zion on coronation day to establish the sonship of the Davidic king to Yahweh (Ps. 2:7). By its application to Jesus (which occurs previously at Jesus' baptism and elsewhere in the New Testament) the formula identifies him both as "son of God" and as Christ/Messiah, which are identical in meaning in the Hebrew Bible. Such an announcement from the cloud would thus confirm Peter's confession at 8:29.

However, the coronation formula at Ps. 2:7 does not include the qualifying term "beloved" in relation to "son." In fact, in the entire Septuagint there is only one passage in which the combination *huios agapētos* appears, and there three times: the story of the sacrifice of Isaac at Genesis 22 (verses 2, 12, 16). There Abraham is commanded by God to take his only beloved son "to the land of Moriah and offer him there as a burnt offering on one of the mountains of which I shall tell you" (v. 2). Isaac, the beloved son, was the long-awaited child of God's promise on whom the further promise of God for many descendants depended. In what seemed to be a complete contradiction, God commanded Abraham to sacrifice the son on a mountain in Moriah. The use of the combination *huios agapētos* on the Transfiguration Mount in reference to Jesus seems to transfer this entire motif to Jesus, the long-awaited son of God whose death would apparently contradict the promise of God for his kingdom. That the expression *huios agapētos* refers elsewhere in Mark to a son who is to be killed can be seen in the parable of the vineyard (Mark 12:1–11, esp. v. 6).

The entire christological announcement from the divine voice thus confirms Peter's confession that Jesus is the Messiah/Christ and at the same time corrects the prevailing view of the Messiah by confirming also Jesus' own understanding of himself as one who must suffer and die. Strikingly, both aspects of this announcement are related to Mount Zion.

The location of the coronation formula is explicit in Psalm 2. "You are my son" occurs immediately after the speech of God that he has "set my king on Zion, the mount of my holiness." As for the "beloved son" aspect of the announcement, Genesis 22 tells only that the event took place "on one of the mountains" in "the land of Moriah." No one knows where such a land is located, and so the early versions of the Old Testament changed the difficult reading to the similar sounding "land of the Amorites" or the like. The Septuagint understood the Hebrew word to be related to a term meaning "high" (*rāmâ*) and so rendered Moriah as simply *tēn gēn hypsēlon*, "the high land." However, Moriah does stand in the Hebrew text both here and in one other passage: 2 Chron. 3:1, where Mount Moriah is the name of the hill on which Solomon built his temple. In other words, by the time of the Chronicler about 400 B.C.E., the mountain in Jerusalem which was once named Zion became known as Moriah, and that terminology persists to this day for the name of the mount on which the Dome of the Rock now stands. Later, because of the Christian concern for the Old Testament traditions, the name Zion was transferred to the mount west of the original location. Thus, in the first century the Temple mount was Mount Moriah, and in all probability the tradition which attaches Abraham and Isaac to the Rock under the Dome was already connected to that hill by the name Moriah. When one couples that new name with the frequent mention of Zion in the Old Testament, especially in the psalms, it is clear that in tradition Zion and Moriah were one and the same. Thus the entire announcement from the cloud, "This is my Son the Beloved," has its roots in the holy mount traditions of Zion/Moriah.

Earlier we had demonstrated that the *narrative* of the Transfiguration was based on the traditions of Mount Sinai. Now we have seen that the *announcement* from God concerning Jesus' identity is based on the traditions of Mount Zion/Moriah. With these two holy mountains from the Hebrew Bible providing the allusion for the entire story of the Transfiguration, it is understandable why the mount is called *oros hypsēlon*. It is indeed the space which possesses the quality for serving as the navel of the earth, for it provides God's answer to the debate over the identity of Jesus. (See figure 3, page 176.)

Within the entire Gospel according to St. Mark, the Transfiguration story occupies a key position, and its role can be seen by Mark's use of the title "Son of God." First, the title appears in the super-

FIGURE 3

The Quality of the Transfiguration Mount

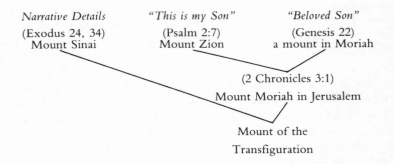

Narrative Details   *"This is my Son"*   *"Beloved Son"*
(Exodus 24, 34)   (Psalm 2:7)   (Genesis 22)
Mount Sinai   Mount Zion   a mount in Moriah

(2 Chronicles 3:1)
Mount Moriah in Jerusalem

Mount of the
Transfiguration

scription of the book: "The beginning of the gospel of Jesus Christ, the Son of God" (1:1). Second, the title is part of the announcement given to Jesus alone at his baptism: "You are my Son, the Beloved; with you I am well pleased" (1:11). The identity announcement is identical to that of the Transfiguration, but at the baptism no mountain is involved. Third, the unclean spirits whom Jesus encounters near the sea cry out "You are the Son of God"; they are commanded by Jesus to keep this information to themselves (3:11–12). Thus, fourth, it is not until the Transfiguration event on "the mount" that human beings learn Jesus' true and full identity—and then only selected and invited disciples. Finally, the title appears on the lips of the Roman centurion who stands beneath the cross: "Truly this man was the Son of God" (15:39). For Mark's development of the title, the Gentiles come to the knowledge of Jesus' identity on the basis of the crucifixion. In this scheme the understanding of the Transfiguration Mount is consistent with what we have seen in the traditions: the mountain is the space at which divine identity is revealed to those humans who are invited (see especially Exod. 3:1–15).

While the use of the Transfiguration story in Matthew is quite similar to that in Mark, Luke effects some changes which are significant for our concerns. First, perhaps not understanding the impact of the Semitic literary device, Luke changes the "after six days" to "about eight days after these sayings" (Luke 9:28). Clearly, however, the author does relate the mountain experience to the discussion which precedes. Second, Luke changes *oros hypsēlon* to "the mountain," and by so doing surrenders nothing; the importance of "the mountain" as the space of secret manifestation to the disciples

throughout his Gospel does not require the adjective *hypsēlon*,
"high." Third, typical of Luke's use of the mountain elsewhere, Jesus
ascends in order to pray, and the whole transformation of his appearance occurs while he is at prayer. Fourth, the content of the conversation among Jesus, Moses, and Elijah is reported: they speak of Jesus' *exodos*, his departure, which is to be accomplished at Jerusalem.
Fifth, the disciples are falling asleep and can barely keep awake, but
they do manage to receive the intended revelation. Sixth, the announcement from the cloud tells that Jesus is "my Son, the Chosen"
rather than "the Beloved" and thus calls to mind the image of the
servant in Isa. 42:1–4, where that figure is described as bringing justice and God's *tôrāh* to the Gentiles. This typical concern of Luke replaces the allusion to Moriah, but the suffering aspect has already
been achieved by the reference to Jesus' *exodos*. A number of these
changes from the Marcan account establish the mount as a foreshad-
owing of the Mount of Olives, where likewise in connection with Jesus' praying, the disciples keep falling asleep and need to be awak-
ened (Luke 22:39–46). It is significant in this connection that, for
Luke, the Mount of Olives is the place of prayer and ascension, as
well as of the arrest (not the Garden of Gethsemane). Thus the Passion motif is common to both mountains: the Transfiguration
Mount and the Mount of Olives.

THE UN-MOUNTAIN QUALITY
OF GOLGOTHA

According to legend Golgotha is the holy hill, the *axis mundi*,
where the Second Adam died over the grave of the first Adam. Indeed, the "Skull" is said to refer not only to the shape of the hill but
to that part of Adam's skeleton which is often depicted in medieval
art at the foot of the cross. The tradition is attested in the Church of
the Holy Sepulchre in Jerusalem where directly below the altar
marking the place of the cross is an ancient tomb called the Chapel of
Adam.

The understanding of Golgotha as a hill plays a considerable role
in Christian poetry and hymnody, to say nothing of pictorial representations on the walls of museums and in modern films. So intent
on elevation are some pilgrims to Jerusalem that Golgotha has been
located elsewhere than its traditional location. Indeed, it is difficult to
establish that the site in the Church of the Holy Sepulchre was once a
hill. The entire area might once have been a depression instead.

The evidence in the New Testament presents Golgotha in terms
quite opposite to those of the common legend. Nowhere in the Gos-

pel accounts or elsewhere in the New Testament is Golgotha called a hill or a mountain. Rather, in every reference to Jesus' crucifixion, the site is simply named "the place" (*ho topos*).

In contrast to "the mountain" as the space to which selected followers are invited for special commission and revelation, "the place" (*ho topos*) represents that space where Jesus seeks solitude but is besought by others and disturbed. These disturbances lead to opportunities for Jesus to teach publicly (Luke 4:42; 6:17; 11:1) and to perform such public miracles as the feeding of the multitudes (Luke 9:12 and parallels). Such a disturbance at "the place" also leads to Jesus' arrest (Luke 22:40). In other words, "the place" is where no one is invited, but where crowds come seeking him. Yet in those disturbances occur the opportunities for the public ministry of Jesus. It is no wonder that Golgotha is not a mountain but "the place" where Jesus is crucified (Luke 23:33 and parallels). Not even in death is Jesus left undisturbed. Yet there his ultimate public ministry is achieved: he dies for all.

It is indeed possible that in describing the crucifixion, Luke—and to a lesser extent Matthew and Mark—intends to convey a particular impact by recalling the sacrifice of Isaac. Just as Abraham and Isaac "came to the place" (*ēlthon epi ton topon*, Gen. 22:8), so Jesus, along with Simon of Cyrene and the two thieves, "came to the place" (*ēlthon epi ton topon*, Luke 23:33). Moreover, just as Isaac addressed his father with the vocative *Pater* (Gen. 22:7), so Jesus addressed his Father *Pater* (Luke 23:34, 46) at "the place." It seems to the present writer that Luke is consciously employing the Septuagint of Genesis 22 in a more explicit manner than that of Mark and Matthew. By so doing he presents as parallel the death and deliverance of Jesus and the deliverance from death of Isaac, the promised child of Abraham. Apart from the specific use of the Septuagint here, the other two synoptists had already called attention to the story in Genesis 22 through the use of *huios agapētos* in the Transfiguration announcement. Even while dropping that combination, Luke achieves the same purpose as he emphasizes instead "the place."

JOHN'S DESACRALIZATION OF
THE MOUNTAIN

The author of the Gospel according to St. John seems deliberately to desanctify the mountain concept in favor of an enhanced personal relationship to God through Jesus. While the same concern for the role of Jesus appears in the Synoptic Gospels as well, the author of

John seems bent on removing all the props in order to make that personal element stand out sharply.

The story about the meeting of Jesus and Nathanael offers the first example. Having just called Philip to follow him, Jesus spotted Nathanael and declared "Behold, an Israelite in whom there is no guile" (John 1:47). That observation led Nathanael to respond with his identification of Jesus: "Rabbi, you are the Son of God. You are the King of Israel" (v. 49). The confession seems to mark Jesus as the expected Messiah. In any case, Jesus promised the new disciple even more revelation in the future. "Truly, truly, I say to you, you will see heaven opened, and the angels of God ascending and descending upon the Son of Man" (v. 51).

The impact of the latter part of the verse seems to be dependent on the story of Jacob's dream at Beth-El. There the patriarch envisioned a mound reaching up to heaven as the place where the angels of God were ascending and descending. That vision marked Beth-El as the holy mount, the house of God, and the gateway to heaven (Gen. 28:10–17). Such imagery is placed on the lips of Jesus to speak of himself as he will be revealed. By this transformation of the theme, holiness is assigned not to a place but to a person, Jesus Christ. Thus, for John, God is present with his people not at sanctuaries or on mountaintops but in Jesus. In other words, this human being in whom the Word of God is incarnate has that quality of space which mountain sanctuaries possess elsewhere: Jesus is the point of contact between God and humans.

The desacralization trend becomes quite explicit in Jesus' discussion with the Samaritan woman at the well in Sychar (Shechem). The mountain connected with that city had for long been considered "the navel of the earth" (Judg. 9:37; see the discussion above, pp. 140–41). As such, it has continued through the centuries to be the major sanctuary for the Samaritans. The centrality of this mountain in comparison with Zion in Jerusalem, which likewise was considered "the navel of the earth" (Ezek. 38:12), was an issue the woman wanted Jesus to comment upon. His response was unambiguous: "Woman, believe me, the hour is coming when neither on this mountain nor in Jerusalem will you worship the Father . . . the true worshipers will worship the Father in spirit and truth, for such the Father seeks to worship him. God is spirit, and those who worship him must worship in spirit and truth" (John 4:21–24). True to John's contrasts between the earthly and the heavenly, between flesh and spirit, here the author sets as contrasts mountain worship and spiritual worship. Since Jesus himself is the truth in John's Gospel, one might interpret the passage as pointing to himself as the proper "space" in which people worship the Father, just as Jesus himself replaces the Temple in 2:21. By this transformation of the place of worship to Jesus, once again he is understood to be "the navel of the earth," the space where the heavenly and the earthly worlds converge, where humans can experience the holiness of God and his presence.

One can only wonder whether the saying "I am the gate; if any one enters by me, he will be saved, . . ." (John 10:9) is not also related to this same idea. To be sure, the context of the saying is the Good Shepherd image, and so the gate is usually understood to be the sheepgate. Yet if the claim to be "the gate" had its origin apart from the present larger passage, the impact might have been derived from the concept of the "gate of heaven" in Gen. 28:17 and in general mythology, particularly because the author used the Beth-El story from Genesis 28 earlier, that is, at John 1:51.

THE MOUNTAIN IN
ESCHATOLOGICAL/APOCALYPTIC HOPE

According to Hebrew traditions, "the mountain," in particular Mount Zion, was to become "on the day of the Lord" the space to which all nations would come in order to learn his *tôrāh* and to convert instruments of war to those of peace and food production. Likewise, on Mount Zion people would be saved from the awful wrath, and there also was the place of *shalom* (see above, pp. 158–60).

To some extent, these hopes for "the mountain" had already been accomplished in the ministry of Jesus. However, it is in the last book of the Bible, the Book of Revelation, that the apocalyptic hopes for "the mountain" come to full realization. In the final vision of the seer (21:9ff.) John reports that one of the angels had transported him in the Spirit "to a great and high mountain" (*epi oros mega kai hypsēlon*). That he was on a *oros hypsēlon* leads one to think of the cosmic mountain as we have understood those words in Matthew's story of the Temptation and in the Transfiguration. Since his vision was of a heavenly Jerusalem coming down out of heaven, that holy mountain must have been Mount Zion (see Ezek. 40:2ff.), the counterpart on earth of God's heavenly home (see also Gal. 4:26; Heb. 12:22). Like the seventy or more elders on Mount Sinai, this seer stood at the point where the worlds converge, the navel of the earth; while those ancient elders saw the feet of the God of Israel on a jeweled footstool, he saw the glory of God in terms of a many-jeweled city. As in John's Gospel, the Temple is replaced by a person: there the person of Jesus, here the persons of the Lord God Almighty and the Lamb (v. 22). Like the mountains in the Hebrew Bible and like "the mountain" in Mark and Luke, only those who are invited may enter: "only those who are written in the Lamb's book of life" (v. 27). Then, as in the prophecies of Ezekiel (chapter 47) and Zechariah (14:8), so here in the vision life-giving waters flow forth from the navel of the earth: there from the Temple, here from the throne of God and of the Lamb, "for the healing of all nations" (22:1ff.). Here too the universal hope of pilgrimage is realized, for all nations and kings (see Isa. 60:1–7) shall bring their glory and riches into this city. Thus, on the one hand, the seer's experience on "a high mountain" is quite similar to that of Ezekiel who, however, saw the Temple. On the other hand, the seer's vision of a city without a Temple sounds very much like the word of Yahweh in the preaching of Third Isaiah.

> Thus says Yahweh,
> "Heaven is my throne,
>   and the earth is my footstool;
> what is the house which you would build for me,
>   and what is the place of my rest?"
>
> (Isa. 66:1)

According to the author of Revelation, the eschatological day will settle the issue: the heavenly Jerusalem will descend upon Mount Zion and there will be no Temple. No such structures will be necessary for the worship of the Lord by those who are invited.

SUMMARY OF "THE MOUNTAIN" IN THE NEW TESTAMENT

We have seen different evaluations of the mountain motif in the New Testament. For Mark, and even more for Luke, the mountain is the space of revelation to invited disciples and the commissioning of those chosen to preach and exorcise unclean spirits, that is, to demonstrate by word and deed the presence of the kingdom of God. Matthew opened up the mountain to the crowds who both heard Jesus' *tôrāh* and experienced his healing there.

It is important to ask about the reason for this understanding of the mountain. In the ancient Near East the basis for the sacralization of the mountain was the creative and orderly power which was established at the space in *illo tempore* or in the natural cycle of the seasons. The mountains in the Hebrew Bible, particularly Sinai and

Zion, were "holy" to Israel because of what Yahweh had done in the history of the people's experience. For the synoptic writers, "the mountain" takes on special, even cosmic, impact only in relation to the identity of Jesus.

The Transfiguration Mount, wherever it is, was the place of Jesus' identity as the Son of God who would be sacrificed and delivered. Thus that mountain has about it the sense both of Passion and of Victory. Elsewhere in the synoptics "the mountain" is the space where Jesus, before and after death/resurrection, commissions his disciples with the work of the kingdom of God: preaching and healing/exorcising. By such commissioning of others on "the mountain" Jesus is identified as the Son of God, for Yahweh is the one who had performed those same functions on various holy mountains. Further, as *tôrāh*-giver on the mount, Jesus again takes over the function of Yahweh as the one who speaks with authority. Thus it is the issue of Christology which transforms the mountain motif in these writings, and the sanctity of "the mountain" is directly related to the space where Jesus' identity and mission are revealed during his ministry.

The author of John not only ignores but actually rejects the role of the holy mountain in order to elevate beyond any doubt the holiness of Jesus. The evangelist's contrast of the earthly and the heavenly necessarily leads him in that direction, and so "the mountain" plays no positive role in his Gospel. Again, however, it would seem that issues of Christology lay at the basis of his decision, particularly by his replacing the Temple with Jesus.

Finally, all sorts of mountain images come together in the Book of Revelation, particularly in the final vision, where the hopes of the Old Testament prophecies are fulfilled and simultaneously transformed. The mountain to which all nations will make pilgrimage is the one on which is situated the heavenly city whose Temple is not a building but God and the Lamb. It is from this sacred space that all the earth will receive the gift of life, and experience that Eden-like existence which God intended from the beginning. Thus only through the eschatological fulfillment of the redemption and victory accomplished in Christ does "the mountain" return to its mythical relationship with Creation.

Summary and Some Implications for the Church

My presupposition throughout this study has been that biblical writers quite intentionally used religious motifs and images from a variety of mythological sources and that their constant transformation of such images provides a means of unifying the component parts of the Bible, even the two testaments. Moreover, the uniqueness of Israel's testimony to God and that of the church's proclamation about Jesus Christ are highlighted by observing how writers in each of the testaments reinterpreted traditional material. For the authors of the Hebrew Bible that material was derived from the mythological systems of Mesopotamia, Egypt, and Canaan, while the New Testament writers drew from those already transformed traditions in the Hebrew Bible or more often perhaps from its Greek translation, the Septuagint.

The motifs chosen for discussion here—the battle between order and chaos for the rule of the universe, the cycle of life and death in nature and in humanity, and the quality of the holy mountain—were closely related to one another in the mythology of ancient Israel's neighbors. The first two are based on the natural cycle of the seasons, a cycle which corresponds to the defeats and victories of the deities in their relationships with one another. The third theme is subsequent to the success of the chief god, for on the basis of his victory over his enemies or on the basis of his ordering of the universe, "the mountain" becomes sacred for all time. The interrelatedness of these three motifs derives directly from the purpose of mythology, which was to deny change in favor of maintaining a static and secure system. Indeed, this security was founded upon a structure consisting of temporal, spatial, and personal correspondences through which the struggle for survival could make some sense.

183

The *temporal correspondence* is demonstrated most clearly in the regular cycles of nature by which order overcomes chaos. Whether the opponents be Marduk and Tiamat, Baal and Yamm, or Re and Apophis, the opposing forces are deities who represent natural phenomena. The victory of the god of order assures that the structure of the universe established at creation or in the primordial period will continue. This connection is seen best in the Babylonian story of Marduk and Tiamat, for the ritual enactment of that battle each New Year time effects the correspondence between creation and the present.

The poetic theologians of ancient Israel demonstrated much awareness of the conflict mythology, even to the point of proper names such as Leviathan, weapons such as nets and arrows and wind, and monster descriptions such as twisting, fleeting, or multi-headed serpents. At times the Hebrew prophets used such mythological imagery to describe Yahweh's victory over historical kings and nations, thereby interpreting as cosmic Yahweh's victories and his reign. On other occasions the poets of Israel left the imagery in the realm of the primordial, particularly to support the Davidic covenant and the election of Jerusalem.

In comparing Israel to her neighbors in regard to this motif, we have seen that the tension between myth and history was not the issue which made Israel unique. Rather it was the removal of the correspondence between the god and natural phenomena which set Israel apart. It was therefore not myth but mythology—not a means of describing God but the very understanding of God himself—which made Israel different. Such a radical change, it seems, was due to a special revelation from God, the precise time or nature of which is now impossible to determine. That new revelation caused a radical transformation of the ancient myth. Although some official Jerusalem theology would seem to support the status quo on the basis of some mythological tendencies, most of ancient Israel's theologians recognized that Yahweh was a God of dynamic change, a mover of history who effected his will on his own and on other nations.

The New Testament contains some striking transformations of this mythological motif. While the Hebrew Scriptures portrayed Yahweh as coming down from heaven to defeat the historical representatives of chaos, the Gospel writers left the chaos agent mythical and historicized instead of the one who brings order: Jesus, the Son of God. That he fought and brought under control ("rebuked") the sea, unclean spirits, and Satan indicates that the cosmic victory over chaos rather than one more minor conquest had been achieved in preparation for the kingdom of God. Thus while the New Testament rarely uses the word "God" (*theos*) to refer to Jesus, the use of this mythological theme transfers from Yahweh to Jesus the divine authority to bring under control the power of chaos and to accomplish what is necessary for the kingdom of God to be realized. Thus does the mythological cycle of defeat and victory come to an end when the historical Son of God subdues chaos in its universal dimensions. That victory—confessed now by the church—will be experienced by people everywhere only at the last day, when the sea will be no more.

The church must be careful that in its proclamation of the cosmic victory of Christ it does not ignore God's continuing battle against the oppressions and injustices which people experience in the world. That Jesus did not fight the Roman army but the chaos of the universe does not excuse the church from involvement in the world. Indeed, if the church is serious about a two-testament Bible, then it can never ignore the many faces which even defeated chaos wears in its opposition to God's reign. The church's Old Testament demonstrates repeatedly that God sets out in battle array against all powers and institutions which represent the ugly monster of chaos. The universal or cosmic nature of Christ's victory prevents any nation or institution, including the institutional church itself, from excluding itself from the Warrior's judgment. While the decisive "rebuke" has already occurred, all the world's structures stand unworthy before God. The task of the church then is twofold: first, to announce to the world that God's victory has been achieved, and second, to strive to demonstrate by its own deeds and style that God's reign has already begun. Such a representative of order, even in the midst of chaos, can serve as a foretaste of the age to come.

The *personal correspondence* of mythological structures was seen in the study of fertility and sterility. To be sure, the correspondence of deity and natural phenomenon was evident in much of this theme as well, for the descent into the netherworld of the Canaanite Baal and of the Babylonian Ishtar corresponded to the demise of vegetation and sexual potency for a season. At the same time, however, the role of sacred prostitution in Canaanism seems to relate directly the persons of the deities and the worshipers in the temple precincts who fertilize one another for the sake of the community's survival. Moreover, the person of the king and of the queen corresponded to the fertility god and goddess in several Mesopotamian texts. In Egypt the pharaoh, as the incarnation of the god Horus, procreated himself for all eternity.

Perhaps nowhere in the Bible is the trend toward demythologization more strongly pronounced than in regard to this motif. In the Hebrew Scriptures Yahweh is portrayed as the husband of a wife, as father of Israel and of the Davidic king, and as mother of Israel, but nowhere does there appear the slightest indication of Yahweh's sexual activity. The familial images of husband, father and mother are used as analogies for the intimate relationship which exists between Yahweh and the people of Israel. That Yahweh's bride is a people rather than a fertility deity completely removes any mythological connections. Yahweh is indeed responsible for the fertility of plants and of humans, but his action is that of benefaction rather than participation. The closest Yahweh comes to sexual involvement is the creation of male and female as the image of God; immediately, God blesses them, that they may be fruitful and multiply (Gen. 1:27–28). This bold assertion makes it possible to speak of God by analogies which are male and female; it also indicates an equality between the sexes which God established at creation. However, it does not suggest any sexual activity on the part of God. Since Yahweh in not involved in such activity, sex has no cultic significance for ancient Israel. Human sex is the gift to men and women alike from a God who does not experience its pleasures.

The New Testament comes dangerously close to mythology in the discussion of the conception of Jesus in Mary's womb. That a representative of the deity and a human woman are the actors in this drama brings to mind some of the personal correspondences of Egyptian mythology. However, the precise choice of words to describe the conception enables the writer of Luke's Gospel to avoid the pitfalls. No sex takes place, and the characters do not play the necessary roles for mythology. The Holy Spirit causes a virgin to conceive. Such precision in describing conception here is not intended to denigrate sex but to explain the basis for the claim that Jesus is the Son of God. The account of the virgin birth is more a matter of Jesus' identity than of a moral evaluation of sex. Likewise, we have suggested, the absence of any reference to Jesus' own sexual expression is related to his identity as the eschatological Messiah rather than to an argument for asceticism. The only sexual relationship in which Jesus is said to be involved is his wedding (present or future) to a bride who is not a woman but the church. This relationship between Christ and the church continues the image from the Hebrew

Bible in which Yahweh's bride is the covenant community of Israel. As for the sexes, Jesus befriended and cared for women and men, and his ministry of reconciliation abrogates any inequality wrought by human sin. Thus sexual equality/inequality is a theological issue in the Bible and not simply an assumed cultural phenomenon.

People within and without the church today seem to make human sex more of an issue than it ought to be. There are those who "demonize" sex, that is, consider sex to be a taboo far more important for morality than any other issue. Apart from its necessary role in procreation sex is considered to be evil, and Gen. 1:28 is sometimes quoted to prove the point. Yet there are others who "divinize" sex, who make it the primary focus of interhuman relations, who use sex as an object of devotion and satisfaction and even as a measure of self-worth. Our study of the Bible's response to the mythology of fertility and the corresponding ritual role of sex renders both these positions inappropriate. Since sex has no cultic significance, it cannot be elevated to the status of divinity. On the other hand, since God granted to humans a pleasure beyond even his own experience, a pleasure in the mutual affection between male and female, one can hardly consider sex to be demonic. Sex is a gift which, like other gifts from God, can be abused by human sin, but as a gift sex can also be enjoyed to the glory of God, provided it occurs as the expression of a committed intimacy between two lovers. We have seen that on the basis of God's asexual/bisexual nature, Yahweh has a committed intimacy with Israel without the accompaniment of sexual activity. Such should be possible—even encouraged—in human relationships as well. However, sexual activity without committed intimacy leads one to the danger of mythology: sex is used to accomplish some purpose other than the communication of a relationship.

As for the issue of sexual equality, the church needs seriously to look at its hermeneutical stance. Are all parts of the Bible equally important in prescribing Christian behavior and attitudes? We have cited numerous passages from the law codes in the Hebrew Scriptures and even some excerpts from New Testament epistles which assume male domination of the female. To be sure, such passages are to be examined thoroughly and not apart from their cultural and canonical context. Culturally, most of the ancient world shared the view that woman was subordinated to the man, but that commonality in itself does not establish a hierarchy normative for Christians. Canonically, Genesis 1 and 2 both indicate in their own ways that at creation God made male and female as equal counterparts to each other.

It is only with the disruption of God's intended *shalom* in Genesis 3 that the hierarchy begins. The inequality caused by human sin continues in the Bible until the creation of a new community by the redemptive act of God in Christ: "in Christ" there is neither male nor female. Now the question for the church is: On what basis does it make its judgments and set its standards? On the basis of human sin or on the foundation of God's creation and redemption? That we still live in a sinful world is no excuse to maintain an inequality which has been abrogated in Christ. To do so is a denial of redemption and of the reality of the new community, the kingdom of God, which began with Christ. Whatever each denomination decides regarding the ordination of women must be based on its own theology of ordination and not on the basis of an assumed insufficiency or unworthiness in the female half of the Christian community.

The *spatial correspondence* of mythology was examined in terms of the sacred mountain. Our discussion of the quality of "the mount" in Egypt and in Mesopotamia concentrated on the act of creation: the sacred hill was established for eternity at the time the cosmos was formed. Thus the mountain in these mythologies was holy in an unchanging, absolute sense. While no creation story exists from ancient Canaan, the absolute quality of the mountains sacred to El and to Baal seem to be related to the perpetual cycle of the seasons, and so their quality as holy is as firm as the rhythm of nature. In every case, it seems, the earthly holy mountain corresponded to the home of the chief god in heaven and served therefore as the point of communication between the divine and human worlds.

That ancient Israel was familiar with the imagery of "the mountain" in the mythologies of her neighbors is attested to by the use of specific data from their stories: the group of seventy which eats and drinks on the mountain's summit, the use of theophany signs reminiscent of storms and volcanic eruptions, the application of the name Zaphon from Baal's stories to Yahweh's Mount Zion, the notion that God or his angels descend from heaven at the mountain, the terminology of "navel of the earth" to describe the connection between heaven and earth in a three-storied universe.

We have observed, however, a major transformation of the motif in the Hebrew Bible, for the quality of Yahweh's mountains was determined not on the basis of creation but according to the uses Yahweh had ordained in history. Thus the mountains were holy in a relative sense rather than absolutely. When Sinai had served Yahweh's purposes, it ceased to be important for Israel. Even Zion was desacralized by the Deuteronomistic school when the people exiled to Babylon had no apparent access to God's presence. In each case, Sinai and Zion, functions rather than quality determined the significance of the sites. Only those invited could ascend these mountains, but to those who were so called God revealed his identity and purpose, commissioned leaders to execute his will, and instructed people in his law. Ultimately, the mountain (Zion) would be the space to which all peoples would flow to learn the will and Word of God.

The Gospel writers of the New Testament differ on the use of the holy mountain motif. John completely rejects any notion of sacred space in order to assert the exclusive holiness of Jesus Christ. Matthew picks up the hope that the mountain is the space where the eschatological community is revealed, but Mark and Luke interpret the mountain as the space where Jesus invites certain followers to the summit in order to receive special information concerning his identity as God's Son and to be commissioned as heralds of the kingdom of God. Strikingly, all four Gospel writers avoid the word "mountain" in reference to Golgotha; instead they call the site of the crucifixion "the place" (*ho topos*). The function of this space too needs to be examined. In contrast to the mountain to which a selected few are invited for special revelation and commissioning, "the place" is that space to which no one is invited but the crowds intrude anyway, disturbing Jesus who usually has some other plans for his time. Jesus' response, however, is always to welcome the crowd and to let them set the agenda. "The place" was, therefore, that space in which Jesus' public ministry occurred—a ministry of teaching, healing, feeding, and ultimately of dying for the sins of the world.

It is perhaps natural for the church to raise the banner for John's Gospel, in which space is desacralized in favor of the sacred person. We tend to applaud any approach which is people-oriented rather than space-fixated. Even Matthew's eschatological explosion of the mountain theme seems more applicable to our theology than does the tradition in Mark and Luke which continues the functions of the mountain as found in the Hebrew Bible. Yet their understanding of the functions of the mountain and the place provides an interesting balance for the church's understanding of space. If "the mountain" is the space to which some are invited to hear the special announcements about the identity of God and his Son, to learn his instruction for living, and to be commissioned as proclaimers of the kingdom, then I suggest that Christians can enjoy mountaintop experiences whenever they gather as the family, particularly in worship where the Word of God is proclaimed and the sacraments administered. Without the experience of the mountain the church cannot exist, and so that space in which the family is fed with the Word and commissioned to be priests is "the mountain."

On the other hand, the church—like Jesus—must always go downhill after the mountaintop experience, and there it finds itself at "the place." Such is any space where the church allows itself to be vulnerable, where the crowds set the agenda and where public ministry occurs. There the church through all or any of its family members presents itself to the world as servant. Thus "the place" is anywhere the church does not complain about interruptions but welcomes them as opportunities to feed, heal, teach, and announce the reconciliation which occurred at "the place called Golgotha."

These three themes from ancient mythology illustrate the need to use mythical language to speak about God. Such an attempt to describe the Indescribable and to explain the effect of the gospel necessarily causes us to employ myth even when we have given up mythology. Indeed, if myth is an expression of reality which can be described in no other way, then myth will be an essential part of the church's theology until that day when God creates a new heaven and a new earth. Only then will myth—like the sea, like death, and like holy temple mounts—be no more.

Notes

1. Humphrey Carpenter, *Tolkien: A Biography* (Boston: Houghton-Mifflin, 1977), p. 147.

2. James Barr has set forth this understanding of mythology as a series of correspondences in "The Meaning of 'Mythology' in Relation to the Old Testament," *Vetus Testamentum* 9 (1959): 1–10.

3. For a historical treatment of myth/mythology in relation to the Bible, see J. W. Rogerson, *Myth in Old Testament Interpretation* (New York: Walter de Gruyter, 1974).

4. Ephraim Speiser, "Ancient Mesopotamia," in *The Idea of History in the Ancient Near East*, ed. Robert C. Dentan (New Haven: Yale University Press, 1955), pp. 35–76; Hartmut Gese, "The Idea of History in the Ancient Near East and the Old Testament," in *The Bultmann School of Biblical Interpretation: New Directions*, ed. James Robinson et al. (New York: Harper & Row, 1970).

5. J. W. Rogerson provides some helpful discussion on the differences between the evolutionary and diffusionist approaches to the study of comparative cultures in his book, *Anthropology and the Old Testament* (Atlanta: John Knox, 1978).

6. James B. Pritchard, *Ancient Near East in Pictures*, 2d ed. with supp. (Princeton: Princeton University Press, 1969).

7. Thorkild Jacobsen, "Mesopotamia," in *Before Philosophy* (Baltimore: Penguin Books, 1949; orig. ed. 1946), p. 189.

8. The rendering "Rahab who sits still" (*RSV*) is an attempt to translate the impossible Hebrew *rahab hēm šābet* which literally means "Rahab they sitting." Without changing the text but simply by joining the final two words and vocalizing differently, the resulting *rahab hammošbāt* = "Rahab who is vanquished" makes more sense.

9. Following Hans-Joachim Kraus, *Die Psalmen* I, "Biblischer Kommentar" (Neukirchen, 1960), pp. 512ff., note n.

10. The Hebrew text reads here, "curse the day"(*yôm*); however, it had already been suggested by Gunkel in 1895 that the allusion to Leviathan in the second line demands a change of vowel to *yam* = Sea, which makes the parallelism as a whole point to the mythological conflict. See the discussion

by Marvin Pope, *Job*, "The Anchor Bible" (Garden City, New York: Doubleday & Co., 1965), p. 30.

11. Following a suggestion by Tur-Sinai (Torczyner), Marvin Pope (*Job*, pp. 185ff.) divides *šmym* = "heaven" of the penultimate line into two words, *śm ym* = "he put Sea" and argues further that *sipra* = "fair" is related to the Akkadian word *saparu* = "net" or "bag." Thus he translates: "By his wind he put Sea (in) a bag." This suggestion, which makes a better parallelism than is evident in the present text, calls attention to the net which Marduk used in order to entangle Tiamat.

12. Frank Moore Cross, *Canaanite Myth and Hebrew Epic* (Cambridge: Harvard University Press, 1973), p. 98.

13. In his study of the term *rebuke* (for which he would prefer a different translation) Howard Clark Kee demonstrates that the background for *epitimān* in Mark and the other synoptics is not the Greek or Hellenistic world but that of the Old Testament and Jewish apocalyptic. The term appears in the Qumran literature in the same way as in the Old Testament and in Mark: as a command which subjugates evil powers and leads to the rule of God. On this basis Kee argues that the christological issue of Jesus as Son of God, while not original in the exorcism stories, is likewise derived not from Hellenism but from Jewish traditions (*New Testament Studies* [1967–68]: 232–46).

14. Quoted from Thorkild Jacobsen, *The Treasures of Darkness: A History of Mesopotamian Religion* (New Haven: Yale University Press, 1976), p. 38.

15. T. H. Gaster, "A Canaanite Ritual Drama. The Spring Festival at Ugarit," *Journal of the American Oriental Society* 66 (1946): 49–76; Marvin Pope, *El in the Ugaritic Texts* (Leiden: E. J. Brill, 1955), pp. 37–42.

16. Quoted from H. Franfort, *Ancient Egyptian Religion: An Interpretation* (New York: Columbia University Press, 1948), p. 43.

17. The following represent a summary from the chapter "They Embraced One Another: Mesopotamian Attitudes Toward Sex" in A. Kirk Grayson and Donald B. Redford, *Papyrus and Tablet* (Englewood Cliffs, N.J.: Prentice-Hall, 1973).

18. See the discussion by Hans Walter Wolff, *Hosea*, trans. Gary Stansell (Philadelphia: Fortress Press, 1974), pp. 13–16.

19. Hans Conzelmann, *1 Corinthians*, trans. James W. Leitch (Philadelphia: Fortress Press, 1975), p. 182.

20. See the discussion by Mircea Eliade, *Cosmos and History: The Myth of the Eternal Return* (New York: Harper & Brothers, 1959), pp. 12–17.

21. Samuel Noah Kramer, *Sumerian Mythology* (Philadelphia: The American Philosophical Society, 1944), pp. 51–53.

22. Pope, *El in the Ugaritic Texts*, pp. 61–81.

23. Pope, *El in the Ugaritic Texts*, pp. 75–81.

24. *Harvard Theological Review* 60 (1967): 411–31.

25. Martin Noth, *A History of Pentateuchal Traditions*, trans. Bernhard W. Anderson (Englewood Cliffs, N.J.: Prentice-Hall, 1972), pp. 179, 186ff.

26. Hand Walter Wolff and Walter Brueggemann, *The Vitality of Old Testament Traditions* (Atlanta: John Knox, 1975), pp. 67–82.

27. Foster R. McCurley, Jr., "'And after six days' (Mark 9:2): A Semitic Literary Device," *Journal of Biblical Literature* 93 (1974): 67–81.